To Miriam + [illegible] —
in friendship —
Reuben Slonim

June 10, 1979

FAMILY QUARREL

Reuben Slonim

Family Quarrel

The United Church and the Jews

CLARKE, IRWIN & COMPANY LIMITED TORONTO/VANCOUVER

Canadian Cataloguing in Publication Data

Slonim, Reuben, 1914
Family quarrel

Bibliography: p.
Includes index.
ISBN 0-7720-1092-7

1. Judaism—Relations—Christianity. 2. United Church of Canada—Relations—Judaism.
3. Israel—Foreign opinion, Canadian. I. Title.

BM535.S56 261.2 C77-001050-4

ISBN 0-7720-1092-7

Published simultaneously in the United States by Books Canada Inc., 33 East Tupper Street, Buffalo, N.Y. 14203, and in the United Kingdom by Books Canada Limited, 17 Cockspur Street, Suite 600, London SW1Y 5BP.

1 2 3 4 5 81 80 79 78 77

Printed in Canada

To the memory of Dave,
who would have understood why I wrote this book,
and to his children and grandchildren, inheritors of a humane tradition

ACKNOWLEDGMENTS

This project was aided immeasurably by the enthusiasm and criticism of respondents in interviews and to questions by mail; the cooperation of the staff at United Church House, Toronto, especially Dr. A. C. Forrest, Dr. W. Clarke MacDonald, Dr. George Morrison, now minister of Timothy Eaton Memorial Church, Margaret Pryce and Irene Scott; the help of the staff at the Canadian Jewish Congress, Toronto, particularly Ben G. Kayfetz; Professor J. W. Burbidge, Dr. W. H. Clarke and Professor Vivian Rakoff who read the manuscript and contributed valuable insights; Norma Pettit, who edited the manuscript with unusual skill and devotion; Rena Tsur, who spent uncounted hours typing the manuscript; the members of Asbury and West United Church and Congregation Habonim of Toronto, who provided ecumenical encouragement; the Atkinson Charitable Foundation, which contributed generously to the cost of publication; and not least, the people of Canada who make possible the Canada Council, which provided a grant. The author is deeply grateful.

CONTENTS

FAMILY QUARREL

THE SETTING:

Why I Wrote this Book

The United Church of Canada and the Canadian Jewish community may be described as two opposing camps viewing each other across a Maginot Line.

Viewed from the Jewish side, the United Church is infested with anti-Semites and an almost ineradicable anti-Semitism sanctified in the New Testament and hallowed by the Christian Church for over 1,900 years. This anti-Semitism is seen in a contemporary form as anti-Zionism, or anti-Israelism. This anti-Zionism enables liberals, who are devoted to individual rights, to attack Jews collectively and thus to accomplish the ancient purpose of demeaning Jews and Judaism. Even in democratic Canada, therefore, Jews feel they must be ever vigilant against the detractors of Zionism, which has become a dirty word, and against the opponents of Israel, who spread their views through the general press and exert pressure on the government in Ottawa in the formation of Middle East policy.

From the United Church side, Jewish defensiveness is often seen as clannishness and paranoia, as an inability to assimilate into the general population as full-fledged Canadians, free of the psychological weight of the history of persecution and unhampered by outworn chauvinistic concepts and tribal traditions. Jews are seen as the parochial nation of old, which cannot make up its mind whether to cleave to biblical prophetic ideals and the service of all people or to its fancied chosenness and exclusiveness. This ambivalence renders Jews incapable of recognizing the Palestinians who now suffer in the same kind of Diaspora, or exile from their homeland, which Jews have experienced for almost two millennia.

Involved in these general images are the issues of liberalism, peoplehood, anti-Semitism and anti-Zionism, memories of the Holocaust—the murder of six million Jews under Hitler's tyranny, the rights of the Palestinian Arabs and, not least, the traditional theologies of Christianity and Judaism. The bulk of my discussion will be concerned with these issues, which, in one form or another, have been troubling Christians and Jews for centuries—for the quarrel that broke out between the United Church and the Canadian Jewish community in the late 1960s brings all these issues to the fore.

Some United Church members, and certainly other Canadians, may be unaware that a quarrel—largely over attitudes towards the Middle East—exists, although it has elicited headlines in the daily press and invaded public affairs programs on radio and television. Few Jews have been untouched by it because of the attention given to the dispute by the Jewish press and because of the natural inclination of Canadian Jews to react to any kind of criticism, especially of Israel, from non-Jews. But the quarrel would not really be resolved even if all United Church members were to become unequivocally pro-Israel. Christians and Jews need a continuing dialogue in depth to explore ancient prejudices, old theologies and traditional myths which have always been obstacles between them. The tragedy is that the United Church and the Jews have ceased to communicate even on a superficial level.

To treat adequately the issues underlying the quarrel, one would have to apply the disciplines of the historian, the sociologist and the theologian. I make no such pretensions. Mine is a practical aim: to awaken the United Church of Canada and the Canadian Jewish community to an awareness that they have become alienated from each other, that the alienation is growing through neglect and that an accommodation must be found, and to make a number of practical suggestions as to how such an accommodation might be reached. My purpose is not to be profound and systematic, but rather to be sober and challenging. I write as a participant-observer who has spoken to other participants, presenting their experiences and views as well as my own.

Before considering the underlying issues, I shall provide a brief history of the quarrel itself. What is it? When did it begin and how has it escalated? I shall then look at Canadian Jews, how they organize themselves, how and why they react to criticism with admitted passion. The Jews of Canada are like Jews in other parts of the world, with a difference. The similarity and the difference are both factors in the quarrel with the United Church.

It will also be necessary to consider the views of the official United Church and of the magazine, the United Church *Observer*, on some of the issues, particularly the Middle East. The Church does not regard *The Observer* as its spokesman; Jews find it hard to separate the two. Any judgment on the quarrel, therefore, will have to consider the respective positions of the Church and of *The Observer*. To do so will necessitate an examination of the records. While accusations were being hurled back and forth in the years since 1967, the details of the *Proceedings of the General Council,* the governing body of the Church, and of the editorial policy of *The Observer,* were overlooked. The importance of setting the record straight cannot be overestimated.

A number of factors make it particularly difficult to judge the issues in the quarrel. The relationship between the United Church (3,768,800 adherents, according to the General Council Research Office) and the Jewish community (about 300,000 according to the Canadian Jewish Congress) is that of a majority to a minority. Both the majority and the minority have rights and needs, and these must be taken into account when judging the issues. This task is even more intricate when judging Middle East questions, where Israel (3,000,000 versus more than 100,000,000 Arabs) is regarded as David by the Jews and as Goliath by the homeless Palestinians, who are supported by the United Church.

Another factor that makes judgment hazardous is the difficulty of assessing Jewish nationalism. For a Christian liberal, such as the late Arnold Toynbee, Jews are the symbol of internationalism *par excellence*. Even Jews pride themselves on their cosmopolitanism which is able to leap national barriers. Liberal Christians often find it upsetting, therefore, to face the spectacle of Jewish nationhood, since they think of Jews in terms of the universality of the ancient Jewish prophets. Many Jews, on the other hand, brand the rejection of Jewish nationhood as a double standard. "If Jewish nationalism is a moral nonsense," says Middle East observer Ronald Segal, "what is to be said of Egyptian or Syrian nationalism; or Jordanian, Lebanese or Palestinian? Even the wider compass of Arab nationalism will not bear too close a moral examination. If Israel is a product of conquest, the Arab world was scarcely established by prayer. And the present separate Arab states emerge from a past, near or remote, which adapted the map to the arbitrations of power. In the end, justice is reduced to a matter of chronology. And this is moral quicksand."

I must now outline my own involvement in the United Church-Jewish affair in order to indicate my double role as participant and observer. As a participant, I came to the quarrel very late.

In the 1950s and sixties several rabbis wrote for *The Observer*, rabbis of large congregations who represented the official Zionist or pro-Israel view. That may have been one of the factors that brought *The Observer* into collision with the Jewish community; it sought representative Jews instead of a spectrum of Jewish opinion.

By the late 1960s the quarrel was well advanced, the United Church *Observer* publishing editorials and articles sympathizing with the plight of the Palestinian refugees and condemning Israeli policy toward them, and the Jewish community reacting with increasing hostility. But I continued to remain out of the dispute. My own reorientation on the Middle East had already occurred, that is, I supported Israel's right to exist as strongly as ever but not her government's attitude toward the Palestinian refugees. My views to that effect were being published in the general press. I agreed with *The Observer*'s sentiments on the refugees but was offended by its unbalanced presentation. Thus I agreed and disagreed with both sides in the dispute and could not make an acceptable contribution to its resolution.

But on September 1, 1972, the *Canadian Jewish News* trained its editorial guns on A.C. Forrest, the editor of *The Observer*, in what seemed to me a blatant piece of hypocrisy. It disclaimed any intention of trying to tell the United Church how to conduct the affairs of Canada's largest religious publication but it offered advice nonetheless: "If the Church is content with a woefully biased official journal such as *The Observer*, that is their affair, but they might well examine the pattern established by the CJN."

Then the CJN translated this suggestion into plain talk: "We have jealously guarded our sense of balance and objectivity by publishing, almost every week, articles which describe events from the Arab point of view. In this way our readers can make their own judgments based on the statements of the most competent spokesmen on both sides." If this claim were founded on fact, it would still have been a kind of preening United Church members would have found offensive. But the claim was not fact. The CJN blew up a token treatment of the Arab press and called it an authoritative presentation. The impression given was that the newspapers of Beirut, Cairo, Damascus, Baghdad and Amman were culled and collated for an exhaustive interpretation of the Arab viewpoint.

The truth was that the CJN used mainly the *Beirut Daily Star* for its "Arab sources" and presented a diluted version of a single weekly article, so emasculated that it was often difficult to get the point of the piece, and the material was usually buried in the back pages. Obviously half a column of muddled extract from one Arab paper did not constitute "statements from the most competent spokesmen." Even this half-hearted effort was discontinued after a few months.

I wrote an article in the *Jewish Standard* charging the CJN with giving Forrest powerful ammunition against the Zionists: "We get nowhere with this kind of attitude. The CJN accuses Forrest of masking behind the role of an 'abused crusader,' while it is guilty of similar hypocrisy. It's a cynical game that's being played . . . which helps nobody, not Israel, not the Arabs, nor the cause of Middle East peace . . . . I am embarrassed by the confused notions of the United Church in backing Forrest and chagrined that the CJN should be the spokesman for the Jewish community in tussling with Canada's most influential Protestant denomination."

In the late spring of 1974 I again brushed up against the United Church-Jewish quarrel by writing an article for *The Observer*, at Forrest's invitation, on my return from a trip to Israel and Lebanon. It was clear that just the appearance of my byline in *The Observer* would evoke criticism from the Jewish community. After *The Observer*'s intense pro-Palestinian campaign and its official censure in June 1974 by the Canadian Jewish Congress, the spokesman for the Jewish community, my writing for the United Church publication was sure to be interpreted as defiance of communal discipline. My piece, "The Real Middle East Crisis is Still to Come," was so interpreted.

The Observer's precede correctly noted that I was in Israel and Lebanon when twenty Israeli children were kidnapped and killed by Palestinian terrorists at a schoolhouse in Maalot, and when the Israeli air force in reprisal killed more than fifty persons in Lebanese villages and refugee camps. I had interviewed Moshe Neeman, father of one of the dead Israeli schoolgirls, who said: "I do not believe in revenge. I regret the killing of women and children in Lebanon, but we must be strong. We must seek out the terrorists and rub them out. When peace comes, as it must, it will be hard for me to love the Arabs, but we will at least live without hate." In the village of Kfair, in Fatahland, I had spoken to Kozai Nofal, a Lebanese farmer, whose wife and two sons had been killed by Israeli jets the day before the interview. Israeli planes bombed Kfair again during the interview.

Some critics found my visits to bereaved parents on both sides of the border a sentimental exercise. One said in a letter: "We don't need a rabbi to be impartial; we need him as a partisan for his people."

The problems of a Jewish writer discussing Jewish issues, especially in the context of Christian criticism, are complex indeed (see Notes on

The Setting). Should a Jew, not to say a rabbi, take the role of impartial observer? Is it not his duty to be a public defender of the Jewish people? I have faced this problem for more than three decades, writing for the general press. The non-Jewish liberal may fail to see the difficulty. Surely one does not hide facts or dilute arguments on behalf of a special group; otherwise the writing is worthless. But the answer is not that obvious. Newspapers have often followed the dictates of self-imposed censorship in the interests of national security. The Jewish people has always been on the defensive and expects loyal Jews to be sensitive to its safety. Until recently criticism of Israel by Jewish writers even in the Jewish press was considered unwise.

Debate is more open in the American Jewish community, because it is a larger entity with a more influential political base, and its sense of security is stronger. But even there the fear prevails that non-Jewish Americans do not understand the Jew's political, social and economic problems or his overriding preoccupation with security, and therefore any kind of criticism of Israel by a Jew in the public media is considered ill-advised. In Canada this fear is intensified by the Jewish community's fractional minority status and the forceful presence of active Holocaust survivor organizations. In this country any criticism of Jews or Israel within the Jewish community or beyond is suspect.

Israelis appear to have a less defensive perspective on such matters and write without inhibitions for the general press of Europe and North America. They argue that the Jewish right to exist is on sounder moral ground if criticism is allowed free play, that Jews can only benefit if non-Jews see them in a true light, as a people with all the shadings of right and wrong struggling to find a place in the sun.

The Canadian Jewish community is also strongly committed to ancient Jewish concepts. The idea of *hillul hashem* (profaning the name of God, which was applied to unseemly quarrels within the Jewish community) is still preserved as an important element in the pattern of Jewish conduct. That concept prohibits the denigration of the convenant between God and Israel, the people and its land. A statement which might cause doubt as to Israel's right to her land would be construed by most Canadian Jews as negating the covenant.

At the same time, Jewish tradition is strong on the right of dissent. The Talmud, the authoritative Jewish commentary on the Bible, in particular encourages different points of view in its approach to community problems. In the first century of the Christian Era, during the siege of Jerusalem by the Romans, the militant Jewish war party retreated to the Masada plateau in eastern Palestine and fought to the death. A minority peace party made an accommodation with the enemy, proceeded to a small coastal town on the Mediterranean and founded a school where the Jews developed "a portable homeland," the Torah in which the Mosaic law and Jewish traditions were recorded. Jewish tradition upheld the right of the minority peace party to disagree with those who insisted on continuing the war. Had this controversy not occurred, Jews would have lacked the Torah, the instrument that enabled them to survive for more than 1,900 years without a land.

One can understand the reluctance of Jews in Canada to let down their guard, in the light of their minority status and of the historic persecutions by Christians. But denial of open debate is contrary to the spirit of their own tradition, which always recorded minority opinions on the principle that the minority of one generation may be the majority of the next.

I do not believe that the general problems of Jews and Christians or the particular difficulties between the United Church and the Jews in Canada are irreconcilable. Reconciliation, however, can only progress on the basis of openness and free debate. Only the most fervent partisan of the United Church or the Jewish community would maintain that all the right is on one side and all the wrong on the other. One who wishes to be fair to both will seek rather to understand what each side stands for, what it considers to be at stake, and will neither excuse nor justify biased elements in its defence. The quarrel between the two communities and the necessity of resolving it, and of reconciling the deeper differences underlying the quarrel, should engage the interest of all who are concerned about the integrity of the Canadian social fabric.

CHAPTER ONE

How the Quarrel Escalated

The current quarrel between the United Church and the Jewish community has ironic overtones, because the first public efforts at good will between Jews and Christians in Canada took place under United Church auspices. In the years immediately preceding and during World War II, prominent United Church ministers—E. Crossly Hunter, Stanley Russell, Ernest Marshall Howse, James Bryce, and others—spoke in synagogue pulpits, pleaded with the government for the admission of Jewish war refugees to Canada, and staunchly supported the Jewish right to a homeland in Palestine. In the 1930s Howse and Hunter organized the first Canadian branch of the Conference of Christians and Jews, an affiliate of the American organization, founded to encourage co-operation and understanding among Roman Catholics, Protestants and Jews.

In the late 1930s and forties the refugees from Hitler's tyranny broke upon the conscience of all democratic nations. Canadians and Americans expressed deep sympathy for these hapless victims of the Nazi terror, yet refused to open the immigration doors to them. Howse, Hunter and colleagues took up their cause. In Winnipeg, where he served for a time, Howse became president of the western branch of the Canadian Committee on Refugees. Sidney Smith, then president of the University of Manitoba and later Canadian external affairs minister, and newspaper editor John Dafoe served on his executive.

The committee pressed the federal and provincial governments for action on behalf of refugee orphans, refugee relatives of Canadian residents and refugees with skills needed in Canada. Theirs was no wild demand to open the floodgates to an indiscriminate stream of Europeans, which many Canadians feared would be the result of any relaxation in immigration regulations. It was rather a balanced request, with both the needs of the sufferer and of the country in mind.

The committee felt the government could do more; in all conscience it could not do less.

The foremost Nazi victim was the Jew, and Howse stood up for him. On October 11, 1942, in Winnipeg's Civic Auditorium, he electrified an overflow audience with an address still remembered in that city, "I Speak for the Jew":

> Now the suffering comes to the Jew first, and to the Jew it comes most terribly. The scourge has fallen upon defenceless people as perhaps earth has not seen since at the siege of Jerusalem a savage soldiery in one night ripped open the bellies of two thousand Jews to see if they had swallowed the gold of the Temple. After two millennia of history it becomes the loathsome distinction of the Nazi Party again to shame the memory of man with the degenerate ferocity of those bygone days. . . .
>
> So I speak for the Jews. But I speak not as for someone different from myself. When I read the dark and bloody record of what, in these very days, just beyond a curve of this good earth, is happening in Nazi lands, I think not of Jews and Jewesses: I think of men, women, and children, of young lovers and little babies, of homes and families. And when I plead for the Jew I plead for my own family and yours, and the families of all mankind.

This passage from Howse's speech is typical of the kind of thinking that led him and other United Church leaders of the 1930s and forties to support Zionism, the movement to establish a Jewish home in Palestine, then a British mandate. (After World War I the League of Nations had divided much of the territory of the defeated Ottoman Empire, including Palestine, into mandated territories governed by the victors.) Two months after Howse's speech, in December 1942, *Fellowship*, the journal of the Canadian Conference of Christians and Jews, carried a plea for the admission of Jews to Palestine to which "Jews have an ancient moral claim, never relinquished in all their history." The statement was signed by Hunter, Howse and other United Church clergymen and laymen. Its appeal for Jewish political self-determination was bolstered by arguments that came from the blossoming Zionist organizations in Canada: the Arabs benefited socially, economically, culturally, medically and hygienically by the presence of Jews; a larger Jewish settlement could only mean an increase in the potential resources of the land and would, therefore, be a blessing to Arab and Jew alike; with the support of democratic nations, no difficulty would be encountered in producing a political formula, fair and just not only to Arabs and Jews but to the three religions concerned about sacred sites in the Holy Land.

All this had the shine of pre-war Zionism, the conviction that good will was sufficient to make peace and create justice, and many United Church leaders were, at this point, starry-eyed Zionists.

With the establishment of the state of Israel in 1948, however, "the bias for Israel," as Howse phrased it, changed to what was considered evenhandedness. The United Church *Observer* did not hail Israel's independence. It cautioned the Israelis editorially to de-emphasize nationalism and concentrate on religion.

In the years following the founding of Israel, the position of the United Church and of *The Observer* grew increasingly ambivalent. On the one hand, they continued to support Israel's right to exist; on the other, the Church and, in particular *The Observer*, grew more and more concerned about the plight of the homeless Palestinians, who had fled during the Arab-Israeli war which followed the establishment of Israel, and began to criticize Israel's seeming indifference to them.

During these years, most Jews were barely aware of the United Church *Observer*. They had no reason to read it because in the main it treated subjects beyond their area of interest. Only the professionals of the Canadian Jewish Congress, organized early in the century as the spokesman for the Canadian Jewish community, and the Zionist organizations noted its editorial content and direction. In the 1950s and early sixties, there was a general awareness among Canadian Jewish leaders that the United Church was divided in its loyalties between Israel and the Palestinians, but passions had not yet exploded. Then came June 1967.

In the weeks before the outbreak of the Six Day War, when the state of Israel was surrounded on three sides by hostile Arab armies and the only open side was to the sea, into which Arab leaders were threatening to push Israel, a sense of gloom pervaded world Jewry; the prospect of "a second Auschwitz" loomed. Words of support for the right of Israel to live, say Canadian Jews, might have provided the comfort the Jews of Nazi Germany yearned for and did not get from Christian leaders. In the United States, the Christian community as a whole was indifferent. In the aftermath of the war, Rabbi Marc H. Tannenbaum of the American Jewish Committee indicated why a response from Christians was important: "It was the moral and human issue of the potential massacre of two and a half million Jews that demanded a spontaneous outcry from those authorized to speak for the Christian conscience in the nation."

A few American theologians did respond to the mortal Jewish fear: John C. Bennet, Robert McAfee Brown, Martin Luther King Jr., Reinhold Niebuhr, Daniel Poling and others. But even their voices had to be awakened by the pleas of the Jews. Hertzel Fishman, in his book *American Protestantism and a Jewish State*, says that most liberal Christians in the US were content merely to offer prayers.

What about the United Church of Canada? At least one clergyman, Bruce McLeod, who was later to become moderator of the Church (head of the General Council, the law-making and policy-making body of the Church), responded in a way that made Jews feel they were not alone. He was a minister in Hamilton, Ontario, at the time. His relations with the Jews had not yet crystallized, though he had friends among them. He had just returned from Vietnam and was immersed in the problems of Southeast Asia which were simmering and soon to boil. He says he "didn't know a thing about the Middle East" or who were "the bad guys and the good guys," and that he was "insensitive to the depths of emotional attachment of Canadian Jews to the state of Israel." He had read the newspapers but thought it too early to make judgments of the facts as he had them. Then he heard from a neighbour and friend, Rabbi Bernard Baskin, who told him of the emotional involvement of Hamilton Jews, and how they expected the Church to respond.

Within three days, a statement, expressing concern for the survival of Israel, was signed by four hundred people from eight denominations and twenty-five congregations, was published in the local paper and transmitted across the country. Often Christians are silent, McLeod was to say later, because accusations are hurled before there is awareness of the problem. In this instance no letters were written to the newspapers in condemnation of the silence of the Church. Rather, a rabbi triggered a response on a person-to-person basis. It was not a nationwide awareness, but it indicated to Jews that some Christians cared.

The official United Church, however, responded on another plane. On June 6, 1967, at the outbreak of the war, the then moderator, Wilfred C. Lockhart, joined the president of the Canadian Catholic Conference and the Primate of the Anglican Church of Canada in a call to prayer "for a just and honourable peace." Not a word appeared in the message regarding Israel's right to life and security. Words do matter, as those who are occupied with religious concerns are aware—the right kind of words, timely words, words that are more than just an offering to propriety. Since Christians and Jews are part of the same historical family, the words, as Jewish tradition phrases it, should have come from a heart of understanding and would have entered the heart straining to hear them. The 1967 war, as it turned out, ended in delirious triumph for Israel and today only the "history-ridden" Jews remember the tense weeks when a people's life hung in the balance.

The Six Day War produced a critical shift in relations between the United Church and the Jewish community; the quarrel had begun. Jews were angry and disappointed with what they considered the United Church's "non-stand" on Israel's right to exist in the weeks preceding the war and during the war itself. These feelings of hostility towards the Church were aggravated by *The Observer*'s increasingly outspoken sympathy towards the Palestinian refugees and condemnation of their treatment by Israel, a sympathy that was not balanced by equally strong expressions of concern for Israel's survival.

When the general press drew attention to *The Observer*'s strong sentiments on Jewish issues, masses of Jews in Toronto, Montreal, Vancouver and Winnipeg turned their resentment on the United Church's publication. A. C. Forrest became a household word. Most Jews could not name the moderator of the United Church, but *The Observer* editor achieved notoriety through an editorial policy that challenged the strong pro-Israel stand of the Canadian Jewish Congress and the Zionist organizations of Canada.

A long and painful history has given Jews patience and perspective and reason to remember their haters, but it has also provided facile parallels that pass for explanation and understanding. Forrest became another in the seemingly unending line of "enemies of the Jewish people."

Had the issue been left to professional administrators of the Canadian Jewish Congress, complaints to the United Church or *The Observer* would probably have been limited to meetings behind the scenes. The Congress follows a careful and deliberate technique in dealing with Christian and Gentile groups.

This technique was demonstrated by the fact that although *The Observer*'s pages had been crowded with vigorous Middle East themes since the Six Day War, the Congress did not condemn this development until seven years later, when its June 1974 plenary session expressed "sorrow that known racists and bigots (were) given a platform to voice their hatred and venom" in the publication of the United Church of Canada.

The B'nai B'rith (a Jewish fraternal organization), however, which has been in the business of anti-defamation (its own phrase) on this continent for more than a century, has generally taken a livelier and more open approach. In recent years it has been acting with the Congress through the National Joint Community Relations Committee, but control over programs of its local lodges is tenuous.

By the early 1970s the lodges were chafing at the bit to bring grievances against *The Observer* into the open. Nineteen seventy-two was barely two weeks old when the Toronto Lodge *Digest* published a column by its president, Alfred Green. His first paragraph reflected the pent-up feelings of masses of his co-religionists: "We Jews have controlled our emotions for centuries. A hush-hush policy . . . stifled our inner feelings, forcing us to carry the yoke of brutal persecutions [in silence]."

Then he rushed on: "From biblical times there has always appeared a Pharaoh, or in plain language, an anti-Semite, who attempts, for ulterior motives and by nefarious means, to besmirch and throttle the Jews. Such a character is Dr. A. C. Forrest, the editor of the United Church *Observer*, a paper which reaches the home of every United Church member in Canada. . . . Dr. Forrest is constantly taking advantage of his position as editor to attack Jews and Israel. The Church, by its silence, condones these attacks."

Alfred Green's gift for exaggeration—*The Observer* devoutly wishes it did indeed reach the home of every United Church member (with a Church membership of over 3,000,000, *The Observer* has a circulation of only about 300,000)—was exceeded by his candidness. He was speaking his heart and at last putting into bold print what Congress and B'nai B'rith leaders were too cautious to say.

Green's original concept for settling accounts with *The Observer*'s editor was more prudent and, perhaps, would have proved more effective. Initially, he had invited Forrest to address the Toronto Lodge; the invitation, according to Green, was "eagerly" accepted. But after consultation with a Toronto rabbi, who argued that Dr. Forrest's appearance before a Jewish audience would give undesirable weight to his views, the invitation was withdrawn.

As a consequence of the column in the *Digest* of the Toronto Lodge, Dr. Forrest served notice of libel against Green and the editor of the *Digest*.

The Digest outburst came in the wake of earlier charges of anti-Semitism against Forrest, *The Observer* and, by implication, the United Church. Until November 1971, Jewish critics accused Forrest mainly of anti-Zionism, but in that month's issue of *The Observer* the editor wrote an editorial in defence of the World War II record of Christians and the Church.

Forrest did not go quite so far as to repeat "the anti-Semitic canard that the allies fought the war in defence of Jewish interests," as charged by Professor H. Weinberg in the Toronto *Globe and Mail*. The phrase "Jewish interests" is an open-ended formula that does not appear in the editorial. Had Forrest used the term, his accusers might have had solid evidence for the charge of anti-Semitism.

Here is the editorial:

> At meetings of the Associated Church Press in Philadelphia some time ago, we heard two speakers making reference to the failure of Christians of the West in dealing with the Hitler regime in Germany.
>
> One speaker, a professor of some eminence, said, "No one did anything." The other speaker expressed the same sentiment in similar words.
>
> We hear this slander repeatedly, especially from Christian Zionists who emphasize that the Church did so badly by the Jewish people in times past it must now throw all its support behind Israel. This is pretty faulty reasoning, but that seems to be the way it goes. Just for the record it should be remembered that in order to stop Hitler, a good many hundreds of thousands of Western soldiers, sailors and airmen died.
>
> In Eastern Europe uncounted millions of Czechs, Poles, Ukrainians and others—Jews and Christians—were slaughtered before Russia brought Hitler's armies to a halt. Twenty million Russians died.
>
> Within Germany itself, thousands of German Christians died in their futile attempt to resist Hitler. For example, 2,771 priests and an unestimated number of Protestant clergymen, including Martin Niemoeller, were imprisoned in the infamous camp at Dachau. About 1,000 of them died in that camp of hunger, ill treatment or disease.
>
> That great Swiss theologian Karl Barth wrote after VE Day in 1945, "In proportion to its task, the Church has sufficient reason to be ashamed that it did not do more. Yet in comparison with those other groups and institutions, it has no reason to be ashamed; it had accomplished far more than all the rest."
>
> Whenever we hear a Western clergyman, forgetting his Church history, say of the Hitler era, "No one did anything," we are reminded of the famous statement by Jewish professor Albert Einstein who said: "Being a lover of freedom, when the [Nazi] revolution came, I looked to the universities to defend it, knowing that they had always boasted of their devotion to the cause of truth; but no, the universities were immediately silenced. Then I looked to the great editors of newspapers, whose flaming editorials in days gone by had proclaimed their love of freedom; but they, like the universities, were silenced in weeks. . . .
>
> "Only the Church stood squarely across the path of Hitler's campaign for suppressing the truth. I never had any special interest

> in the Church before, but now I feel a great affection and admiration for it, because the Church alone has had the courage and persistence to stand for intellectual and moral freedom. I am forced to confess that what I had once despised I now praise unreservedly."

Anti-Semitic is not an accurate term for the editorial. It did, however, display a lack of sensitivity to a tragic era, opening a Pandora's box of associations—Hitler, the Holocaust and Christian guilt, the silence of the Roman Catholic Church, as Ralph Hochhuth charged in his play *The Deputy*, the seeming indifference to the plight of the Jews by the war strategists, the closing of immigration doors to Jewish refugees by democratic governments, the feeling of inadequacy and guilt of Jews themselves for not having done enough for their own brethren.

The journalist's word for this kind of editorial is flip. It lacked shading, subtlety and moral nuance. On first reading it is simply maladroit; one wonders what all the fuss was about. A second reading reveals a lack of feeling on an issue that has touched the soul of Jew and Christian since the Nazi period. Much has been written about the Holocaust (see Chapter 8) and religious responsibility, but it has not helped to dispel the bewilderment over the Hitler manifestation. Both Christian and Jew are still unsure of what the response should have been. The editorial overstated, and overheated, an agonizing memory.

Reverend Donald Keating resigned from the United Church in protest, asking: "Is not Forrest lighting candles that stoke the fires that turned to smoke and ashes the bodies of six million Jews in the Holocaust?"

Since there was a lack of precision in Forrest's argument, it is not surprising that the quotations from the editorial were also careless. Rabbi Gunther Plaut wrote in the *Canadian Jewish News*: "The editorial . . . stated that the Church had little or no share of guilt in bringing on the Holocaust." It stated no such thing, but it was possible to draw such an inference.

Jay Jacobs in the Toronto *Sun* also misquoted *The Observer*: "Forrest has been editorializing without regard for truth, including his latest gem, 'Hundreds of thousands of Western soldiers, sailors and airmen gave their lives in World War II to save European Jewry.'" That was a shortcut to prove a point. The editorial said they died to stop Hitler.

Rick Cardonne, also in the *Sun*, in effect wrote the prologue for Alfred Green's column in the *Digest* of a few months later: "The fact is that Forrest vehemently opposes Israel because Israel is a Jewish state. The fact is that Forrest is an anti-Semite, a bigot. . . ."

All these reactions appeared beside a reprint of the editorial in the March 1972 issue of *The Observer*. Doubtless this was done to present both sides of the argument in an effort to bring down the temperatures of the United Church and Jewish communities. Here are the facts, *The Observer* was saying, judge for yourself.

For Canadian Jews the editorial transformed an anguished controversy into a black and white confrontation: "You say Christians failed the Jews in the Nazi period and I say they didn't." Many Christians did fail; some did not. The books on the subject are voluminous. To this day the contradictory opinions make lugubrious reading. To cite two examples, Guenter Lewy in *The Catholic Church and Nazi Germany* condemns official Christianity. Anthony Rhodes in *The Vatican in the Age of the Dictators, 1922-1945* defends it. Both books are carefully documented. It was futile for *The Observer* to try to resolve the issue in a short, tendentious editorial.

Deplorably, the March 1972 issue, in which the reprint of the November editorial and the reactions to it appeared, also contained an article by Rev. John Nicholls Booth entitled "How Zionists Manipulate Your News." The effect of the Booth article was to raise temperatures in both communities to fever pitch. This former Canadian and Unitarian-Universalist minister of Gainesville, Florida, and Long Beach, California, was known to the Canadian Jewish Congress and B'nai B'rith because his byline had appeared in the American periodical *The Cross and the Flag*, considered by both organizations to be overtly anti-Semitic.

The article provided ammunition for the protagonists on both sides. For Forrest and his supporters it was proof that one could not criticize Israel without being branded anti-Semitic; for Jews it was a clear demonstration that anti-Zionism and anti-Semitism belonged to the same family of ideas.

Aside from boosting fevers, the Booth piece was bad journalism. Its motivation was largely personal pique. Obviously, as Booth admits, he was waging a private war against B'nai B'rith's Anti-Defamation League (ADL), an organization founded to combat racial and religious prejudice and discrimination, particularly against Jews. The ADL had been monitoring Booth's speeches and broadcasts and pressuring his church members and the American media to stay clear of him. A large segment of his article was devoted to his experiences with ADL.

Indeed, the article struck out at B'nai B'rith in such a way as to elicit from the Jewish fraternal organization a notice of libel against *The Observer*, its editor and the United Church. In the course of his diatribe, Booth accused B'nai B'rith of using its tax-exempt status as a charitable organization for promoting "political" activities on behalf of Israel.

Here, then, were two legal actions arising from the verbal incontinence of Jews and Christians—from Forrest against B'nai B'rith officers and from B'nai B'rith against Forrest and his principals.

Forrest was the first to cut through this demeaning exchange. In the June 1972 issue of *The Observer* the word "Apology," in box-car type, appeared at the top of page 17. The Booth article in the March 1972 issue had been relegated to page 24ff. Nobody could claim that Forrest was eating his humble pie in a hidden corner of the magazine: "We are advised that B'nai B'rith Foundation of Canada was incorporated in 1968 for religious and educational purposes. We are sorry if the article in question has caused offence to B'nai B'rith. . . ."

It is time to let Forrest speak for himself. His words have been transcribed from a taped interview, with editing only for written clarity.

> I was startled when Alfred Green's accusation of anti-Semitism was brought to my attention. I had been, I felt, slandered and libelled a number of times [in regard to the Zionist question], but usually shrugged my shoulders and let it go. But that was the nastiest piece of obvious libel I had seen.
>
> I took it up with a couple of friends, one a former lawyer for the United Church, and with some of my fellow editors in the US. Each of them said: you've got to stop this thing; it's getting out of hand.
>
> I believe that there's a way by which a forthright discussion, debate or even controversy may be carried on, and the law provides certain limits. This violated the limits. The only protection you have against this sort of thing in Canada is to sue for libel or lay a charge under the Criminal Code prohibiting the dissemination of hate literature.
>
> I don't agree with the hate literature law. I was advised to initiate a libel suit. There are several stages to such a suit: you serve notice of the action, you give the other side a chance to reply, apologize or correct things, then if you don't act on it within a year, it's dead.
>
> So I initiated it, and there was great excitement around. I was told from the start that I would probably make my point and let it go. I decided to do that.
>
> Very deliberately we gave no publicity to it at all [in *The Observer*]. Any publicity came from the other side, if I remember correctly.

About that time we carried an article in *The Observer* by a Dr. Booth—an American Unitarian and left-winger—which was very critical of the Zionists of America. I think it was titled, "How Zionists Manipulate Your News."

A counter-suit was leveled against me, only it also included *The Observer* and the United Church of Canada. That brought a different group into it. My case was simply personal against this B'nai B'rith publication [the *Digest*] and Mr. Green.

Now I was told by pretty good counsel that I'd win the case against Green; that damages would be practically nil—it wasn't a very important publication, just went to a few people; that B'nai B'rith would lose the case against us; that our position was not libelous, but in order to remove any possibility that it could be found libelous I was advised by a lawyer and United Church people to apologize.

I apologized, I recall, in language that was advised by legal people to the effect that if any Zionists felt they had been offended we were sorry. And this is true, because I know there are Zionists and Zionists. I am more sensitive to that than I was, and I do not want to hurt any Zionists. Some of the Zionists had been pretty rough on me, but there are a lot of good Zionist people, very gracious. I realized that the article may have been too general.

So the thing sat there. Eventually my suit was dead. This was quite deliberate. My lawyer advised me to let it die. After the first month or two I had made my point. The Jewish people got all excited about it. Our people were a bit excited about *The Observer* editor being involved in a libel suit, something that didn't seem the right way for church editors to do things. So I let it go.

There was strong pressure—strong pressure of various sorts—to repudiate the Booth piece. I said if anybody could show me there was anything incorrect or false in it, I'd apologize. To this day, nobody has shown to my satisfaction that there was anything incorrect in it.

Eventually the moderator and the secretary of the General Council came to me with a statement they and some B'nai B'rith people were undertaking to sign. There had been a number of meetings. I read it; it repudiated Dr. Booth for what he said. I said no, I'd have no part of it. I had asked Dr. Booth to write the piece; I had a certain responsibility.

Maybe I should go back here. This piece was written for *The Observer*, but naturally Dr. Booth had put in it a lot of material he had used elsewhere. He preached some sermons saying these things.

Some of his stuff had been picked up by right-wing publications in the US. And there was information put out to the effect that our piece had been reprinted, that I was republishing stuff that appeared in right-wing periodicals and so on.

Well, I simply insist that while Dr. Booth no doubt used the same material in different places, he told me that without his permission, or his knowledge, some of his stuff had appeared in right-wing journals, much to his embarrassment.

I've had some of my stuff appear in right-wing publications and in some Communist papers. Some Zionist papers pick out parts they want.

Well, I refused to go along with the moderator and secretary of the General Council in coming to any sort of agreement. I was ready to sit down and talk with people. I was very much distressed by the fact that things I had done in *The Observer* seemed to be an attack on Jewish people. I don't mind attacking or criticizing the policies of people with whom I disagree. I don't attack persons. I don't like to be considered one who attacks people.

Eventually B'nai B'rith and representatives of the United Church of Canada in their personal capacity shook hands and issued a statement. The press quoted George Morrison [then secretary of the General Council] as saying this was a kind of agreement that we drop the two libel suits. I just want to point out my libel suit was already dead and had nothing to do with the agreement. I had no expectations they would pursue their libel suit either. We'd have had to defend it, which would have been a nuisance and a costly thing. But I had every confidence we'd win.

Starting again, I suppose I'd simply ignore what Mr. Green said.

Thus the apology over the Booth piece came from concern not to hurt Zionists personally and from reluctance to involve the United Church in costly legal proceedings. But Forrest still maintains that there is nothing "incorrect or false" in the article. As a skilled journalist, Forrest knows that accuracy demands not only the facts but the right tone. No writer can be totally unbiased, but if he is deeply involved in a controversy and his tone reflects that involvement his article is suspect.

Aside from its tone, the Booth piece abounds in inaccuracies. One could go through it gathering mistakes, misleading and misinformed statements like faded rosebuds. It cites a number of scholars who have been subjected to "character assassination" by Jews, among them historian Arnold Toynbee, who once called the Jews "a fossil." True, Toynbee was roundly criticized by the Jewish press and Jewish leaders in Britain, the US and Canada, but he did not consider this criticism character assassination. Indeed, he seemed to take the criticism to heart and revaluated Judaism and the Jewish people in two chapters of his volume *Reconsiderations*, in which he regrets the use of the term fossil. His afterthoughts were also reflected in lectures on the demonic nature of anti-Semitism at German universities and in his speeches to the Tercentenary of Anglo-Jewry and the British section of the World Jewish Congress.

Another error: Booth says Jean Paul Sartre is a Jew. He is not. Anyone who has read his powerful *Anti-Semite and Jew*, an attack on anti-Semitism and a sensitive defence of the Jew, could not escape the fact that he is non-Jewish.

No need to go further to prove that Booth made egregious mistakes. Forrest may have been reluctant to reject the Booth piece because he had ordered it, but he should have checked it for accuracy and judged it for journalistic balance. However, Forrest's insistence that he did not reprint Booth's article from another publication is borne out by the facts. This is an important point, because Forrest's critics accused him of republishing material from an anti-Semitic periodical.

Early in 1971 Booth had preached at least two sermons involving Jews in his California church, "The Dubious Ethics of B'nai B'rith" and "Zionist Myth Examined." Excerpts from these sermons appeared in two issues of the *American Mercury* (Summer and Fall, 1971) with a note that the original texts were available from the Unitarian Church of Long Beach.

The Cross and The Flag, published and edited by the late Gerald L. K. Smith, which specializes in anti-Black and anti-Semitic polemics, reprinted in full one of the Booth sermons in its February 1972 issue, under the title "American Freedom Versus Zionist Power." The precede must have been discomfiting to the Unitarian minister, as Forrest claims, for it describes him as running "head on into the stubborn, dogmatic, tyrannical world-wide institution known as Jew-Zionism," a term popular with the haters. A comparison of Booth's article in *The Observer* with his sermon excerpts in the *American Mercury* and the reprint of the sermon in Gerald L. K. Smith's tract reveals that while the ideas in all four presentations are similar the material is not identical. Evidently Booth rewrote his arguments four times.

As suggested in Forrest's interview above, not all the exchanges between United Church officials and Jews in 1972 were hostile. During the months of the verbal hostilities between Forrest and the B'nai B'rith, two leaders of the United Church and two from B'nai B'rith held a series of luncheon meetings in which they tried to separate themselves from their roles in their respective organizations and look at the situation as friends: Rev. Bruce McLeod, then moderator of the United Church; Rev. George Morrison, then secretary of the General Council of the Church; Lou Ronson, businessman and member of

B'nai B'rith executive; and Herbert Levy, executive vice-president of B'nai B'rith.

On May 4, 1973, they issued a joint statement of reconciliation (see Appendix A). Sydney Maislin, president of Canadian B'nai B'rith, signed in place of Ronson. It was not an official document adopted by the elected boards of the two organizations, but there was a tacit understanding that the libel actions would be allowed to lapse. As we have seen, A. C. Forrest did not sign the statement.

Nineteen seventy-three was a somewhat better year for United Church-Jewish dialogue. On October 19, when the Yom Kippur War, or the Ramadan War, as the Arabs call it, was in full tide, four United Church scholars—B. Robert Bater, now Principal of Queen's Theological College, Alan T. Davies of Victoria University, University of Toronto, and David E. Demson and William O. Fennell of Emmanuel College at the University of Toronto, in company with Roman Catholic professors, published a statement in the Toronto *Globe and Mail* that swept the Jewish community of Toronto and was reproduced for Jews across the country (Appendix B). Professor Emil L. Fackenheim of the University of Toronto said it "put our Christian enemies [Forrest and *The Observer*] on the defensive and made them look sick."

The statement was all that Zionists could hope for. It recognized political Zionism as a reaction to Christian anti-Semitism and as an authentic liberation movement of the twentieth century. It defined Israel as a "resurrection symbol following the crucifixion symbol of Auschwitz." It recognized the tragic plight of the Palestinian refugees but saw them as "a comfort for a troubled Christian [conscience] which, preferring not to dwell on Christian guilt with regard to the Jews, dwells instead on Jewish guilt with regard to the Arabs." It disqualified the churches as potential mediators in the Arab-Jewish struggle in the light of the history of Christian-Jewish relations. It insisted that Christians could not be neutral in a conflict where one side aims at negotiation over disputed issues and the other at the destruction of a government and "if Arab rhetoric is to be taken literally," genocide. Therefore, Christians must stand with Israel "without equivocation."

The participation of United Church ministers did not mean, however, that the statement represented the official Church position. On the contrary, W. Clarke MacDonald, on behalf of the Committee on the Church and International Affairs, wrote a rejoinder as the United Church's spokesman (Appendix C). His was the dual emphasis, developed over more than two decades, upholding the security of Israel and self-determination for the Palestinians. He condemned the statement in the *Globe and Mail* because it "served to polarize local feeling." Professor Emil Fackenheim was astonished. Why object to polarization, he asked, when *The Observer* furthers the same purpose in its anti-Israel policy? Why is it a virtue for A. C. Forrest and a vice for Davies, Demson, Fennell and Bater?

Whatever MacDonald meant by polarization—alienation, intensifying emotions—the burden of his letter is clear: the United Church is concerned about *all* the victims in the conflict. Israel is victimized when her security is endangered; the Palestinians are victimized when they are homeless. This is not an unreasonable stand and is in line with the feelings of many Israelis who oppose their government's policy towards the Palestinians. The question Canadian Jews ask is: May the Church take such a position? Israelis, yes, but Christians, living outside Israel? Especially against the backdrop of the entire Christian record regarding Jews?

Another letter to the *Globe and Mail* (Appendix D), signed by Lorne M. Kenny, chairman of Islamic and Near Eastern Studies, University of Toronto, and thirteen other professors of the department, also challenged the statement of the Roman Catholic and United Church clergymen and asserted that the Palestinians have rights. But their stand was mainly accusatory, raising the rather eccentric question as to whether hostility to Arabs could be called anti-Semitism. Perhaps this was what MacDonald meant by polarization—the Department of Islamic Studies of the University of Toronto versus Emmanuel and Victoria Colleges of the same university.

Charges of anti-Semitism flared for a third time in March 1974, when *The Observer* published an advertisement (Appendix E) by G. J. Salter of the British-Israelite Federation, which the Canadian Jewish Congress and B'nai B'rith have long suspected of having anti-Semitic leanings. But while the Jewish press noted the appearance of the ad without much surprise, vigorous reaction against it came from the daily press and United Church ministers.

What helped to keep the resentment of the Jewish community in check this time was the indignation of United Church members toward their own publication. This may be one of the lessons in United Church-Jewish relations. Jews seem to feel they can mute their protest if others will do the shouting for them.

The Salter ad, as it has come to be known, was a mixture of obscure biblical interpretations, old fictions about a world Jewish conspiracy and anti-Catholic bias. Most publishers would have rejected it on grounds of incoherence.

But it slipped through at *The Observer*. The "anti-sieve" mechanism, as then General Council secretary George Morrison put it, was not working. To make amends, Forrest devoted a page in the May issue to critical opinion of the ad. It must be said of *The Observer* editor that he tries to follow the journalistic rule of being fair to the opposition. The Salter ad occupied a full page in a box on page 38 in the March issue; the refutations were also given a boxed page in an even more favourable position in the later edition.

In his editorial precede to the letters (seven opposing publication of the ad and one in support), Forrest took his cue from the daily press and acknowledged that if he had been more careful he would have rejected the ad "on grounds of taste" (see Appendix F). He was not aware, he said, of British Israelite anti-Semitism. Nor did he seem to detect anti-Jewish hatred in the ad. He checked with Salter who assured him that the ad was philo-Semitic, "for it shows that God has chosen the two tribes of Judah [the Jews] and the ten tribes of Ephraim-Israel [presumably Britain and others] all of whom are Semites, as a special people unto himself above all the nations of the earth."

But the advertisement insisted that "official Judah, with many individuals of the ten tribes and non-Israelites as their willing tools and collaborators, controls the money of the world." Anyone with even a superficial knowledge of the hatemongers would recognize this passage as ancient anti-Semitic claptrap.

At least five United Church ministers recognized it as such. Rev. William O. Fennel of Emmanuel College found it "in bad taste . . . theologically irresponsible . . . anti-Semitic . . . anti-ecumenical." Rev. C. H. Parker of Queen's Theological College considered it "an invitation to join in the worst kind of anti-Semitism" . . . having "no place in the paper—or any paper where attempts are made at truth and decency." In a witty reply, Rev. Robert F. Smith of Richmond Hill, Ontario, described it as "Salter's Unclarified Anti-Semitic Balm." And Rev. R. G. Nicholls of Lucknow, Ontario, saw it as "literalist, illogical, without scholarly foundation . . . also strongly anti-Jewish in flavour."

Only Rev. Herbert S. Blezard of Morrin, Alberta, supported the decision to publish the ad: "I believe one of the marks of a Christian is that he will be a man willing to listen. He tries to understand the point of view of those with whom he may differ, even those he considers his enemies. How are we going to understand the thinking of others, such as Mr. Salter, if we stifle the expressions of their opinions?"

Yet even for freedom-lovers, there are limits to free opinions. The law has fixed them—libel, slander, sedition and most recently hatemongering against groups. But the law would have difficulty going after the Salter ad because of its fuzziness.

Still another dispute erupted after the plenary session of the Canadian Jewish Congress in June 1974, when Gunther Plaut of Holy Blossom Temple in Toronto reported on the Jews and Canadian churches. He judged that "in the last two years there has fortunately been a maturing of attitudes." The optimism was unwarranted.

It was reported in the *Canadian Jewish News*, June 21, 1974, that the rabbi of Holy Blossom Temple had told the Congress that United Church leadership had held "a great number of meetings . . . in an attempt to stifle 'the more and more raucous fulminations of *The Observer* and its editor.' " On the basis of this report, the August *Observer* denied that such meetings were ever held and rejected Plaut as a spokesman for the Jews "when he attempts to stifle *The Observer* or anybody else."

Then on August 23, the *Canadian Jewish News* reported *The Observer* as "attacking" Plaut and the latter, in turn, as denying he ever made any statement regarding the stifling of *The Observer* editor in his report to the Congress. The text of that report bears him out.

Forrest wrote a letter to the CJN: "If Dr. Plaut did not write or say in his speech or somewhere what you said he did, then your report was inaccurate. Why didn't you or the rabbi deny it soon after it appeared in your paper? For let's face it, your story has made me look unfair in the eyes of your readers. If Dr. Plaut did not say or write this, then I owe him an apology, you owe him an apology and you owe me an explanation. If Dr. Plaut did write or say this, and your report was accurate, then your story of my 'attack' on him seems like a Nixonian attempt to cover up."

Plaut wrote to Forrest saying he did not know on "what the reporter based himself." When I asked for an explanation by letter on August 26, 1974, Plaut did not reply. A CJN reporter said the statement about "stifling Forrest" did appear in an early draft of Plaut's Congress speech; it must have been deleted in a later version. Another possible explanation is that the statement was made during discussion at the Congress meeting after the formal address.

The affair remains a mystery. Forrest was at fault in not checking out the CJN story before commenting on it. But it seems clear that Plaut and the CJN maintained a concerted posture against him and denied him the facts. Relations had reached the point where leaders in the Jewish community deemed it important not to make explanations to the editor of a publication which enters about 300,000 Canadian homes.

The breach between Forrest and Plaut was especially unfortunate because both had been founders of *Ferment '67*, a thoughtful magazine designed for dialogue among Catholic, Orthodox, Protestant, Jewish, Muslim and Buddhist leaders in Canada. Plaut became chairman of its editorial advisory board and Forrest its publisher. The United Church's Ryerson Press paid the bills. The venture foundered after ten issues because of money problems, but it had brought Jewish and United Church leaders together on a meaningful level at a time when differences were exploding.

The Canadian Jewish Congress has been talking to Roman Catholics and the Canadian Council of Churches in the years since 1967, but the gap to be spanned with the United Church itself remains as wide as ever. Generally, the attitude of Canadian Jews has hardened toward Christian liberals (see Chapter 5) and especially those of the United Church. Orthodox Jews have rarely paid attention to "what the 'goyim' [Gentiles] say." Liberal Jews are now beginning to adopt a similar stance. Leave us alone, they plead, maybe dialogue will have a better chance after a period of "benign neglect."

But Jews can no longer isolate themselves. That was possible in the older, harsher society of the European continent, when they were a community within a community. Today they are an integrated entity in Canada, as in all democratic countries. The United Church and the Jews are bound together in a spiritual and historical affinity and in a common bond of Canadian nationality.

Scholars have called Judaism and Christianity "mother and daughter" or "elder and younger brothers." But their differences over the centuries have been deep. They often seem unable to live either with or without each other. Theologian Alan T. Davies, citing the German Catholic writer Karl Thieme, underlines the special Jewish-Christian connection: "The encounter of Christians and Jews today has the strange pathos of a meeting between estranged members of the same family after a great lapse of time. Only dimly do they perceive in each other the once close brother or sister of the past. No other encounter between the great religions has this character."

Bringing the current United Church-Jewish quarrel out into the open and fearlessly examining it in all its aspects will not only provide background and information necessary for a successful resolution of the dispute; it may also serve as a first step towards a deeper Jewish-Christian reconciliation.

CHAPTER TWO

The Plaintiff

In this chapter I shall probe the collective spirit of the Canadian Jewish community, the masses of people with whom I have been in contact since childhood. I shall be as open as possible in my comments, as though I were speaking to Jews alone.

Some of my Jewish readers may have doubts about such an approach, wondering whether it does not provide fuel for anti-Semitism. But I believe Jews are in error when they suppose that their human faults are alone responsible for stimulating the haters. As a minority, Jews are disliked in the same way as some people dislike the Irish, the Blacks or the Poles. But anti-Semitism is more than dislike; it is hallucinatory hatred which is as much horrified by Jewish virtues as by Jewish faults. No one would suggest that Jews hide their virtues because of the anti-Semites, and it would be similarly irrational to try to hide faults which Jews, as human beings, are heir to.

Moreover, as a Canadian I do not feel constrained to present to my neighbours a polished exterior that conceals the character, good and bad, within. In boyhood and adulthood I have met anti-Semitism in Canada, but I have also been made to feel secure by the wholesomeness that springs from the libertarian traditions of this country. In some respects, Canada is like Denmark, where in pre-World War II years Jews did not fear to bring their internal disputes into the general community and have them reported in the general press. This openness created a strong rapport between Jewish and Christian Danes, and when the Nazis invaded, the Danes rallied to the Jews as "our own people." An open Jewish stance may be misunderstood by the anti-Semites, but it would be folly to allow them to deter legitimate Jewish attitudes.

I shall, therefore, discuss frankly some of the factors that make the Canadian Jewish community defensive and cause it to react passionately to statements which deal with Jewish issues. The main reason for the Jewish community's defensive posture is, of course, fear that anti-Semitism may take hold of the Christian Church, including the United Church, as it has in centuries past. In Canada, this posture is given added dimension by the fact that an active group of Canadian Jews are survivors from Hitler's Holocaust. I shall consider both these factors in detail in later chapters. In this chapter, I shall concentrate on other factors in Jewish defensiveness: collective decisions by consensus and the loss of the ancient Jewish principle of dissent, the problems of assimilation and intermarriage and the difficulty of devising educational measures to cope with them, and finally the lack of a vigorous, independent press to keep watch on Jewish community leadership so as to keep it sensitive to current Jewish needs.

My open critique does not mean that I am not aware at all times of "the saving remnant" in Jewish homes across Canada where the enduring spirit of *Yiddishkeit* (Jewishness) still prevails, where Jewish ritual and practice provide an atmosphere of warmth and security. In these homes children still feel the deep impress of Passover, Yom Kippur (Day of Atonement), shiva (seven days of mourning for the dead), Yahrzeit (annual memorial day for a departed loved one), Sabbath candles, the Ninth of Ab or Black Fast (commemorating the destruction of the ancient Jerusalem Temple), kashrut (dietary laws), tefilin (phylacteries—small leather boxes containing Hebrew texts, worn by Jews at morning prayer to remind them of their spiritual obligations) and mezuzot (doorpost receptacles containing the *sh'ma*, the central theme of Jewish liturgy, "Hear, O Israel, the Lord is one"). I am a liberal Jew and do not speak for orthodox Judaism, yet while finding no identity with its formal beliefs I do feel at home in its spirit and devotion to the Jewish people which, with its unpagan attitude toward life, is the same as my Jewish liberal aspirations.

A man, say the ancient sages, must always "speak the truth in his own heart." For if he does not, if he conceals from himself the presence, in his spirit and in the spirit of others, of aggression and pride, he will be busy doing all things except that which needs to be done first and urgently. At all costs, then, the truth, no matter how grim and discouraging.

But is the truth about Canadian Jews so discouraging? It is not as pleasant as many are accustomed to believe, but there is nothing of permanent discouragement in it. If weaknesses in Canadian Jews are deep, their strengths can be very high. If they can fall into indifference, they are also capable of robust awareness. If they are often quickly irritable, as United Church leaders have discovered, they are as often gentle and patient. Frequently they not only forget self-centred interests but sacrifice them to the common Canadian welfare.

In this spirit, then, I describe Canadian Jews.

The structure of the Canadian Jewish community may best be understood in contrast to that of British Jews on the one hand, and American Jews on the other. In Britain the Jews function on a wondrously unified basis—one Board of Deputies of British Jews (the governing body), one chief rabbi, one *beth din* (chief rabbi's court for internal disputes and ritual questions), one Jews College and one orthodox United Synagogue network. Liberal synagogues exist, but their influence is minimal. With American Jews dissonance is king. Rivalry flourishes among the defence organizations (those who counter anti-Semitic attacks on Jews)—the American Jewish Congress, the American Jewish Committee, B'nai B'rith and the American Jewish Labor Committee. Three prosperous religious establishments vie for community support—the Orthodox Rabbi Isaac Elhanan Yeshivah and University and its lay affiliates; the Jewish Theological Seminary and the United Synagogue of America, the Conservative wing; and the Reform institutions embracing the Hebrew Union College-Jewish Institute of Religion and its federated temples. Numerous orthodox divisions dot the Jewish landscape.

British Jews stress unity; American Jews diversity. Canada's Jewish community is a unity of diversities. It is not so disciplined as the British model, nor so chaotic as the American pattern. It has no rabbinical chiefs but as many religious splinters as the American community with which it is affiliated. Typically Canadian, its establishment or governing bodies—the United Jewish Welfare Fund and the Canadian Jewish Congress—strive for consensus and order among differing ideologies. Their decisions are usually made on the lowest common denominator of mass sentiment and virtually exclude dissent. In his 1975 study of the Toronto Jewish power structure, sociologist Ya'acov Glickman noted that anti-establishment elements are simply ignored.

In these circumstances Canadian synagogues have to a large extent become the instruments of "the Jewish power elite" for philanthropic fund-raising. Rabbis proclaim on Yom Kippur eve, the most sacred moment of the ritual calendar, that support of Israel through the purchase of bonds is a sanctified act. They do this because for them the European Holocaust, which took the lives of six million Jews, was a kind of crucifixion and the birth of the state of Israel a kind of resurrection. But community consensus reinforces the act.

As with non-Jewish Canadians, Jews—except for the orthodox minority—no longer turn to prayer and worship to the extent their ancestors did. These things function as a dimming memory of an ancient exercise in the psyche of Jewish suburbia. Rabbis, cantors and choirs perform before a passive audience which thirsts for something spiritual but has been estranged from it by the skepticism of the age. The state of Israel, however, is something tangible and visible and near enough to religious aspiration to provide a substitute for traditional piety. "Holy Land" is not just an expression with Canadian Jews; it carries a sanctified aura as a haven for the persecuted.

American Jews are not that romantic about Israel. There is a growing sense among them that something is wrong with the relationship between the Jews of Israel and those of other countries. The unease stems from tension over religious definitions in Israel in which only orthodox Judaism is recognized, from the specific issue of the direct involvement of Israeli officials in the 1972 American elections and from the competing needs of an increasingly active American Jewish community. The tension rises every year when allocation of priorities is considered: Which should come first, Israel or domestic Jewish needs?

Canadian Jews also face this agonizing choice but rarely allow open challenges of Israel's policy to enter their considerations. In the United States, not only inactive Jews but the positive activists have been apprehensive regarding Israel's policies toward peace and apparent lack of imagination in the pursuit of a Middle East settlement. Canadian Jews are, perhaps, as deeply torn by their commitment to Israel on the one hand, and their doubts about the state's policies on the other; but as a smaller and more homogeneous community, they have a greater fear of speaking out lest they add to the strength of Israel's enemies.

In 1974 important changes occurred among American Jews in their relations to Israel. A wide spectrum answered the old Israeli government slogan of *Ein Breira* (there's no choice) by creating a new organization called *Breira* (choice) to promote independent-minded approaches to Middle East peace. *Breira* has been joined by such groups as Tzedec Tzedec (Justice Justice) of Washington, D.C., Yozma (Initiative) of Los Angeles, Hutzpah (Audacity) of Chicago and the Middle East Peace Group of Boston. Speakers from Israel, who disagreed with Premier Itzhak Rabin's decision to ignore the Palestinian refugees and deal directly with King Hussein of Jordan (who ruled the territory occupied by the majority of the refugees) came to the United States offering unconventional alternatives for peace. Even the American B'nai B'rith has sponsored lectures by dissenting members of Israel's parliament, the Knesset.

In Canada few synagogue-goers and other Zionists hear such views. Before World War II, Reform rabbis in Canada were the vanguard for new ideas and alternative solutions. This is no longer true. Canadian synagogues and rabbis generally cling to Jewish establishment patterns of thought and behaviour. This makes it easier to close ranks and discourage dissent in disputes with non-Jewish groups. In the Canada of today, the ancient Jewish principle of dissent is thus severely muted.

United Church members who condemn Jews for their inability to accept criticism should understand that the Canadian Jewish community, like its sister communities in other lands, is fighting a desperate battle against the corrosive effects of a lessening identity, what Jews call assimilation. This struggle is not simply a matter of inculcating in Jews spiritual values, as with Christians; it involves the survival of the Jews as a distinct group through the Hebrew language, customs and folkways, in short, the survival of the Jewish way of life.

Jewish education of children, stressed in Judaism as no less important than prayer, is perhaps the Jewish community's most urgent task—without it they are sure to disappear. Yet in Canada today the Jewish system of education seems on the brink of bankruptcy, spiritually as well as financially. The evening and synagogue schools, designed specifically to transmit Judaism, are in the private view of schoolboard members already insolvent, and no longer serve either individual needs or communal hopes, paying rather lip-service to outdated forms and producing alienation among pupils (see Notes on Chapter 2).

Nor is the Jewish parochial school (Day School) producing the creative loyalist for which many had hoped. Jewish civil service has difficulty finding personnel—administrators, educators and fund-raisers. It may be too early to tell, but even Day Schools are not generating in young people the same pride in Jewish communal careers as in business and professional careers in the general community. Even a Day School graduate does not seem to consider himself a success until he has proved himself in the non-Jewish world.

Clearly, if the Jewish educational system is to carry out successfully its function of transmitting and maintaining the Jewish identity, its content and structure will have to be radically reorganized to bring them in line with the needs of Jews living in Canada today.

Without such a change in the educational system, there appears to be nothing but assimilation in store for the majority of the Jewish community in Canada. Intermarriage (where the non-Jewish partner converts) is now roaring over the Jewish community like a forest fire. In most of these marriages Jews feel that they are the losers, the suspicion being that converts will return to the majority. Mixed marriage (where Jew and non-Jew retain former identities) is becoming an increasingly popular life-style, and in these the Jewish partner is certain to be assimilated, as happened in France before World War II.

Orthodox Jews have no difficulty in coping with assimilation. To them the Jewish heritage is based on supernaturalism and meta-history. They hold the same faith in the advent of the messiah and in the bliss of the world to come as did their fathers. Orthodox children live out their entire lives within the social framework of the endemic community. So long as they observe the proprieties of that social life, they develop an awareness of being rooted, of belonging, of being cared for. They gain both social security and social status. Orthodoxy gives its children the ancient mental, moral and spiritual orientation, coupled with a belonging feeling, and thereby supplies them with a plan for life. With few exceptions, intermarriage is not their problem, and mixed marriages are almost unheard of.

For another group of Jews, who cannot accept the orthodox constrictions, there is no prospect of a future for Judaism outside the state of Israel. They see anti-Semitism not just as a passing madness but as a chronic disease of the whole of Western civilization. And even when anti-Semitism is held to a minimum, assimilation remains a real danger. They maintain, therefore, that it is quixotic to expect even democratic countries like Canada to give Jews the sense of security necessary for leading a normal life. Logically, then, for them the principal aim of Jewish education should consist of fostering in the child a yearning to live in Israel. Otherwise, if he is not to live there, if he is to live in the Diaspora, exiled from his ancient homeland, he will have to develop a heroic resignation to a life of self-denial and sacrifice, made necessary by dangers inherent in the attitude of the dominant population in his host country toward the Jewish minority group. But there is not a single school in the Canadian Jewish community that adopts such aims. The negators of the Diaspora, those who feel Judaism cannot survive outside Israel, are many, but when it comes to translating their philosophy into educational terms they are uncertain and hesitant.

Even greater uncertainty reigns among all other Jews, those who are neither orthodox nor Diaspora-negators. They believe in the Canadian democratic system and also in the state of Israel. They are eager to be integrated into Canadian society, yet they refuse to disappear as an identifiable group. In 4000 years of Jewish history only the modern Jewish communities of Western society have faced this problem.

The problem consists of finding economic and social security in Canadian citizenship and, at the same time, moral and spiritual security within the Jewish people and its tradition. Jews have been rather successful with the former but are still searching for the latter. The failure has been due largely to the community's tendency to patch and sew up the seams of the old Jewish order instead of building a new one to meet new conditions. Canadian Jews need a radical change in the content and structure of their community. But this process of internal change is impeded by the ongoing Middle East crisis and its demands. Preoccupied with these demands and with concern over increasing erosion of loyalty to the Jewish people and believing that in free Canada there was no necessity to carry on the ancient battle with the Church, Jews see the quarrel with the United Church not only as an unwelcome intrusion but as an addition to their already complicated identity burdens. The old fear of anti-Semitism and the new problem of assimilation combine to make them sensitive and impatient.

A crisis of the spirit, combined with worry about Jewish survival, gives Canadian Jews the jitters. One manifestation of such nervousness was their reaction to Key 73. Launched in 1973 by more than 130 church bodies and denominations, Key 73 was a continent-wide drive to win converts to Christianity. There was at once the feeling among some Jews that they must man the ramparts because the Christians had ganged up to convert them.

Key 73 did not garner much support from the United Church, and Jews had no reason to quarrel with the Church on this score. But missionary activity on a grand scale is always frightening to Jews, and this fear, combined with the quarrel over the Middle East, drowned out the United Church assurances that it was not bent on capturing Jewish souls. In the United States the Synagogue Council and the American Jewish Committee lectured the evangelists, especially those on high school and college campuses, that "the right of religious liberty involves the duty of respecting the conscience of others who do not feel the need to be witnessed to." In Canada, the Toronto Board of Rabbis, among other Jewish groups, issued a statement of concern "over the obvious missionary activity towards Jews in the Key 73 program."

Suspicion of Christian intentions dies hard with the Jews, especially the orthodox. Early in 1975, two liberal Canadian rabbis, returning from meetings of the World Council of Churches and the Vatican Commission for Religious Relations with the Jews, reported that the Vatican no longer regarded Jews as potential converts. They were criticized in a letter to the *Canadian Jewish News* (January 14, 1975) by orthodox Rabbi Immanuel Schochet, who contended that "at the bottom of all diplomatic doubletalk the Church's unequivocal reiteration (is) the duty to missionize and convert." He cited a dialogue between Cardinal Willebrand of the Vatican and the American Talmudic authority Rabbi Joseph Baer Soloveitchik, who challenged the Pope's representative to deny that the Church's aim was to missionize "the Jews first." The Cardinal, said Schochet, provided no adequate response.

Christian missions to the Jews are not a new phenomenon in Canada; they have been going on since the British conquest of Quebec in 1759 when only about ten Jews were living in this country. In this century "Hebrew Christians" and other missionaries have been trying to persuade Jews by letter and pamphlet that "God's word ends not with the prophet Malachi but with Revelations."

Generally Canadian Jews before the 1970s were able to take missionaries in their stride. They seemed to understand instinctively that religious liberty implies the right to proselytize, which is not much different from advertising. TV commercials also "bear witness" to the worth of a product or an idea. So long as there was no contravention of libel laws, Jews accepted the fact that missionizing is permissible in a free country. The Grits do it; the Tories do it; the NDP does it; Lever Brothers and General Motors do it. And Christians have a right to do it, if they are so inclined. In Chapter 10 I shall discuss the meaning of of missionizing in a modern context and how it may be counter-productive.

In fact, Canadian churches did not focus Key 73 on the Jews. The campaign was an American import, promoted by Carl F. H. Henry, a former editor of *Christianity Today*, evangelist Billy Graham and others who conceived the idea in 1968 at a motel near Washington's Francis Scott Key Bridge; hence the name Key 73. The United Church of Canada found aspects of Key 73 "less than compatible with (its) present belief and practice." In its official statement, it dissociated itself from any tendency to single out any group of people as a target.

The Canadian Roman Catholics, although associated with Key 73, were marginal in their participation. Most of the bishops stood with the late Father John Keating of Toronto's Catholic Information Centre: "A conversion drive toward the Jews would be unwarranted aggression. The basic drive to steal sheep is in contradiction to the whole spirit of the age. . . . The Church must have ideas in the marketplace, but they must be marketed without pressure or proselytism in the pejorative sense."

Even the evangelically minded Christians insisted that Jews were not the target. Dr. Leslie Hunt, principal of Toronto's Wycliffe College (Anglican) and chairman of Key 73's executive committee in Canada, said: "I am horrified that this activity should have been picked up as an onslaught upon the Jews. . . . We are concerned with the thousands of people who do not believe in anything. We have great love for the Jewish people and what they have done through the centuries." These comforting statements were to no avail. All Christians were suspect, including the United Church.

Key 73 was perhaps beneficial for the Jews of Canada in the sense that it acted as an alarm bell. It indicated that Jewish consciousness is geared to all things except their inner lives. They support Israel, build and operate Hebrew schools, administer charities and join synagogues. But they depend on rabbis to do their studying for them, on Israel for their identity and on the schools to implant in their children "the Jewish micro-dot." They are preached at from pulpits, harangued from annual meeting platforms and anti-defamation conferences, but few voices speak to their inner, personal needs. They rarely give thought to their own sense of value in Jewish communal life. It's enough to raise the funds that build the institutions that keep the Jewish machinery going.

This lack of spirituality is a disease of the age and not confined to Jews alone. What differentiates many Jews from adherents of other faiths is that they confuse "busyness" in Jewish communal activities with spiritual living. The clatter of federations, United Jewish Appeals, welfare funds, hospitals, homes for the aged, fraternal orders, public relations agencies and Zionist organizationalism is not necessarily the advance of inner forces. There is ample reason to believe that, by and large, the contribution of the vast network of Jewish agencies toward keeping alive in the young the desire to carry on as Jews, if not altogether negative, is negligible. Hence the reason why Canadian Jews cling to their hope symbol, the state of Israel, and why they fight like tigers when they think it is being maligned by United Church leaders, for Israel gives them what they find difficulty producing in their own lives, faith and aspiration as Jews.

There are some Jews within the synagogue—a fractional number—who do not soliloquize like Hamlet about their Jewishness, confident that it represents a link with the past and the future. If they are orthodox, they believe that God revealed his special concern in their ancestors. If they are non-orthodox, they accept the ethical and spiritual truths underlying the ancient traditions as inherently worth preserving.

There are some Jews outside the synagogue—another fraction—who find in the creative possibilities of Jewish life sufficient reason for maintaining it. They are convinced—on the basis of what Jews have been able to achieve as individuals in all fields of human endeavour, economic, social and cultural—that if Jews were permitted to live in peace they would contribute to the world more than their share as a people.

But most Jews seem unconcerned about creative Jewish values. They may be rich, of the middle income group or in the lower economic brackets. They may be presidents of Jewish organizations, institutions and agencies. Yet they are all alike in one respect; they lack a deep spiritual connection. They are motivated by philanthropy but not by the momentum of history and the beckoning of the Jewish future. They are for Israel more as a haven of refuge than as the flowering of the Jewish spirit.

In his voting habits the Jew also demonstrates defensive loyalty to his people. Occasionally one hears the denial that there is such a thing as a Jewish vote. There is a Jewish vote, and there should be no embarrassment in owning up to it. Jews know it, Canada's political parties know it and the Canadian Jewish Congress, which usually takes the high road on the subject, knows it.

Admittedly Jews in Canada do not vote *en bloc,* but group loyalty is a factor when a Jew enters the polling booth. It would be unnatural for him to leave his Jewish connections outside. Like other citizens, he is concerned about taxes, inflation and unemployment. Unlike them, he also worries about which political party would do more for Israel and for the right of Soviet Jews to emigrate.

A Jew just cannot say: I vote as a Canadian or as an American, period. He votes as a Jewish Canadian or a Jewish American. He approaches an issue or a candidate with the ancient query: Is it or he good or bad for Jews? Because of our system and population distribution, the question is of minor importance in Canada; political strategists reckon with it but do not underline it. In the US it looms large; it can mean victory or defeat for either of the major parties, and it worries those who manage campaigns (see Notes on Chapter 2).

In the whole of Canada there may be only two ridings—Mount Royal (represented by Prime Minister Pierre Trudeau) and Toronto-Eglinton (former External Affairs Minister Mitchell Sharp's bailiwick)—where Jews can swing the vote. In the US if a presidential candidate can make inroads in the Jewish vote in the crucial states of California, New York, Pennsylvania and Illinois, his election prospects are considerably enhanced.

Only in one instance have Jews figured in the Canadian politics of recent decades. In the summer of 1975 the premier of Ontario, who was embarking on a provincial election with diminishing prospects, withdrew support for a United Nations conference on crime which was to be held in Toronto, because Palestine Liberation Organization representatives were to be present. Leaders of the opposition parties agreed with this decision, and the federal government requested the UN to change the conference site. Jewish officialdom regarded the decision as a moral triumph for the nation, but many Canadians considered it the result of ethnocentric pressure, setting an unwelcome precedent.

This incident was an exception to the general rule of Jewish political powerlessness in Canada. Nevertheless, although Jews as a group may not be a potent political force in Canada, they are sensitive to political nuances which concern them as Jews and they will vote defensively on them.

The defensive character of the Canadian Jewish community—reinforced by fund-raising, the fight against assimilation, anti-Semitism and Christian missionizing, and voting patterns—is further enhanced by a submissive Jewish press. The Jewish weeklies in Toronto, Montreal, Winnipeg and Vancouver are generally spokesmen of the established Jewish institutions—the Welfare Fund, the Congress and the Zionist organizations. The function of a newspaper in a free society is to be a watchdog, and when it fails to warn and criticize it becomes a house organ. The world of the Anglo-Jewish and Yiddish press in Canada is populated by house organs, except for the Toronto *Jewish Outlook* and the *Wochenblatt* (Weekly News), both leftist publications. Toronto's biweekly *Jewish Standard* considers itself another exception. In the past, it has generally taken a stand in opposition to Welfare Fund decisions in matters of policy and in line with the Canadian Jewish Congress; this line has now been blunted with the merger of the two organizations in cities like Toronto and Winnipeg. The *Standard* also takes a hard-line stand on Israel, with a correspondent in Jerusalem who is often to the right of the Israeli government. For a period of about two years it published articles critical of Israeli policy, which I wrote, but compensated for this concession with militant pro-government editorial rebuttals.

The most flourishing papers are in Toronto and Vancouver

(*Jewish Western Bulletin*), with Montreal served by the Toronto operations. Far and away, the weekly with the greatest influence and largest circulation (about 30,000) is the Toronto-based *Canadian Jewish News*, once owned by a transplanted New York newsman who edited a colourful product with an outspoken orthodox bias, often to the exclusion of other communal points of view. Yet it had the virtue of generating controversy.

Today the *CJN*, which until recently also published the *Chronicle-Review*, is financed by the "big givers," who have tied it into a deal with the central fund-raising agency, the United Jewish Welfare Fund. The arrangement involves the exchange of editorial space for subscriptions, paid for by the Welfare Fund on behalf of its contributors. The Fund finds it cheaper to take space in the CJN than to publish its own paper. At the same time, the arrangement affords the CJN "guaranteed circulation."

Theoretically Canada's strongest Jewish newspaper may argue that its deal with the Welfare Fund does not influence editorial policy or handling of the news, in the same way that metropolitan newspapers claim to be independent of advertisers. What redeems the general press, however, as the Davey Report on Canada's Mass Media indicates, is that it does not depend on a single organization for its core of subscribers and it employs a highly professional staff. Such a staff will often oppose the publisher on a question of the priority of news or profit. But an ethnic newspaper cannot afford that kind of staff. In a subscription deal with a dominant communal agency, its efforts at independence are doomed from the start. (See Notes on The Setting regarding freedom of the press in the Jewish community.)

Inevitably we must look at the *Canadian Jewish News* and the United Church *Observer* side by side. The contrast in their respective roles is another factor promoting misunderstanding between Jewish and United Church leaders. Both periodicals claim freedom from interference with editorial content. The Jewish paper's editor, however, is responsible to a board of directors which is in effect the publisher. *The Observer* combines the editor and publisher in one person, A. C. Forrest, who is answerable to a board but who has greater leeway in policy decisions. The result is that the *Canadian Jewish News* reflects the character of the Welfare Fund-Jewish Congress while *The Observer*'s style mirrors the character and convictions of its editor-publisher.

In sum, the *Canadian Jewish News* is somewhat less than what its masthead legend says—"an independent community newspaper serving as a forum for diverse viewpoints." It serves the community but not independently, and the diverse viewpoints it presents do not violate the limits imposed by Jewish self-defence. *The Observer*, on the other hand, represents more than its statement—"published monthly under the authority of the General Council, The United Church of Canada." The Council has authority but seldom exercises it for fear of offending the principle of free thought. This gives the editor-publisher great authority, an arrangement Jews find difficult to understand because it could not prevail in their own community.

While Jews complain about the United Church and are on the defensive, the conclusion should not be drawn that they live with an attitude of mistrust toward everything non-Jewish. Obviously they have a part in the social, economic and cultural life of their country, something their ancestors on the European continent did not have, and like other citizens, they give to the common welfare of the Canadian people the best in their power to give. For activist Jews, the best they have to give is to be found in Judaism, the repository of centuries of Jewish spiritual experience. As convinced Jews and loyal Canadians, they struggle to incorporate into Canadian life the universal values of Judaism and to utilize the Jewish way of life as an inspiration to preserve these values. If they could succeed at this, it would mean renewing in Judaism itself its universal significance and enriching at the same time their Canadian home. How to do this while maintaining ties with the state of Israel, beleaguered and looking inward, is the problem today.

The Canadian Jew cannot live, as philosopher Mordecai Kaplan has said of the American Jew, "with his loins perpetually girt for a hasty departure for Eretz Israel." That would not inspire his neighbours with confidence in him or with respect for Judaism. He must live positively with faith in his future in Canada while fighting for his security and identity both here and abroad. That is a complicated and excruciating way to live, but historically the Jew has always lived in crisis. "It's hard to be a Jew," said the Yiddish storyteller Sholom Aleichem, and Marc Chagall, the artist, pictured him as a fiddler playing while balancing on the roof. Not infrequently there is glory in being Jewish, and that is what justifies the fiddler's precarious perch.

No different from his ancestors, the Canadian Jew believes his existence is always precarious. Any pressure from without could topple him from his hazardous position. When *The Observer* publishes articles he considers anti-Semitic or anti-Israel and United Church leaders fail to announce their displeasure with *The Observer* stand, he reacts passionately, because he is firmly convinced that his security and status are at stake.

CHAPTER THREE

The Accused

There is a widespread impression that had A. C. Forrest been more cautious in his comments on Jews, the European Holocaust, the role of Israel and the plight of the Palestinian refugees, the quarrel between the Jewish community and the United Church of Canada might have been avoided. That is a misleading assumption. Forrest did help to precipitate the quarrel and gave it shape. His editorials and articles sparked editorial comment in the general and the Jewish press and aroused Christians and Jews alike to write letters to the newspapers. He wrote with emotion, and it is no surprise that the response was emotional. But the quarrel was not only of Forrest's making; the seeds of dissension between the two communities existed from the founding of the United Church in 1925.

Many in the United Church insist that Forrest does not represent their views. Many say he does. Certainly the emphasis in the *Proceedings of the General Council,* the governing body of the Church, does not always square with *The Observer* editor's viewpoint. Why, then, Jews wonder, does the Church empower him to make policy decisions for its publication?

The question touches basic differences in the history and character of the two communities. One reason for misunderstanding is the Jewish fear that the majority is in a position to take advantage of the minority. It is the centuries-old suspicion the Jew has for the Church; it is the lesson about Christians history has taught the Jews (see Chapters 7 and 10). As a minority, Jews think in terms of self-protection and organized, unified action. The momentum of Jew-hatred persists for them even in a free society like Canada. There is no official anti-Semitism here as there once was in Europe, but Jews still meet social anti-Semitism, and fear, with good reason, that the full-blooded kind is just beneath the surface.

The questions Canadian Jewish leaders ask of the United Church reveal these ancient suspicions. If the United Church is concerned about its Jewish neighbours, why is it officially silent when *The Observer* publishes an insensitive editorial on the Holocaust? Why official silence when *The Observer* permits the publication of a patently anti-Semitic advertisement by the British-Israelites? Why silence in the face of Arab attacks on Israel?

No such defensiveness or ancient suspicion exists among members of a majority group like the United Church. Most of them find it hard to understand Jewish insecurity, often regarding it as parochialism or paranoia. They have the self-confidence to survive a public wrangle. That is what free speech is all about, they say, and that is the prevailing attitude in the United Church: "I may not like what Forrest says, but by the ghost of Martin Luther's ninety-five theses, he sure has the right to say it, especially in a magazine like *The Observer* which represents the spirit of the Church, a spirit that is enhanced by controversy." This statement is not a direct quotation, but it reflects the attitude of a large segment of United Church members.

The Canadian Jewish community does not understand the vital influence this emphasis on free speech and free thought has on the relationship between the official United Church and *The Observer*. George Morrison, former secretary of the General Council, who probably knows relationships among United Church subsidiaries and agencies as well as anyone, defines *The Observer* as "a publication of the Church in the field of religious writing, freed from the policies of our education people." Forrest is "not writing a curriculum of theological education." The aim of the Church through *The Observer* is to produce a kind of *Christian Science Monitor* in Canada, "something that will be holding up Christian values, a quality of life." Former moderator Bruce McLeod says: "*The Observer* remains an untamed and vigorous voice within our Church. It is not a house organ like, say, the *IBM Weekly News*. Its editor is both loved and respected (if not always agreed with) within our community. Nor will any statement questioning either the responsible use he makes of press freedom or the integrity of his continuing concern for justice in the Middle East and elsewhere ever be signed by me." In short, the official United Church vigorously defends *The Observer*'s right of free speech.

But Jews do not accept this defence. Jewish theologian Emil Fackenheim says: "Ever since the Six Day War the most visible and powerful groups in the United Church have behaved toward the Jewish people as though this Church were, indeed, a monolithic body, and their behaviour has been hostile. To be more specific, *The Observer* has shown an ever-increasing anti-Jewish bias, and United Church officials, while seeking refuge behind the editor's freedom of speech, have either themselves kept silent or else used their own freedom of speech only to defend the policies of the editor, or even to attack, often vociferously, those who opposed these policies, be they Jewish and especially should they be Christian. No official I know of has made use of his freedom of speech to oppose the anti-Jewish policies of *The Observer*."

The president of the Canadian Jewish Congress, Sydney M. Harris, goes further. Like most Jews, Harris does not, or cannot, accept the separation of *The Observer* from official United Church policy. He thinks of *The Observer* as having the same relation to the official church body as the Congress *Bulletin* has to the Congress executive. If the editor of the *Bulletin* published material contrary to the policy of the executive, he would be removed. "It is the attitudinal climate in the office of *The Observer* that permitted the Salter ad to be printed," says Harris. "That ad is anti-Semitic. If that's the kind of ad they will print, they're living in an atmosphere of anti-Semitism in that editorial office. The sooner the United Church does something to clean its own house, the sooner we will be rid of that kind of problem."

For the Jews the issue is clearly defined; they demand a clear-cut, definitive stand from the Church.

For the Church the problems are more complex. *The Observer* is not the official organ of the Church, and may oppose church policy so long as it gives expression to contrary opinions. Fackenheim may be justified in his charge that United Church officials do not stand up to *The Observer*'s editorial positions, but that is a comment on the disposition of the officials, not on the policy of the official United Church. It is the General Council, the governing body, and not *The Observer*, which sets policy for the Church. On issues like anti-Semitism and the Holocaust, the Council has no trouble taking an unequivocal stand. When it comes to the state of Israel, however, the Church's position is not as simple and sometimes gives an impression of non-support of Israel. Most Jews would agree with Albert Rose of the University of Toronto who thinks the United Church has failed Israel. "One wonders what the United Church would have said," muses Rose, "if Tel Aviv had been encircled and occupied by one or more Arab armies. There would have been a lot of carnage; we know this from what the Arabs have said, and I no longer ignore what they're saying. I doubt very much whether we would have heard more than some pious remarks about the Geneva Convention."

It is this tendency to expect the worst from the United Church that makes it imperative for Jews to be clear on the Church's official position toward the Middle East. It would be tragic for United Church-Jewish relations for Jews to conclude that because the Church does not react quickly and vocally on behalf of Israel it is indifferent to the Jewish state's fate.

Bruce McLeod has explained the choices facing the United Church. He says the Church can react to the plight of Israel in one of three ways. "One way is to reason that Israel must be publicly supported, come what may. Another way is to argue that any criticism of Israel is inconceivable because it may encourage anti-Semites, even if well meant; but since Israel makes errors, the only course open is to be silent rather than critical." The second way is "a copout" to McLeod. It means in effect sacrificing concern for Israel, which is unthinkable.

As between criticism, which may be misinterpreted by the anti-Semites, and unequivocal support, the latter has greater risks and should be avoided. The main risk, argues McLeod, is that one may overlook the interests of the Palestinians, who are homeless in part because of Western Christian attempts to solve the problem of anti-Semitism at their expense.

"I have to believe and do believe," says McLeod, "that there is a third way. There is a way of being sensitive to each other, of hearing each other's memory and guilt and talking about the Middle East in mutual respect; not just scoring points off each other, but listening to the feelings that are really there."

During the Yom Kippur War of October 1973 he tested this method. He wanted to give consolation to both Jews and Palestinians in Toronto, and brought to each in turn his statement of concern:

> We recognize and appreciate the memories and fears that are yours in the Jewish and Palestinian communities, as war once again engulfs the Middle East. We want to identify with you in re-affirming Israel's right to live and to live in peace; and in declaring concern for the rights of the refugees, once more caught up in violent conflict.
>
> We join in condemning the inhumanity of war which, as always, is claiming innocent victims on both sides; and we pray that it will cease. We join in hoping for early negotiations which will guarantee Israel her safety within clear and agreed borders, which will deal justly with the refugee problem, and which will inaugurate a time when Israeli and Arab shall "sit under his vine and under his fig tree and none shall make him afraid."

McLeod quickly discovered that middle ground is a notoriously exposed, dangerous and thankless position. Neither community welcomed his words. Each scheduled its separate rally. Each took the traditional attitude of the antagonist in any war: If you are not with us, you are against us. McLeod did not react as Jews wanted him to, yet it is impossible to argue that he was unconcerned about Israel's welfare.

As a practical consideration, John W. Burbidge of Trent University wonders whether it is fair for Jews to expect an institution to protest. "Is moral action the responsibility of institutions or individuals? How would the United Church as an institution protest? Some leading individuals might, and some did I suspect, but the mills of institutional decision-making grind exceedingly slowly. Can you talk about the Canadian Jewish Congress protesting about the counter-revolution in Chile at the time it happened?"

For almost three decades the Middle East has been an agonizing issue for the United Church. Over the years it has considered the Israeli side, then the Palestinian, and back again, writing position papers and battling the problem in and out of the Committee on the Church and International Affairs. It is important to be precise about the United Church's stand, to review the reports of General Council resolutions, to trace their development and to be aware of how definitive conclusions were reached. Without such details, Canadian Jews cannot hope to comprehend where the United Church stands and why. The why is as important as the where.

We are ready to look at the *Record of Proceedings of the General Council* of the United Church of Canada, where the Church's official position is defined. The record consists of general expository statements or background papers, and resolutions. The former are far more instructive regarding the Church's motivations. A resolution is the lowest common denominator of opinion, the bare bones left from the meat of a nutritive discussion; the general statements reveal attitudes, doubts, bias, faith and a sense of inadequacy about a complex human situation.

The General Council bases its resolutions on surprisingly little christology and only the most liberal theology, an important consideration for Jews. The Council asks why a Christian thinks he has something to say on international affairs. Its answers could be accepted by most Jews without reservations: men and nations have a duty to use wisely their God-given powers; a thread of purpose runs through history; Jesus, in line with biblical prophecy, revealed the technique for reconciliation, rejecting physical power and choosing dedication; corporate evil is as real as the individual brand; every nation has the right of existence so long as it grants the same right to others and refrains from maltreating minorities; the Christian interest is not identical with the nation but goes beyond national borders to touch and serve all mankind. Perhaps the most incisive perception is to be found in the *Proceedings* for 1960: "No cause and no state can be completely equated with the kingdom of God."

From these answers it is plain that intensely liberal concepts, rising above narrow theological concerns, prevail in the official Church in the area of international affairs. Our concern is with one area of these affairs, the Middle East, and here the humanist element prevails over theology. There is hardly a hint of the special scriptural relationship between Jews and Christians, a relationship that does not apply to Christians and Muslims. Jews and Palestinians receive equal treatment as actors in a historical drama.

Briefly stated, the official position of the United Church on the Middle East is that it seeks the welfare and security of the state of Israel and at the same time a solution to the plight of the Palestinian refugees, condemning acts of injustice on both sides. However, while Arab refugees are of primary concern, no support is given to compensation for Jewish refugees from Arab lands except in one background paper. The status of Jerusalem receives little attention, and the Jordanian government escapes censure for barring Jewish access to holy sites in the eastern section of the city during the period 1948-67.

The definitive resolution on the Middle East was adopted by the General Council in 1968. It reaffirmed the stand, "stated and restated" since 1948, that "the state of Israel should be recognized by the Arab nations and be permitted to live in peace, secure from threats or acts of force." It urged Israel to withdraw from territories "occupied by force since June 1967, with minor boundary changes," and called upon her to permit displaced Palestinians to return to their homes or be compensated for loss. All this is covered in the first five sections of the resolution.

Section (6) of the resolution appears to be in response to reaction in the Jewish community over a rash of articles in the United Church *Observer* in the months following the Six Day War, condemning Israel for her policies towards the refugees. It is a defence of *The Observer*'s right to self-expression: "We deplore suggestions that those who criticize Israeli policies are necessarily anti-Semitic and that critics of Arab policies must be unsympathetic to the plight of the Arab people. The policies of Arab and Israeli governments are always open to the judgment of public opinion."

This was an evenhanded judgment since it also included the Arabs as fair targets for criticism. But the Arabs were not feeling the effects of *The Observer*'s criticism, and their inclusion seems somewhat contrived. Evidently the Council was steering a mid-course between *Observer* supporters and opponents within the Church.

More to the point is section (7) which envisions meetings of Christians "with representatives of both the Jewish and Arab communities in Canada, in order to seek ways to improve understanding and promote justice and peace." Sadly this kind of United Church leadership has not been carried out extensively on the Canadian scene, where it might have helped to reduce domestic tensions. Arabs and Jews in Canada constitute two solitudes, and little attempt is made to get moderates talking to moderates.

Section (8) was an obvious yet prophetic warning, fulfilled five years later in 1973, that "if Arabs continue to refuse to recognize Israel and maintain a threatening posture, and if Israel continues to occupy the lands she took and insists on unilateral arrangements with Arab nations without United Nations assistance, there is likely to be war again. . . ."

Throughout all the *Proceedings* on the Middle East, the General Council is eager to be associated with guidelines laid down by the World Council of Churches and the United Nations, a natural inclination for those who stress universalism. The desire to believe in the UN is understandable, but in the UN as it was intended to be, not what it has become. Section (8)'s phrase, "without UN assistance," sounds rather innocent today with the international body weighted prejudicially against the Jewish state. Israel cannot expect UN assistance. The majority of the 140-odd UN members oppose Israel not strictly out of moral conviction (many were aided through Israel's technological programs to Afro-Asian nations) but in great measure because of vote-swapping with Arab oil-producing countries.

Even in 1968, the General Council's criticism of Israel for insisting on making unilateral arrangements with Arab nations without UN assistance made little sense. Israel's demand was not for unilateral arrangements with the Arabs but bilateral agreements based on direct negotiations. Admittedly, continued occupation of conquered lands generates bitterness. But withdrawal from occupied territory, while at the same time creating a climate of non-belligerency, is not as simple as Section (8) of the *Proceedings of the General Council* makes it seem.

Three years later, in 1971, the Council adopted a statement in which it supported the now famous UN Resolution 242 which calls for the withdrawal of Israeli armed forces from territories occupied in the 1967 conflict and "the termination of all claims or states of belligerency and respect for and acknowledgment of the sovereignty, territorial integrity and political independence of every state in the area and their right to live in peace within secure and recognized boundaries free from threats or acts of force."

Resolution 242 has posed a crucial question ever since it was unanimously adopted at the UN in November 1967. Which comes first, Israeli withdrawal or termination of belligerency? Obviously, the fair way would be to tie them together and implement them by stages. This would mean negotiation between Israel and the Arab states, a move the General Council of the United Church was now advocating.

In addition, the Council's 1971 stand called for guarantees of freedom of navigation through the Suez Canal and the Straits of Tiran into the Gulf of Akaba and for the establishment of demilitarized zones as a method of assuring the political independence of Arab and Jewish states, measures endorsed by almost every political group on the Israeli side but which would have to be sold to the Arabs.

The 1971 Council not only repeated its demand for a just settlement of the refugee problem but urged the Canadian government "to back any action of the UN which, while guaranteeing the security of Israel, aims to secure justice and self-determination for the Palestinian Arabs." This carried the United Church into the camps of the moderates on both sides of the struggle. In effect, it supported the partition of the old British Mandate territory into two states, Jewish and Palestinian.

Both Israeli extremists and the Palestine Liberation Organization—if Yasser Arafat's demand at the UN in November 1974 for a secular, democratic state is to be taken at face value—are opposed to the creation of two states. Each group feeds on the other, the Israeli "hawks" pointing to the PLO as proof of Arab intentions to destroy the state of Israel and the PLO, in turn, getting fuel from Israel's right-wing groups for the argument that expansionist ambitions are inherent in Israel.

In Israel the "doves" are more organized than their opposite numbers in Arab states, and are less intimidated and more vocal. They include the Zionist Left and most of the liberal element. Most Israelis would be reconciled to the Palestinian claim to statehood on the West Bank if they could be assured that such a state would not be used as a base for attack against Israel. This is one reason why Israeli moderates have little political influence; they cannot offer such assurance.

While the resolutions of the General Council attempt to define the stand of the United Church on Middle East issues, the biennial reviews of events, or background papers, are more revealing, providing an opportunity to follow the attitudes and decisions that led to the resolutions.

In 1954, in its review of events, the General Council was worried that five years after the armistice agreements at the end of the first Arab-Israel war, there was no movement on either side toward a settlement of the issues. It also expressed concern that the Arab case was not as well known as the Israeli arguments, that the Israelis enjoyed "an immense propaganda advantage" over the Arabs, especially in North America.

In the Council's view, this Israeli propaganda blamed the Arabs themselves for the refugee problem and Arab intransigence as the only barrier to peace. But there are other facts not to be ignored, said the Council—that the refugees lost their homes because of the partition of the country and as "the direct result" of the establishment of the Jewish state by force of arms; that the UN Assembly's decision on partition was not ratified by the Security Council; that Israel subsequently added by force of arms twenty per cent more than the territory assigned her by the UN; and that UN resolutions on repatriation of refugees and the internationalization of Jerusalem were rejected by Israel.

The Council was right in noting that the Israel story received better coverage on this side of the Atlantic than the Arab case, but that was due in large part not to Israeli propaganda but to the romance of the rebirth of the Jewish state after almost two millennia. It is only in recent years that the government of Israel has been propagandizing. In the early 1950s there was no need to; journalists themselves were starry-eyed.

The Council failed to achieve objectivity when discussing access to the holy places. It stated that Jews, Muslims and Christians had the right to visit their respective holy sites, most of which at the time were in Jordan. There was no recognition of the fact that while Christians and Muslims did enjoy free access to Jerusalem Jews were barred from such visits.

Nevertheless, the Council's 1954 review realistically summed up the situation: "As the Arabs must accept the existence of Israel and learn to live with her as a neighbour, so Israel must accept her actual share of responsibility for compensation to the refugees who now cannot be reabsorbed by Israel in their old homes for political and psychological reasons."

Two years later, the Council's review of events once more responded to the concern of delegates that the Arab case was not getting a "fair shake." In 1956 the opening paragraph said: "As a Church we must be careful not to take a partisan position. Our policy cannot be less than that of a 'just and impartial friendship' to *all* peoples of the Middle East." For the first time the *Proceedings* dwell at some length on the Jewish refugees as well as on the displaced Palestinians: "The grim fact must now be realized that large numbers of [Palestinian] refugees will never be able to return home. Their places are already taken by the large numbers of immigrants brought to Israel, many of them likewise refugees from other countries. But two wrongs do not make a right." And here the Council hits Western countries hard for "shamefully" evading their responsibility to the Jewish displaced persons. One looks in vain for a reference to Jewish refugees from Arab lands. It was to be fifteen years before the governing body remedied this blind spot.

In its unrelenting search for balance, the Council in 1958 turned, for the first time, to an almost affectionate look at the accomplishments of the state of Israel. This was shortly after Israel had withdrawn from the territories she captured in the 1956 Sinai campaign. She had bowed to Soviet Chairman Nikita Khrushchev's threats and hearkened to US President Dwight D. Eisenhower's assurances, and this evidently made her a co-operative international citizen in the eyes of the Council.

> On the Israeli side we find a game little nation which has opened its doors to a million Jewish refugees from every part of the world to come and build a home.
>
> With money and service and brains from the West it is building farms out of the desert, a magnificent university and splendid government buildings out of the bare rock of the Jerusalem hills, highways along the valleys, a shipping trade on the sea, and an industrial and agricultural economy out of the labours of people who until their return have been the shopkeepers of the world. In Israel today it is more dignified to farm or build than to buy or sell.
>
> The Hebrew language and history must be learned by little children and urbane immigrant Jews from Europe and America. No Jew and few Christians can help but thrill at what is being accomplished in Israel.

At last United Church leaders had begun to understand why the Jewish state had been getting most of the Middle East exposure in the North American press. The Zionist organizations of Canada could not have said it better.

Still, the Council had a "small" reservation; "It is recognized, however, that this is a national more than a religious movement." Here the General Council makes the common error of the liberal

Christian who generally fails to grasp the religious origins of Jewish peoplehood. It should not be equated with contemporary ideas of nationalism. The first modern Zionist settlers in Palestine in the late nineteenth century called themselves *Bilu* (a Hebrew acronym for the prophet Isaiah's words: "Come, let us go up to the mountain of the Lord"). Even Theodor Herzl, the first political Zionist, and Chaim Weizmann and David Ben-Gurion, the first Israeli president and prime minister respectively, all secular Jews, conceived of Jewish peoplehood in the biblical sense, as an instrument for the establishment of universal justice and peace. The Hebrew word *am* (people) has none of the implications of national sovereignty which characterize modern nationalism. The *am* must reflect God's moral law, which alone is sovereign. Thus, even in a mood of acclaim, the General Council was unable to understand the essence of the Zionist revival.

For almost the whole of the following decade the General Council paid little heed to the Arab-Israeli struggle. In 1968, the year the Council passed its definitive resolution on the Middle East, four paragraphs recounted events since the Six Day War, without any attempt at analysis. In 1971, the *Proceedings* presented an objective treatment by Professor W. S. McCullough, obviously a summation authorized by the Council, and on which the governing body based its resolution of the same year. The paper reiterated support of UN Resolution 242, defined the Palestinian guerrillas as a "disturbing element," and addressed the Arabs for the first time in firm tones:

> The governments of Jordan, Egypt, Lebanon and Syria must be prepared to acknowledge the existence of the state of Israel and to accept its borders as they will be determined by negotiation. This is a most difficult question, for the issue is charged with high emotion and it involves a complete *volte-face* in the traditional Arab policy. The border lines agreed upon would have to be internationally guaranteed, both to guard Israel from the necessity of waging recurring defensive wars and to allay Arab suspicions that Israel aims at territorial expansion. Furthermore, Egypt must assent to the right of passage for all ships through the Gulf of Akaba and the Suez Canal. Finally, the Arab governments concerned must be prepared to co-operate fully with whatever commission is set up to supervise the resettlement of refugees. As part of the refugee picture, those Jews previously domiciled in the Arab world, who became refugees after 1948 and many of whom settled in Israel, must be included among those for whom suitable compensation should be worked out.

At last, one meets concern in the United Church for Jewish refugees from Arab lands. It took decades for the General Council to arrive at this kind of plain talk to both sides in the Middle East conflict. Since this background paper is part of the *Record of Proceedings,* it reflects the developing concepts of the General Council and must be included in any judgment of the Church's Middle East posture.

McCullough's background paper in the 1972 *Proceedings* was also fair, though he had to deal with the controversial report of a UN Human Rights subcommittee which investigated Israeli practices in the occupied territories. Arab spokesmen had complained of mistreatment of Arabs, dynamiting of their houses and group penalties for individual crimes (the Israelis called it "administrative punishment"). Israel insisted the investigations were one-sided, unless they included maltreatment of Jews in Arab countries, and refused the subcommittee permission to visit conquered areas. In March 1972, the subcommittee condemned Israel for violating human rights. McCullough wryly commented: "If we take for granted that all UN commissions do their work responsibly, then neither Israel nor the rest of the world can avoid paying serious attention to the findings of this particular commission."

On the basis of this background paper the General Council in the summer of 1972 adopted Resolution 5(c) on the Middle East, which challenged a proposed loan to Israel of up to $100 million from the Canadian Export Development Corporation in light of the UN subcommittee's findings. It urged a meeting with the Prime Minister of Canada to discuss the loan. It further suggested a joint delegation from the Canadian Council of Churches, the Canadian Catholic Council of Bishops and the United Church, or failing such a combination, that the United Church go to Ottawa alone.

Zionists argued that the Council's resolution was faulty because it was based on the report of a subcommittee, albeit representing the United Nations, but which did not even visit the occupied territories. How, then, could its findings have been accurate? Should not the General Council have been concerned also with the condition of Jews in Arab countries? Why the haste to make a decision denying Israel aid? Why the recognition of Israel's alleged sins and not those of the Arabs?

Actually no rush ensued to implement the resolution. Many months passed, during which United Church people developed reservations, the *Canadian Churchman* (an Anglican journal) accused the Canadian Council of Churches of foot-dragging and counsel was taken with the Canadian Jewish Congress. In the end, the resolution was overtaken by the Yom Kippur War and became one of its casualties. Had it lived, said the then moderator Bruce McCleod, it would have been handled "with a new attitude, a new responsibility and an awareness of sensitivity required in the Canadian context."

The new spirit permeated the background paper on the Middle East in the 1974 *Proceedings.* It is a solemn document, supporting an independent state for Palestinian Arabs, reaffirming Israel's right to security, and condemning the Palestinian terrorists, though they were not called that but rather "fanatics who in desperation resort to appalling acts of violence both against Israelis and friends of Israel." The statement added: "More sober Arabs know that such violence is non-productive and cannot lead to a solution of the basic problem." It also observed that the oil embargo during the October war helped the morale of the Palestinian refugees. Again and again the struggle to maintain concern for two just causes in conflict is implicit in the words.

The General Council's resolutions of 1974 reflect the anguish of the background paper, with two additions: the Palestinians should be represented at the proposed Middle East peace conference in Geneva, and the Soviet Union should abide by the UN Human Rights Declaration and allow Jews to emigrate "without hindrance." The first demand is a logical step from the long-standing defence of the Palestinian right to self-determination. The second is significant because many Soviet Jewish immigrants settle in Israel, swelling the population, a cause of Arab anger. Seemingly contradictory, the two demands are compatible within the Church's search for balance and justice.

It was said above that the General Council's background papers reveal self-doubt and a sense of inadequacy. Nothing marks out the character of the official United Church more distinctly than self-questioning, the desire to be righteous but not self-righteous. Perhaps that is the appropriate note on which to end this chapter. The General Council concludes its 1974 *Proceedings* with a prayer, a natural enough exercise for a religious community. Yet nowhere else among the Middle East resolutions is there resort to explicit supplications. The prayer reads: "O God, who has made of one blood all nations to dwell upon the earth, forgive us, we beseech you, for any act or attitude of ours that may have caused disharmony or added to injustice. . . ."

It is clear that the General Council's emphasis is a dual one—on the right of the state of Israel to live and on the need of an identity for the Palestinians. Over and over again in its *Proceedings,* the Church insists that the Arabs must accept the existence of Israel, that Israel's security must be guaranteed—a fact of which many Canadian Jews seem unaware.

Does A. C. Forrest stress the two identities, Israeli and Palestinian, with the same clarity? It is time to turn to the record of *The Observer*.

CHAPTER FOUR

The Untamed

In the United Church, A. C. Forrest's image is that of the untamed editor; in the Jewish community it is that of the anti-Semite. Which is the more authentic? Let us explore the record.

Many have criticized Forrest; few have taken the trouble to wade through the files of *The Observer* since 1955, when he took over as editor from A. J. Wilson. Writer-editor Arnold Ages is one of the few. He examined *Observer* issues for a twenty-five-year period from 1945 on behalf of the Anti-Defamation League (ADL) of B'nai B'rith and produced in August 1969 a "Basic Document" called "The United Church *Observer* and the State of Israel." The stated purpose of Basic Documents is "to serve as the data in the development of ADL policy." The Ages study was the only analysis by a Jew of *Observer* policy on the Middle East and helped not only to develop the ADL stance but to shape general Jewish attitudes toward Forrest, his publication, and the United Church. It was widely distributed in the Jewish community. Since it had such a widespread influence on Jews, it must act as a Rosetta Stone in my investigation of *The Observer* files.

Examining old magazine copies is an unenviable job; it is always possible to miss a crucial point and to be accused thereby of being selective. Without questioning his motives or sponsorship, it is a fact that Ages omits a number of *Observer* articles from his consideration, omissions that affect his judgments and conclusions.

He makes three general observations:

> Even before the period of the current editor, *The Observer* editor had a peculiarly ambivalent attitude toward the question of Jewish nationalism and a Jewish state.
>
> The problem of Israel and the Arabs has never been a preoccupation with the magazine and has never been more than a peripheral concern; that is, until August 1967.

> Since that period, a kind of forum has been presented on the Arab-Israeli question, but from a purely statistical angle it has been so heavily weighted in favour of the Arab viewpoint that the word forum has been denuded of all sense.

The last statement is accurate; the first two are not. Editor-in-Chief A. J. Wilson, Forrest's predecessor, was not ambivalent on the issue of Jewish nationalism; he was against it, just as he was opposed to the concept of a Vatican state. On April 1, 1948, a month before the establishment of Israel, an editorial (missed by Ages) appeared in *The Observer*: "At a time when small nations are being absorbed into large national units, it seems contrary to historic processes that a new sovereign state should be set up for the Jews in Palestine. We have one politico-religious sovereign state in the world, and the Vatican has confused political and religious issues time and time again. Another in Palestine is bound to increase national and racial tensions."

Wilson admitted that the Jews "have done a phenomenal job in Palestine, building up the waste places and making the desert blossom as the rose." But why statehood? "If they would be satisfied to live, and work, and to enjoy the prosperity they have wrested from the soil, without fanatically insisting on the status of a sovereign state, all would be well. For the sake of the peace of the world, the Jews should renounce their claims for an immediate sovereign state."

Nothing could be less ambivalent. Forrest was not the innovator of anti-Zionist sentiment in *The Observer*; he was merely carrying it on.

As for Ages' second conclusion, on its face the contention that the Middle East was only of peripheral concern to *The Observer* before August 1967, appears incredible. Implicit in Wilson's 1948 editorial was deep concern for the fate of the Middle East: "One of the ironies of history is that Palestine, the home of our Christian religion, should after twenty centuries be at this time a scene of bloodshed and hatred. . . . All Christendom has reflected on the passion, death and resurrection of our Lord. The journey he made during his last week on earth was followed in imagination by devout Christians. . . . In the city where those very scenes were enacted, along the dusty roads he travelled, and on the hillsides where he taught peace and love and good will among all people and nations, Jews have been killing Arabs, and Arabs have been bombing and destroying Jewish property and life."

Peripheral concern? It is simply not accurate to say that until August 1967 *The Observer* had only a marginal interest in Israel and the

Arabs. From 1955, when Forrest succeeded Wilson, until just after the Six Day War, at least thirty-six issues carried articles, editorials or letters on the Middle East, and thirteen other issues dealt with related subjects of Jews and Judaism. In the same period, *The Observer* published only four articles on Roman Catholicism, including two on Vatican II, a historic meeting which affected half a billion Christian adherents. On December 15, 1955, three months after he took over, Forrest gave notice of his policy on Israel:

> Strong and influential pressure is being brought to bear on the Canadian Government to send arms to Israel. But we can't believe that those who advocate this want to see Canadian men follow Canadian guns. . . . This is a great complex problem. . . . All we have space to say here is that there are two sides to it. But Canadians are hearing mostly one side. And we are in danger of becoming victims of a smooth propaganda campaign. . . . . We even forget that there are three times as many Christians in Egypt as there are Jews in Israel. We fail to understand that recent treatment of the Arabs has created more misunderstanding than anything the West has done since the days of the Crusades. . . .To raise even a quiet voice to say, let us look at the other side of this hot situation which may lead to war, is to run the danger of being called anti-Semitic . . .

So it goes; the whole litany of charges *The Observer* aired after August 1967 appears early, with the added scare that Canadian boys might follow any guns shipped to the Jewish state. Forrest does not hide a thing. His 1967-69 campaign was not something sudden or mystical, a secret antagonism coming to the fore, as the ADL document implies.

Interest in the Middle East accelerated with the appointment of Forrest as editor and continued unabated through the years. On February 15, 1956, the late Claris Edwin Silcox, who had been employed by the Jewish community to fight anti-Semitism and had broken with it over Zionist policy, appeared in *The Observer* warning that the "Zionists Ask Too Much," that the West needs the friendship of "the Islamic nations" and that "a man may be anti-Zionist without being anti-Semitic."

Several months later, in July, Abraham L. Feinberg, rabbi of Holy Blossom Temple in Toronto, was invited to write in *The Observer* so that, as Forrest said in his editorial "Observations," "those who expressed interest in the recent article by Dr. C. E. Silcox will understand how a very distinguished leader of the Jewish community feels about the matter." Feinberg felt as any Zionist would: "The universal Arab will to erase Israel has been intensified, many impartial reporters suspect, by the romantic, Hitler-like dreams of Nasser. . . . Although I deem the preservation of Israel . . . a worthy aim for a Christendom conscious of Jewish suffering, sensitive to moral imperatives and acquainted with the potentialities of a secure focal centre for Jewish spiritual renascence, yet it is for the sake of peace, primarily, that I bespeak from Christian piety an open heart and mind—and its active intermediation." He then proposed a Muslim-Christian-Jewish Society to embrace the Western and Arab world, "beginning with Christians in the centre to serve as a link between Muslim and Jew!"

It was a challenge the United Church never took up, although the General Council, as we have seen, referred to it once in its Middle East resolutions. In his article, Feinberg expressed compassion for Arab refugees but coupled it with concern "for our own people driven from Nazi-dominated Europe, who became our financial responsibility to this day; hundreds of thousands perished because the world had no welcome for them."

The Observer's involvement with Arabs and Jews continued in 1958 when E. L. Homewood, managing editor, visited the Middle East and produced a series of five articles on the Christian holy sites, the refugee camps in Jordan and the developing cities and farms of Israel. The last article was the feature of the November 1, 1959, issue with a cover in Hebrew print titled "Ben-Gurion's Plan for Israel's Future." It sparked an exchange of letters stretching over several months. Rev. G. W. Goth of London accused the managing editor of having been brainwashed by Israeli propaganda and Rev. L. E. Smith of Ancaster, Ontario, who was on the tour, defended Homewood. Goth: "May I suggest that you ask Dr. Ernest Howse to give us the Arab side. . . ." Smith: "We were well aware of the danger of propaganda, and met plenty of it on both sides of the border."

In 1960, *The Observer* showed an apparently impartial hand by advocating the admission of a thousand Palestinian refugee families to Canada (March 1) and tendering a tribute to Jews on the two hundredth anniversary of their settlement in Canada. Pictures of the new Beth Tzedec Synagogue and Holy Blossom Temple in Toronto accompanied journalist Gordon Donaldson's piece on April 15, which described this country's Jews as "slightly apart, slightly different, glorying in what Benjamin Disraeli called 'the sublime instincts of an ancient race'." For *The Observer*, a Canadian home for Palestinian refugees and Jewish residence in Canada are a combination demonstrating a common concern for both Arabs and Jews.

In 1961, *The Observer* continued its interest in the Middle East and in the Jews of another part of the world, where they were forbidden to emigrate—the Soviet Union. Rabbi Stuart Rosenberg, then of Beth Tzedec Synagogue, who had just returned from a visit to Russia, told *Observer* readers in July that "democratic rights—under the Soviet constitution—are not accorded to the Jewish people and to its religious and cultural institutions." Thus *The Observer* provided a forum for the defence of the Soviet Jews' right to emigrate. It did so despite the fact that many of these immigrants settled in Israel, a matter of displeasure to Palestinians and other Arabs.

Even in the comparatively calm Middle East years of 1962 and 1963, *The Observer*'s interest never lagged. It criticized the federal government for cutting in half Canada's annual contribution to Arab relief, "one of the worst things Diefenbaker has done," and opened its pages to Dr. Ernest E. Long, then secretary of the General Council, who focused interest and sympathy on Jordan and other world spots where refugees languished. Yet touring editor Grace Lane was permitted to register disappointment over the parched landscape of Jordan and the lack of hygiene (October 1, 1963), and was perked up by Israel where "one feels a mystical sense of purpose" (October 15, 1963).

The year 1964 was a critical one in relations between *The Observer* and the Jews. In a long article in the February 15 issue of *The Observer*, illustrated in colour, Stuart Rosenberg told "Christians What (They) Don't Know About Judaism": "If Christians of all denominations can learn to hold hands, and they in turn can come to value the religious power which still thrives among Jews, then there may yet be hope for religion in a world where it is so direly threatened." This courteous scolding foreshadowed an explosive controversy in *The Observer* in June of that year.

The controversy arose from a speech to a Beth Tzedec audience by University of Toronto Professor Marcus Long, who labelled J. S. Thomson's textbook, *God and His Purpose*, anti-Semitic. He was supported by Emil Fackenheim who saw the book as slanderous to the Jews. United Church members were to study the book with the opening of the fall season, and on June 1, 1964, *The Observer* editorialized on the Beth Tzedec incident. It reprinted the passage that particularly offended Long and Fackenheim:

> The most terrible example of religion gone wrong is the crucifixion of Jesus Christ. It was religious men who demanded his death. The leaders of Jesus' own people had made their religion into an idol.
>
> What Jesus taught and did provoked the hostility of Pharisee and scribe. They hated him with such fury and rage that their eyes

were blinded. So when God came to them in the person of his son, they killed him.

Forrest thought it incredible that anyone should find hostile to Jews these words of former moderator Thomson, "whose whole life and ministry has breathed intolerance of bigotry" and who led a church "which continually insists that race discrimination, religious arrogance, prejudice and intolerance are among the major moral and social lessons of the time."

It should be obvious, Forrest insisted, that when Thomson writes of Pharisees he refers to the religious leaders of Jesus' day who demanded the death of Christ. That is anti-Semitic? The United Church has finally arrived, he stated, at a point where it can talk with Roman Catholics, "but it's difficult to have dialogue with our Jewish friends without being charged with prejudice."

In his editorial, Forrest acknowledged "the dark chapters" in the Christian treatment of Jews over the centuries (see Chapter 5, 7 and 10). "Most members of the United Church don't know about them," and he said he was grateful to Jewish leaders for pointing them out. "But we've got to have some realism here." Pharisaism has become a dictionary word, connoting hypocrisy. It is used innocently. Either Thomson's book is anti-Semitic or it is not. If it is, "then we'd like this pointed out to us clearly and in a brotherly way by spokesmen for the Jewish community."

Finally, the editor lost his patience: "But they can't expect us to soft-pedal history or manage the record, or edit the New Testament to protect the sensibilities of descendants of sinners of two thousand years ago, whether they be Jew, Greek, Hebrew, Roman, Jute, Angle, Saxon, Pict or Scot. History should never be distorted for anyone or anything. We say these things knowing that many United Church people are tired of being tight-lipped, white, Anglo-Saxon Protestant majorities, afraid to say what they think for fear they will offend a minority. . . ." The editorial was titled WASPS.

Since the incident occurred at Beth Tzedec, Forrest demanded of Rosenberg that he comment on the charge of anti-Semitism and the *Observer* editorial. In his reply, July 1964, Rosenberg thought the Thomson book was "most engaging" but unscholarly: "After reading his book, I am afraid I could not trust him to produce an authentic, accurate description of Judaism." As for the editorial, Rosenberg added, it would have been better had Forrest not written it.

The seeds of a later quarrel were planted in this controversy of 1964. In later years *The Observer* editor was to criticize the then rabbi of Beth Tzedec for equating anti-Zionism with anti-Semitism. While

Forrest separates anti-Zionism from anti-Semitism, most Jews do not, and they related *The Observer*'s post-1967 anti-Zionist campaign to *The Observer*'s partisanship in defending Thomson's book. To overlook this connection is to miss an essential point in the United Church-Jewish quarrel—that for Jews those who oppose the Jewish state are also insensitive to the historic role of the Jewish people.

With the Marcus Long-Fackenheim-Rosenberg dissonance still ringing in his ears, Forrest led a tour to the Middle East in the summer of 1964. Of this trip he wrote: "I don't think one can ever understand his Jewish neighbour until he has been to Israel. . . . I can understand why most Jews thrill to the story of Israel. Here a scattered people finally found a home. They have restored a dead language in less than two decades. They are restoring a desert land very quickly . . ." (*Observer,* December 15, 1964).

Even in this tranquil mood, the editor insisted on considering both sides. He met some Palestinian refugee boys in Hebron (then in Jordan) who objected to picture-taking because of their poverty, which would thereby be exposed to the folks at home in Canada. And the guide added: "They know you will go to Israel and take pictures of great irrigation projects, tractors turning the desert into a garden, and you will say, compare that—the lazy, backward Arabs and the Jews." The ADL document refers to this piece, describing it as "a straight-forward account of the suffering and bitterness which the author encountered during his visits to the (refugee) camps." Not a word about Forrest's appreciation of Israel's progress!

The only year the Middle East receives no treatment in the two decades of Forrest's editorship at *The Observer* is 1966. Yet the Ages-ADL paper says that before 1967 "the state of Israel . . . never loomed very large in the *Observer*'s optic. . . ." As we have seen, B'nai B'rith uses Basic Documents as guides in the formation of policy. With Ages' misreading of *The Observer* files, it is no surprise that the Jewish fraternal organization clashed with the United Church.

Yet Ages is right in his conclusion that from 1967 to 1969 the United Church *Observer* lost its sense of proportion on the Middle East. In the eight years since 1969 (beyond the purview of the Ages study) the perspective has not yet been recaptured. The compounded wounds resulting from disagreement succeeding dispute, almost without letup, have kept the United Church-Jewish quarrel festering, and little has been done to allay, bandage or heal it.

If a reader since 1967 were to obtain his information on the Middle East from *The Observer* as his only source, the picture would be distorted beyond recognition. The fault is not, as Ages charges, that Forrest favours the Arabs; he has a right to the Arab viewpoint just as the Zionists have a right to the Israeli view. The error, most grievous, is that the editor interposes himself between his readers and the situation to be covered. *The Observer*, as a monthly, offers a greater proportion of opinion as against hard news than does a daily publication. But even a monthly magazine has a responsibility not to diffuse the dividing line between opinion and fact. In the years 1967 to 1969 that line almost disappears.

One has only to juxtapose a piece of April 1, 1968—"What Happened When I Criticized Israel"—with one of January 1969—"Dear Jews"—to see the extraordinary effect. The former is an article by the editor in the body of the magazine; the latter an editorial identified by the initials P. C., associate editor Patricia Clarke. The only difference between them is that the former uses the first person singular and the latter the editorial "we." The burden of both articles is the same: Israel should be subject to criticism, as is any other political entity, and to label such criticism anti-Semitism is unjust. The point is well taken but not well given. The impression of the two pieces is of a monolithic promotion, trumpeting the editor's obsession.

One of the reasons for the rich diet of Middle East reports in the late 1960s and early 1970s was that Forrest, on his sabbatical in 1968-69, resided in that region. He took a personal interest in Palestinian problems and became a familiar figure among the inhabitants of the refugee camps in the West Bank and in Lebanon. His *Observer* articles and his book, *The Unholy Land*, based on his experiences, were manna to the homeless, and he was swept along by their praise and his enthusiasm for their cause. But, unlike the General Council of the United Church, which constantly kept in mind the injustices done to both Jews and Palestinians, Forrest seemed to forget that two just causes were involved, those of Israel as well as the Palestinians.

The weight of material on the Middle East in these years was indeed heavy for *Observer* readers to bear. From March 15, 1967, to July 1, 1969, twenty-four issues contained articles, editorials, the editor's "Observations" and letters on Israel and the Arabs.

There was a decided effort to promote the fact that not all Jews are Zionists. In the issue of May 15, 1968, Bill Gottlieb, public relations director for the American Council of Judaism, told "The Other Side of the Zionist Story." The Council was correctly described as "a national organization of Jews with an anti-Zionist viewpoint," but nothing was said about its almost total lack of influence in Canada. In recent years the Council has lost so many supporters that it has ceased to be a force even in the United States.

As noted, most of the 1967-69 material was on the Palestinian refugees, and the question persists: Why the massive coverage tilted toward the Arabs? Because, as Forrest often explains, it is important to balance the pro-Israel coverage of the daily press. Such an argument was valid in the fifties and early sixties because of the romance of the Zionist experiment, aided by Israeli public relations techniques. One has the feeling, certainly from reading the Toronto *Star*, that in the later sixties the press became more objective on Middle East issues. Yet even assuming that in these years it remained markedly pro-Israel, did *The Observer* strike a balance?

What is balance in the journalistic sense? Does it mean that a publication pours out coverage for one side after it has poured out coverage for the other? Or taking a stand for one side because other journals have opted for the opposite side? Or does it mean trying to be fair, balanced, in every article and editorial published? The last is the most desirable, because readers, unlike editors, do not assess an article by considering what has gone before and what will come after it. A reader does not say: Today *The Observer* is for the Arabs, but remember yesterday it was for the Israelis. Because the Arab-Israel struggle has developed its own illogic over the years, an editor needs special care in applying logic and balance to every single thing he publishes on it.

A shining example of balanced journalism on the Middle East appeared in *Newsweek*, December 2, 1974. It was reprinted and distributed by Beirut's Lebanese Association for Information on Palestine. Jerusalem-born Edward Said, professor of English at Columbia University, wrote an "Open Letter to the Israelis"; and Abba Eban, former foreign minister of Israel and also a professor at Columbia, wrote an "Open Letter to Palestine Arabs." The two letters were placed side by side.

Neither Said nor Eban minced words. Said: "When the PLO is recognized in the world as our people's sole legitimate representative, your leaders say only that the PLO is a bunch of terrorists who do not represent Palestinians, that Jordan is Palestine and that you are not about to discuss the Palestine question."

Eban: "The unsolved question is whether Arab nationalism will come to terms with the rights of the Jewish nation to live securely in its original and only home. Nothing in Arafat's squalid tirade [on behalf of the PLO at the UN in the fall of 1974] was more ludicrous than his assumption that there can be twenty Arab states and no Jewish state in the Middle East."

But Said also said: "I know . . . that we must be open to each other's reality. Our representatives, yours and ours, after all are *ours*; they must be made to respond to what, as human beings, sick of war, persecution, suffering and exile, we feel, you Jews and we Palestinians. Together we must make the present and the future: equality for Arab and Jew in Palestine, no war, no persecution for anyone."

And Eban also said: "Surely it is time for the peaceful, lucid voices of Palestine Arabs to be heard. . . . History has decreed that you and we give our love and devotion to the same skies and hills and earth. For all others, this region is an object of interest or controversy. For you and us, it is home. It is only as sovereign nations within a regional harmony that we can make it the abode of peace and sanctity."

One reads the *Newsweek* presentation and says: The Middle East difficulties are mountainous, but there are possible breakthroughs. One reads *The Observer,* particularly during 1967-69, and says: The problem is insoluble. Balanced journalism generates hope; one-sided coverage to make up for one-sided coverage elsewhere produces hopelessness.

As one examines *The Observer* issues from 1967 to 1969, one finds a few obvious efforts to balance the arguments. Ages says these attempts are "both insipid and inconsequential." Yet the following statement from an *Observer* editorial, January 1969, is not inconsequential: "The United Church's General Council has stated since 1948 that Israel should be recognized by her Arab neighbours and permitted to live in peace. Far from condemning Israel for the June 1967 war, *The Observer* called her victory 'a necessary defensive action against continued military threats'."

Nor is this statement unimportant: "I have spent enough time in Israel and the Arab countries to believe that the common people of all countries want peace" (*Myths and Facts* by Forrest, June 15, 1969). It was not inconsequential when *The Observer* published a letter by the Israeli ambassador to Canada, Gershon Avner, which said: "Israel has again declared that in the context of honest peace negotiations, which we advocate day in, day out, there can be a full regional and international solution of the refugee problem to which Israel will contribute by way of both repatriation, compensation and aid in resettlement" (November 15, 1967). It was not inconsequential when, in the same issue, an article by Rabbi Gunther Plaut appeared under the title: "Israel Wants Justice, Too."

The error in Forrest journalism is that it wants balance yet insists on proving a point. In the October 1, 1967, issue, which is almost wholly devoted to the Arab refugees ("Injustice, In Her Present Policies Israel Stands Condemned Before the World"), the most incomprehensible presentation is the picture of a pitiable little Arab girl, hit by napalm, titled "That's War," with comment that is particularly insensitive. It recalls the days of Joshua, when Israel fought "a nice, quick, decisive war; the army marched around Jericho for a week and the walls came tumbling down. This time the strategy was even more brilliant, and all the people of Jericho fled across the Jordan. From the air a new ghastly dew has been added. Napalm!" The last paragraph: "But after all, people said, 'That's war.' And it was, as wars go, short, decisive, relatively cheap in casualties to both sides. And things such as napalm help to get it over in a hurry—even more quickly than marching around a city blowing trumpets."

The piece is filled with contradictions, and one is left with the following impression: Israel is a war-maker and conqueror, in ancient times and today. She is very efficient in war. She herself sustained casualties, but she caused the suffering of this little girl.

Surely logic and balance called for a statement that the real enemy is war, not Israel, that children suffer on both sides. And if pictures were needed, why not of Israeli and Arab children side by side? The ADL document makes much of this insensitivity.

Forrest sometimes violates another journalistic principle, the quoting of anonymous sources. Occasionally, this is permissible, as when an official refuses to be identified. But there are enough anonymities in the Forrest pieces to make the reader question. One need not go as far as the ADL in saying that "the writer was quoting himself," but one wonders at the point of it all. *The Observer* editor told of meeting "a man [a Jew] in the King David Hotel" in Israel who spoke of getting those "fat friends of ours [Jews] who go down to Florida and sit on their fannies for six months every year to come here [Israel] and spend some money and build up the country." In order to avoid the impression that he was using an anti-Semitic stereotype, Forrest should have identified the man.

The story was all over the Jewish community in Toronto at the time. The typical Jewish reaction was: "The fat, Florida Jews are wealthy; why make a point of it in connection with Israel?" Sensitive Jews? Perhaps, but they are insecure even when wealthy; they cannot forget history and their minority status. Anti-Semitic Forrest? That is the question to be answered.

The ADL-Ages document says the question is irrelevant, then goes on to quote a definition of anti-Semitism by E. M. Howse: "For the essence of anti-Semitism is not in the person against whom it is directed. It is in the nature of the hostility. It is in the fanaticism, the distortion, the emotional enmity, the resort to smear, the desire to injure." Every Jew will have to make up his own mind about Forrest, says Ages. After attempting to demonstrate the distortion and hostility of *The Observer*, and then posing Howse's definition, it is naive to believe Ages expected anyone would say Forrest is not an anti-Semite.

Father Gregory Baum of St. Michael's College would probably argue that Forrest is afflicted with "false consciousness," which is about the same as saying he writes anti-Semitic things but is unaware of doing so. Certainly Forrest is often confused about Jews; he does not understand them, despite his many Jewish friends; he knows little about Judaism except what he reads in the New Testament, an unreliable source on the subject. But he is not an anti-Semite. The word comes too quickly, though understandably, to suffering Jews.

There are various degrees of hostility to Jews. Polite social dislike is one; the "higher anti-Semitism" of the nineteenth-century "higher biblical critics" is another; Nazism is still another. Anti-Semitism is not simple dislike. Drumont in *La France juive* and Hitler in *Mein Kampf* have shown it to be more than resentment; it is no less than loathing, terror, horror and hallucination. Forrest does not fit any of the above categories.

Moreover, he has grown in understanding of the problem of anti-Semitism. "I wasn't very familiar with its tradition," he says. "I didn't know how bad Christians had been, that Martin Luther was an anti-Semite. Then I became aware of the kind of Jew-hatred that has functioned in this country where curling and yacht clubs discriminate against the Jewish people. I wouldn't belong to such a club knowingly. On the whole, we've been better at criticizing the Americans for their treatment of Blacks.

"I remember seeing that movie 'Gentleman's Agreement' [where a Gentile learns about anti-Semitism by passing as a Jew] many years ago, how angry I felt about it. At the same time, I studied the *Merchant of Venice* in high school and wasn't at all disturbed by it. Then I saw it a few years ago in London and was appalled by it. I still don't like it for its treatment of Shylock."

As for the Jewish right to a state, Forrest says: "To me there's no question about the fact that Israel has a right to continue to exist and that Christians have a responsibility to help it exist. I'm ready to say that. But if I were just to come out with a bold statement like that after all the things I've said, I would also have to say Christians have a heavy responsibility to work for peace with justice in the Middle East." The Jewish reaction might have been different had he said it in just these words, as the General Council repeatedly did.

Forrest is groping for some kind of definition of his relationship to Jews. Like others in the United Church and in sister Christian denominations, he is in the dark about them; therefore, he stumbles. It is folly to turn away from him, as some Jewish activists are doing. He belongs to the Jewish-Christian family.

CHAPTER FIVE

Why do Liberals Rage?

The United Church-Jewish quarrel has underlined disillusionment with the concept of liberalism. For Jews this disillusionment had its roots in the nineteenth century; for United Church members it is more recent. Generally in the decades before 1939 the liberal label was borne proudly by Jew and Christian alike. As history demonstrates, a faith is more fervent when it has an enemy than when it is propagated for its own sake. The enemy of the liberal in the 1920s, thirties and forties was the totalitarian or dictator, who was resisted and ultimately defeated in World War II. In the process of resisting, liberalism became a standard and a creed for Christian and Jew. When the war was over, it was thought that tolerance, deepened by its encounter with intolerance, would be the order of the day and most issues would find their resolution under its umbrella.

Our mistake was in confusing liberalism with the absence of "envy, hatred and malice and all uncharitableness." We forgot that basic to liberalism, as to all schools of thought, is human nature, and when that is compounded with controversial issues, immensely powerful and by no means understood, the result is passionate conflict.

Before examining liberalism and the differing expectations and experiences with it and how these differences have helped to aggravate the quarrel between the Jewish community and the United Church, it is necessary to attempt to define liberals and liberalism.

Liberals have difficulty defining themselves (see Notes on Chapter 5). The fundamentalist or conservative has definite criteria; he is bound by an ancient text or the authority of a tradition. An essential characteristic of the liberal is that his thought is free, unbound by orthodox tenets or established forms in religious and political philosophy. Liberals do not agree on criteria; there is usually an argument about who is liberal and what constitutes liberalism.

From conversations and interviews with Jews (Canadian Jewish Congress president Sydney M. Harris, social scientist Albert Rose, community relations director Ben Kayfetz and editor Julius Hayman) and United Church leaders (moderators E. M. Howse and Bruce McLeod and theologian Robert Bater), I have distilled a number of signs and symbols which would be accepted by liberals in both groups.

Liberalism for them begins with humility of spirit. The liberal matches himself against the vastness of the world and recognizes how little he can hope to know of the secrets of reality. Minds are liable to error and illusion; he understands that he cannot know everything.

Because fundamentalists and traditionalists also lay claim to a spirit of humility the liberal goes on to a second mark, openmindedness. Since he does not or cannot know everything, the liberal keeps his mind open to obtain new knowledge. The orthodox believer—in religion, economics and politics, or even science—may declare he has the truth in final and perfect form. Such a declaration is not possible for the liberal mind.

A third sign of conventional liberalism is active tolerance. The liberal will not be content merely to endure, or tolerate, those who oppose him. He will seek out dissenters, encourage them, study them. He will do everything in his power to get acquainted with ideas that are contrary to his own.

The liberal believes in freedom—the furthest extension of tolerance in the positive direction. He will defend it even in the case of those whose ideas seem fantastic. He will fight for the freedom of those who do not themselves believe in freedom. "If there is any principle of the Constitution that more imperatively calls for attachment than any other," said US Supreme Court Justice Oliver Wendell Holmes, "it is the principle of free thought—not free thought for those who agree with us, but freedom of thought for those we hate."

Yet a liberal does not mount a steed in his freedom, like Stephen Leacock's famous horseman, "and ride off in all directions." He has direction and control, not through dogma, but through rationality. At the same time, he is loyal to principle as contrasted with expediency. He believes that deep down in the structure of the universe are standards of right and wrong; he will stand for them "though the heavens fall."

Finally, the liberal regards himself as a humanitarian committed to all causes for the betterment of man, not just the Christian or the

Jew, but man, whoever and wherever he is. Perhaps the essential difference between the liberal and the orthodox or conservative is that for the latter truth is a treasure that has been found and for the former it is a treasure that is being sought.

Generally, Canadian Jews profess the liberal creed. They look for openness to differences and progressive social and economic measures. Social scientist Albert Rose of the University of Toronto is the only Canadian Jewish leader I have encountered who describes Canadian Jews as conservative, but he judges them in the light of parochial traditions and defensiveness as a minority. The collective posture of the Jewish community toward issues that are purely Canadian, however, is liberal.

While United Church members can also be described generally as liberal, some, like former moderator Robert McClure, are more so. One might say they are liberal in belief and radical in the way they promote their belief. They are outspoken and self-confident. Except for concepts about God and Jesus, their theology is negligible. In fact, they are usually suspicious of theological systems. Fundamentalism is anathema to them as is literalism of the Bible.

The assertive liberal in the United Church embraces all signs and symbols already described, but he stresses free thought above all else—above openmindedness, humanitarianism, principle, active tolerance and humility of spirit. Because of his emphasis on free thought as the foremost liberal principle, and humility of spirit as secondary, his essential liberalism does not always emerge. He considers himself a force for peace and understanding, yet in his Middle East statements he has often produced contention and misunderstanding.

Reason says that Jewish and Christian liberals should be able to get along swimmingly. Tolerance, compassion for humanity, equality of all men—these are ideas to nourish the soul of an oppressed minority. Jews, therefore, have embraced liberalism from its beginnings, but historically they have always had trouble with liberals.

As the eighteenth century drew to a close, emancipation dawned for the Jews, and they were admitted to the general body politic, from which they had been excluded for centuries (see Chapter 7). This era was known as the Enlightenment, when the human intellect sought to free itself from the dogma of the ages. Jews were given civic rights not because those who despised them suddenly began to love them. Their emancipation was rather the result of turbulent economic, social and religious changes all coming together at one time. The feudal order was overthrown and with it the belief of the masses that a better life could be procured only in the world after death. The desire to improve human life on this earth became too strong to be denied. It spread beyond the circles of the intellectual elite, and the response to it proved so exciting that men lost interest in the promised reward of the hereafter. The American and French revolutions were inspired largely by this switch from other-worldly to this-worldly concerns. Liberalism was born.

The result of the switch to this-worldly concerns was a program of political reforms whereby the disfranchised came into rights to which it was now decided they were entitled and of which they had heretofore been deprived by the nobility in alliance with the clergy. Once it was proclaimed that all the people were to be included in the rights to life and liberty, it would have been a mockery of the principle to exclude the Jews. Almost at a stroke they were freed from the disabilities of the centuries.

Thus did the liberals extend to the Jews a change in status. The first to benefit were the Jews of Germany, France and Holland, where their administrative ability brought them into contact with the rising class of industrialists. What the Enlightenment and its offshoot, liberalism, had wrought for the Christians it did for the Jews. It changed their expectations so that they no longer looked to divine miracles, for another opening of the sea, to rescue them from oppression; the emancipation was miracle enough. They hailed the granting of political, social and economic rights as an end to their exile, as a sign that they were now part of the nations which had formerly treated them as aliens. New economic opportunities, unlimited access to cultural enjoyment and personal self-expression were in prospect. The blessings were rich and emancipating. The messianic age had truly arrived.

Had the liberal democratic movement followed the logic of its beginnings and a serious attempt been made to translate liberty, fraternity and equality into law, the millennium might have come. One can imagine what would have happened to the Jews in such an eventuality. Most of them might have been assimilated into the surrounding population and culture.

But what the liberals gave, they also took away. The liberal dream of the eighteenth and nineteenth centuries turned into a nightmare for the Jews. They were the first to sense the promise of a better world, and they were also the first to experience its disillusionment. It was the nineteenth century, the liberal era, that spawned anti-Semitism, a new word for an old hatred (see Chapter 7). As Europeans threw off the shackles of the Church, they did not spurn the theological rationale for hating Jews; they simply secularized and rechristened it.

Liberals have confused the Jews who fell in love with their emancipating ideas and then were jilted by their anti-Semitic posture. Voltaire and Hegel, leading lights of the Enlightenment, were impassioned anti-Semites. This paradox made Jews incapable of self-definition, at least the kind of definition that would satisfy the liberals. As a result they became an enigma to themselves and to the rest of the world.

The first attempt at Jewish definition to fit into the liberal world occurred at the Sanhedrin or Assembly of Jewish Notables convened by Napoleon in 1806. As a liberal, the little corporal granted rights to the Jews but expected in return that they would renounce Jewish nationhood. The Assembly responded a bit hesitantly but nonetheless like true-blue liberals. It declared itself a religious community with no affiliation to Jewish communities of other countries except in the area of beliefs and practices and pledged not to engage in secular enterprises with those communities. The Napoleonic Sanhedrin's declaration was approved by many Jews outside France and gave impetus to a new movement called Reform Judaism.

In the middle of the nineteenth century the Reform rabbinate in Germany adopted the Napoleonic declaration as part of a program to distil from Judaism all its nationalistic, or particularistic, elements and render it a universal religion in tune with the liberal spirit. Following in the wake of German-Jewish Reform, the Pittsburgh Platform in the US, in the spirit of American liberalism, "denationalized" Judaism in that country.

The advent of Hitler, the climactic expression of nineteenth-century anti-Semitism, restored nationhood to the German Jews by the Nazi redefinition of their status as more than a religion. It also acted as a powerful catalyst for the reversal of the Pittsburgh statement in the US. American Reform rabbis reasserted the peoplehood of Israel at a conference in 1937, reinstated many of the so-called particularistic or nationalistic elements disavowed by their predecessors and reaffirmed the oneness and indivisibility of world Jewry.

Renunciation of particularism clearly did not bring the Jews economic and social equality. Chauvinistic nationalism grew hand in hand with the Enlightenment to defeat the rational idealism which had brought the Jews out of the ghetto. No matter how eagerly Jews sought to merge with the general population, they remained a breed apart. In Central and Western Europe, where liberalism had its start, Jews entered the twentieth century as outsiders and interlopers. In Eastern Europe, where the majority of Jews lived, they remained disfranchised aliens until after World War I, their hopes of political and social redemption, awakened by the Enlightenment in the West, unfulfilled. As these hopes continued unrealized, Jews throughout Europe became convinced that liberalism was a false messiah, that a new method of emancipation from bondage had to be found to make the Jews a normal people free from discrimination and oppression. Political Zionism—the design to establish the Jews as a nation on the ancient land of Israel, where their body and soul could find a home not on sufferance but as of right—was born. It was in Eastern Europe where Jews lived in medieval states and saw the liberalism of Western Europe turn into a broken reed, that the main response to Palestine settlement occurred.

Zionism was conceived out of disillusionment with liberalism. One may properly ask, "Who made Zionists out of Jews?" And properly answer, "The liberals." To answer thus may be deemed an oversimplification, since it does not take into account the hopes and yearnings, the nurtured memory of two millennia of exile. Still, the spur to political Zionism came directly from the liberals' failure to make good their promises. The words of the nineteenth-century liberal Clermont-Tonnerre became a mockery: "To the Jews as individuals, everything; to the Jews as a nation, nothing."

Today, more than two centuries after the Enlightenment and the birth of liberalism, United Church liberals are in the forefront of the critics of the state of Israel, founded on the Zionist ideal. Some of their criticism is justified as it relates to the rights of Palestinian Arabs, but they must take care that their standards of judgment regarding individual and group rights do not repeat the mistakes of the liberalism of the last two hundred years.

A composite image of the United Church liberal would blend into something like the following. He regards nationalism, including Zionism, as a divisive factor; he is for Jewish statehood, if the Jews want it, but not at the expense of the Palestinians; he opposes terrorism and the stated Arab purpose of destroying the state of Israel, but he says he can understand Arab obsession with both; he holds Jews themselves partly responsible for anti-Semitism; his public statements have caused resentment among Jews; he has many warm Jewish friends, yet he has been called an anti-Semite; he staunchly defends A. C. Forrest's right to express his views.

United Church liberalism, which leads to this posture, is founded on two basic concepts: (1) that the individual is the primary unit of human life and therefore the primary object on whose behalf life's meaning is sought; (2) that nationalism menaces the individual and must be restrained to prevent destruction of his spirit and personality.

In keeping with these assumptions, the existence of distinctive groups of people is regarded as an irrelevance. The kingdom of God is conceived as homogeneous, with all people destined to believe and practise one religion. Ancient Christian tradition harboured such a strong suspicion of group loyalties that it regarded even the family relationship as an impediment to the full loyalty of the individual to God. The United Church rejected this asceticism, but it still retains an absolute faith in the inviolability of individual worth and a disaffection for nationalism.

Nationalism, for the liberal, may have normal and legitimate expression in affording the individual an orderly society in which he can find self-fulfillment without limitation as to race, class, education, economic status or religious affiliation. But it is suspect because it easily develops unhealthy and sinister aspects. Albert Schweitzer, one of the most saintly Christian liberals in this century, has defined this development as "an ignoble patriotism, exaggerated until it has lost all meaning. It bears the same relation to the noble and healthy kind as the fixed idea of an imbecile does to normal conviction." In the Schweitzer spirit, the United Church liberal fears group egotism that leads to unjust treatment of other groups. He fears it in the state of Israel which seems indifferent to the rights of Palestinians.

The love of individual worth and fear of the nation-state have been possessions of the Christian liberal since the Reformation and the Enlightenment. He applies them to all situations, including that of the Jews. That is why Jewish particularism has no special meaning for the United Church liberal. If the state of Israel disappeared, he would mourn the death of a living thing, yet he would still be hopeful about the Jew as a human being. But that is exactly where the liberals of the Enlightenment went wrong. They and their successors in the United Church failed to see that the human being is not a self-contained atom, but is the result of the biological, historical and social forces that operate in the group to which he belongs. Individual personality is a product of two factors: the self-generating life principle and the heritage and social environment supplied by the group.

The United Church liberal is right to stress the importance of the individual as an end in himself and not merely as a means to another. It is the only adequate rationale for democratic equality. It is the only safeguard against the tyranny of the state. But the sacredness of the person can mean nothing if we extract from him all the values he has derived from his group. If we are to respect the worth of the human being, we cannot demand that he denounce the sense of worth he has received from his group.

Moreover, the United Church liberal, as the inheritor of a religious tradition, should understand that there are ideals that live on this earth beyond the individual's life span, ideals that seek fulfillment in the future. These are the heritage of the group and they depend on the group for realization; to deny the group the right to perpetuate itself is to cut off the worth of the individual who espoused the ideal. The group character is, therefore, as much entitled to the concern of religious ethics as the individual personality. We respect the worth and dignity of the individual not on the basis of what he is but on the basis of what he can become. The same should be true of the group.

If the United Church liberal is in a constant search for truth and meaning, as his creed dictates, he must not stop where liberalism began two hundred years ago. He must be concerned not only with the most limited definition of the individual and of the rights guaranteed him, but with the latest psychological and sociological investigations. Conviction must be a living, developing thing, or it is simply a prejudice. The acceptance of the group life of a people or a nation as an instrument for enhancing the worth of the individual is a progressive manifestation. It calls for the extension of the principle of equality from individuals to groups.

This means that every cultural and national group should be permitted to function as a milieu in which the individual's right to self-fulfillment may be realized. Its history, its culture, its way of life and social forms should be allowed to operate for all who so wish. This freedom should be shared equally by all groups. No more should the Jew be told that he is clannish because he treasures his own heritage and folkways. Any interference with the freedom of a weaker group by a dominant one should be regarded as a moral violation fraught with danger to the welfare of the human being who is nurtured by that freedom.

In describing the characteristics of a liberal, Bruce McLeod finds the terms "open" and "closed" helpful. Some conservative people are open, he says, and some liberal people are strangely closed. It is the "closed" liberals in the United Church and the Jewish community who rage at one another. United Church and Jewish liberals stand together on other issues—the Soviet Union, world famine and the economy—but the alliance breaks down when it comes to a deeper understanding of tensions between Christians and Jews. Alan Davies of Victoria University believes that both Christian and Jewish liberals are capable of "particularistic assumptions." Liberals do not easily confess prejudice. They say that everyone should be heard, and some will even go out of their way to elicit contrary opinions. They accept the principle of following the truth wherever it may lead, believe themselves to be humanitarian and acclaim the ability to rise above barriers built by limited vision, but like other men they often confuse "subjective ideas with objective truth." In a religious liberal, says Davies, this tendency "frequently produces a self-righteous style, which has been present in the United Church in considerable measure." The style is not unknown in the Jewish community.

Until the "closed" liberals in both camps stop raging at one another and try to understand one another's experiences with and expectations from liberalism, the United Church-Jewish quarrel will continue to fester. An early step in the ongoing education of United Church members and Jews is for each to remove the beam from his own eye before trying to remove the mote from that of his neighbour.

CHAPTER SIX

The "Chosen" People

Canadian Jews, like Jews in other lands, insist on being accepted on their own terms, as a group, a nation or a people, not only as a religion. Many stress the concept of "chosen people." These terms are confusing to the United Church liberal, and one can understand his impatience with them.

Peoplehood is not easy to define. Social scientist Albert Rose says the Jew is indefinable because he does not follow standardized rules. "If anyone asks me what I am," says Rose, "I say I am a Canadian who is Jewish in the sense of my religious faith. But the census taker tells me I can't describe myself as a Canadian; I must go back to the place of birth of my parents, then my grandparents.

"Well, my father was born in London, England; does that make me, in the scoring words of the census, English? I don't think it does. Well, then, I go back to my grandfather. He was born somewhere in Poland. I certainly would not describe myself as Polish by nationality, or Russian if it happened to be under that jurisdiction at the time. 'Put me down as Jewish,' I say to the census taker, 'if you think that's a nationality; I don't.' But then the next question is, What is your religion? And my religion is Judaism. That form of confusion was obviously pretty widespread if the leading statisticians in the country couldn't devise a way of getting around the dilemma. And they haven't yet." Although unacceptable to statisticians, there is no other way to describe Jews than that they are a people.

Rev. George W. Goth of London, Ontario, poses a question representative of the feelings of many in the United Church: "Why must a Jew remain a Jew and an outsider after a thousand years? Other people become Canadians. In two or three generations even the Arabs cease to be Arabs. Maybe, human nature being what it is, if the Jews insist on being different, they should be prepared to pay the price. . . . They are like no other people on earth."

The Canadian Jew appears as an outsider because he is loyal to the Jewish people and to the state of Israel as well as to Canada. He refuses to assimilate because he believes in the worth of the Jewish people and seeks to maintain its existence. Jews throughout the world function as a people through a common tradition, a common language and literature, laws, history, customs and folkways, with religion serving as an integrating instrument. Religious Jews think of religion as the edifying element in Jewish life. Religion has indeed played an important role in the life of the Jewish people. Yet today, as we saw in Chapter 2, most Jews in Canada and elsewhere are not religiously affiliated.

In 1937, Professor E. R. Goodenough of Yale University wrote that "some modern Jews who are intensely loyal to Conservative Judaism, confess that they do not know whether they believe in God or not, and one prominent rabbi, who spoke for the school of modern Jews, told me that no belief, not even a belief in God, was required of a Jew." Not all Jewish authorities would accept that liberal rabbi's assertion. But it is a fact that there are rabbis who do not believe in God, more now than in Goodenough's time, and no one would think of excluding them from the Jewish people.

The secular Jew has the same status in Jewish society as the religious Jew. The Bible and Talmud for him are not sources of revelation but inspiration. They yield principles of morality which he sees as the genius of the Jew. The secularist and theological liberal among Jews are close in spirit.

A veritable rainbow of ideological groups operate compatibly within the Jewish community: Orthodox, Reform and Conservative religionists, Hasidic mystics, Agudat Israel legalists, secular Yiddishists, labour and capitalistic Zionists and even agnostics who create their own ritual observances on the traditional Jewish festivals. The bond that unites them is the sense of being wanted and having something to be proud of.

Peoplehood is different from race, religion, state or culture yet includes them all, with the exception of race. Opponents of Israel describe her as "a racist state" because the definition of a Jew, who is admitted to instant citizenship, follows rabbinic law—one who is born of a Jewish mother. But the same law also recognizes a convert to Judaism, who is as valid a Jew. Blood is no criterion of Jewishness. The ancestress of King David, the most heroic figure in Jewish folklore, was Ruth, a Moabite, who joined the Jewish people. Jews are a mixture of many racial stocks, especially since the Second Exile in the first century following the Roman capture of Jerusalem.

What, then, does the term people mean? It is as undefinable as personality, yet just as real. Anti-Semites will readily accept the term people for the Jews because, unable to define it, they regard it as a mystique akin to a demonic quality. But there is nothing mysterious about the Jewish people. A person becomes an individual when he recognizes himself as such; the Jews are a people because they so identify themselves. They possess group awareness, ethnic consciousness, like-mindedness. This feeling was developed over 4,000 years and was sensed alike by the Jew of the sixth century before the Christian Era, of the first century, of the Middle Ages and of the modern world.

Perhaps, the best way of thinking about the Jews is that they are all kin, a big family whose members have a special feeling for one another, who take pride in each other's accomplishments, joy in each other's celebrations, who weep for one another and speed to each other's aid in a crisis. In short, Jews care deeply about one another. Mordecai M. Kaplan, the American Jewish philosopher, defined this as the "we-feeling."

The ingredients of peoplehood are not the same in every generation. In the ancient kingdoms of Judah and Israel the people were bound together by land, cult and government; in the Babylonian Exile by religion and a body of literature; in post-Babylonian times by land, law, religion and custom; in medieval times by law, religion and community life. But at all times the we-feeling persisted.

The Enlightenment and the Emancipation sent Jews out into the society of many nations. They no longer lived only by the civil law of the Talmud. They embraced the laws and culture of their host countries where they have become integrated but not assimilated. But the we-feeling persisted, as demonstrated today in loyalty to Israel and in efforts on behalf of Soviet Jewry.

Why does the Jew stress peoplehood? Why does he need more, say, than a United Church member whose only people is the nation of Canada? Why isn't he content to be just part of a religious communion?

Jewish tradition teaches that in ancient times, the Jews of Israel made a covenant with God, promising to worship him, to reflect his moral law, and, as a people, to serve as an instrument for the establishment of universal justice and peace. In addition to belief in this covenant, history has given the Jews a 4,000-year consciousness of outstanding events and heroes. This collective memory and their enduring commitment to the covenant and the sense of peoplehood, which the covenant bestowed, have kept them together through exile and persecution. Memory and commitment produced customs to which Jews throughout the world conformed, laws which regulated conflicts of interest and kept peace within the group, and various forms of esthetic expression through literature, music and art.

Jewish memory was also fostered by universal education among males and by adolescent initiation ceremonies. A Jewish boy of five was introduced to the study of the Five Books of Moses, and Torah study was expected of him for the rest of his life. At thirteen he became Bar Mitzvah, which is not similar to the Christian confirmation, although it is often equated with it.

Bar Mitzvah (son of a commandment) is a dramatic and highly emotional occasion when the young Jew becomes a conscious member of his people. In a sense it is a second birth for him, when the range of his experience is enlarged, giving him a share in the greatness of his ancestors and encouraging him to deeds of his own. In recent years the parallel ceremony of Bat Mitzvah (daughter of a commandment) has been introduced to enlist the power of women in the task of perpetuating Jewish consciousness.

Thus Jews find in their people a sense of self and something to be proud of. It is noteworthy that even modern secular Jews, who have no affiliation with synagogues and have surrendered religious ritual, still turn to the Bar and Bat Mitzvah ceremonies. It demonstrates the psychological aspect of peoplehood as a humanizing force in the life of the average Jew. If he lacks it, he feels rootless and nameless.

Before the European Enlightenment, Jews were members of only one people. Their enduring memory and commitment to the covenant made them different and kept them from assimilating into other societies. Through the centuries, because they were noticeable, they were excluded, especially by Christians, from the society of the nations among whom they lived, often becoming targets of persecution and physical attack (see Chapter 7). When they were granted civic rights in the nineteenth and twentieth centuries, they took on the anomalous role of belonging simultaneously to two peoples.

Now the non-Jew may justifiably ask: Is not this divided allegiance? Let the Jew choose between Canada and the Jewish people, and if the latter is his choice let him move to Israel. Robert McClure, a former United Church moderator, says Jews have contributed to the erection of barriers between themselves and other Canadians because they present an image of dual loyalty and nationality. Other immigrants—Italian, Ukrainian, German, Irish, Scottish, Welsh—brought cultural remnants from the old country, but they were assimilated into the Canadian population; Jews maintained separateness in their integration. Since the establishment of the state of Israel the division of loyalties has intensified. "Did you ever hear," McClure asks, "of a Canadian Scot buying government bonds for Scotland, though Scottish municipal and commercial bonds are available?"

We are confronted here with a moral question. Has a person who is born a Jew the right to withdraw from the Jewish people? Is it ethical to transfer complete allegiance from the Jewish to a non-Jewish people and thereby stamp out one's identity? In modern times millions have transformed their ethnic loyalties. Canada and the United States are testimony to the willingness of Europeans to substitute one ethnic fidelity for another. Although Canadians are inclined to deny the melting-pot appellation, individuals from many ethnic groups in this country can hardly be identified after two or three generations. But not so the Jews. Their political allegiance to Canada is unfragmented but, always visible, their ties to the Jewish people, scattered across the globe, are as tight as ever.

These bonds are strong partly because the Jewish people is under attack. Any attempt to escape responsibilities under such conditions by joining another people would be regarded by other Jews as treasonable.

The attack on the Jews has not lessened though they enjoy civil rights in the democracies. It is still true that Jews have not yet attained social and economic equality in all phases of life and work. In the Soviet Union, Jews are admitted to society, but they are not permitted to have any active connection with Jews in other lands. In Latin American countries, under military dictatorship, anti-Semitism is on the rise. In the state of Israel, Jews are under siege. In the United Nations, Zionism, which to many Jews today is the same as Judaism, is decried. In these circumstances it cannot be moral for a Jew to abandon his people.

Aside from these considerations, in a positive sense, a person surely has a moral right to be loyal to the people into which he is born. No one would condemn him if he gives more love and interest to members of his own family than to members of another family. Since the Jewish people, as we have defined it, is the extension of the family, why should not the Jew love it with all his heart? Jews are bone of the Jewish people's bone, bred in its tradition and suckled at its breast. Jews can do for their own people and it can do for them what no other people can give or claim from them.

Trouble arises when ethnic loyalty rules out other valid loyalties. Devotion to one's mother should make motherhood everywhere dear. He is a poor Jewish patriot whose patriotism does not enable him to understand the patriotism of the Palestinians, for example. Ethnic isolationism is no more admirable than national isolationism, which considers every other nation a competitor for the world's goods and a potential enemy and every measure that calls for co-operation with them a menace to one's own nation.

The right of the Jewish people to exist, its uniqueness, has never implied superiority. Some modern Jewish chauvinists contend that the Jewish people fulfills the destiny of human life more adequately than any other, but it would be hard to prove that the mainstream of Jewish tradition supports such a view. If a Jew says his language is the most beautiful, his laws the most sacred, his history the most purposeful and his morals the most humanizing, he is saying, "My people can do no wrong." One has only to turn to biblical prophets to discover the wrongs the Jewish people committed. Jews are no more righteous or saintly than any other human aggregation, despite the popular belief that, divinely chosen, they enjoy a greater share of the creative spirit than any other people.

This brings us to the concept of "chosen people" which is a source of confusion for both Christians and Jews and for the United Church and the Jews of Canada. "Do the Jews really believe, like the Nazis, that they are God's chosen people?" asks London minister George Goth. Let another United Church minister, Robert Bater, answer: "The Jews were not chosen in the sense that God smiled on them in a unique way, that he liked them and no one else. That's the popular misunderstanding of the term. Chosen in the Bible means the people God chose to work with in a very special way, but that choice was as frightening and fearful as it was a blessing. The consequences of being the instrument of the mighty God on the surface of this earth are immense and dangerous." And, of course, Bater adds, the Bible keeps saying all the way through that the Jews are a stiff-necked people, not God's fair-haired children. To Bater, God working through a people to accomplish his purpose in history is a basic biblical concept. "Take that out and you take out one of the cardinal pillars on which the Old and New Testaments rest. I'm not sure what kind of religion you then have. You can have it based on ethical concepts, of course, but that would be something radically different."

Bater's explanation corresponds to the traditional Jewish version. The Jews regarded themselves as chosen through a covenant with God, as being a "peculiar people" with no special benefits in a worldly sense, as having to perform extra duties because of their special position. One ancient legend says that God offered the Bible and its Ten Commandments to other nations before he offered it to Israel.

The others refused the offer, because they thought God was imposing too many restrictions on them. But the Jews accepted the burden of the law and the service of God. Every morning the traditional Jew recites the words of a 2,000-year-old prayer: "Blessed art thou, O Lord, who has not made me a Gentile." Even the modern traditional Jew recites these words. Through them he means to express gratitude for the opportunity to observe 613 commandments and not just the seven conceived to be the duty of the non-Jew. Thus in being chosen, the traditional Jew believed he had to carry extra burdens. Being chosen did not mean being superior.

The question is whether Jews should insist on such a phrase today, particularly in view of the divisiveness created by the modern tendency to equate the term "chosen" with "superior." Chosen people belongs to another universe of discourse. The ancients had one concept of the world; we have another. They believed they were the centre of all life; we know, with Copernicus, Galileo and Einstein, that our planet is just a smidgin of matter at the edge of only one galaxy with billions of stars and that there are millions of galaxies. The Jews were children of their time and as self-centred as their contemporaries, and so they believed that the land of Israel was the navel of the earth, that the Jewish people was the hero of the human drama and all others supporting players.

That idea is no longer tenable. It simply does not fit our thought-world that a people can be the elect of God for all time, thus pre-determining history. Much as I understand Robert Bater's theological thirst and the traditional Jewish interpretation of the concept, I must accept the more rational assessment of E. M. Howse: "The literal acceptance of the idea that God picked out the Jews is incomprehensible. I do not believe that God plays favourites in any way, whether for privileges or responsibilities. My theology is that we are children of God, all of us. This is a vital element that determines everything else."

Even the average Jew in the past was somewhat skeptical of the chosen people concept, as illustrated by Sholom Aleichem's central character, Tevye the milkman, in the play *Fiddler on the Roof*. "It may be true," says Tevye in his dialogue with God, "that we are the chosen people. But isn't it about time you chose somebody else?"

After the sixth pre-Christian century and the editing of the Torah or Pentateuch in the Babylonian Exile, Jews thought of themselves as special or chosen because they possessed the revealed moral law. With the Second Exile in the year 70 and the rise of the Christian Church, the chosen people concept became a bone of contention between the old and new religions. A case can be made that the Church was far more infatuated with the idea of being "chosen" by God than the Jews had ever been. It asserted that since the Jews had repudiated the son of God they were in turn rejected as the elect. It thereby made a distinction between the new chosen people and those who were now damned.

In self-defence, one might say, the Jews through the Christian centuries countered with their own stepped-up theology. As the Church developed its "fellowship with divine gifts," so did the Jews, one claim to superiority clashing with the other. No further evidence should be needed of the futility of the term chosen people in this age than the confusion and ill will it has caused between Church and synagogue for almost two millennia.

The battle has abated somewhat in our day, since theology does not mean as much to the average person as it used to. Modern Protestant theologians, like Robert Bater and Alan Davies in Canada and the late Reinhold Niebuhr in the US, have further softened the rivalry between "old" and "new" Israel by abandoning the triumphal missionizing of the Christian ages and conceding an equal role to other religions. But fundamentalists in both Jewish and Christian camps still hold fast to the literal chosen people concept.

What is astonishing at this stage of the game is that liberal Jews still cling to the term as though it were the only justification for maintaining the existence of the Jewish people. They do not accept the concept literally as in the traditional belief, but they still find it meaningful in a reinterpreted version.

This version was first promulgated by Jewish intellectuals of the nineteenth century in Eastern Europe and Germany—the *Maskilim* and the historical school of Zechariah Frankel. One of their propositions is that the Jews were chosen because their forefathers were the first to recognize the ethical and social ideals which in time all men will embrace.

To give the Jews sole credit for acquainting mankind with the goals of a better world is still arrogance. Such a claim overlooks the religious philosophies of the Hindus, which preceded all others. It excludes the spiritual and moral contributions of Confucius, Buddha, the Greek philosophers, the Stoics of the Roman period, the humanists of the Renaissance and the rationalists of the eighteenth century. Even if Jews had been first in the field of humane teaching, traditional Jewish modesty would enjoin them not to boast about it.

Another modern explanation of chosen is that the Jews possess natural traits in the realm of the ethical which raise them above the rest of the world. But this is an unwarranted biological assumption the Jews themselves have decried in others who claimed hereditary qualities that set them above other men. Sociologists would reject the contention that ethnic characteristics are determined more by hereditary selection than by historical or geographic factors.

A third interpretation of chosen to which some liberal Jews subscribe today is that the quality or content of Jewish ideals is purer or superior to all others. It is, however, only a short step from saying that we have the best quality to saying that we have the greatest truth, and that goes right back to the claim of monopoly which is offensive to all rational men and women.

Because it implies self-righteousness and bars the way to peace and harmony among all peoples and religions, chosenness is not an acceptable doctrine today. The concept can be discarded because it is not indispensable to the survival of the Jewish people. Other concepts, also claimed to be indispensable, have been eliminated and the Jewish people did not come to an end. Fundamentalist Jews have argued for a century and a half that if you take away the belief in the divine authorship of the Torah, which permeates Jewish tradition from beginning to end, the structure of Judaism would collapse. Liberal Jews no longer accept this assumption, yet the Jewish way of life is as meaningful for them as ever. Why, then, should Jews insist that if they were to surrender their claim to moral and spiritual preeminence over the rest of the world, they would give up the struggle to remain Jews?

Certainly, continuity of Jewish memory or consciousness demands that as many of the Jewish traditional values as possible be retained. But some have been impossible to retain. In the process of living and in the necessity of meeting historical change, they have had to be discarded. So the Temple sacrifices, with the incense and blood sprinklings, are gone. But adjustments were made. Synagogue worship and learning took their place. The Jewish people manages to survive the abandonment of outdated concepts because it is a living organism. It will survive the rejection of the chosen people belief.

How does the state of Israel fit into the concept of peoplehood? For most of their four millennia Jews were without a land. That did not disturb their sense of being a people. The Jews proved that a people does not need its own territory in order to maintain a meaningful existence.

In a real sense, however, Jews were not without a land even in exile, even after they were dispersed throughout the known world in the year 70. Their retentive memory kept the land theirs. It is not true, as historian Arnold Toynbee claimed, that the statute of limitations entered to separate the Jews from their ancestral real estate. Such a statute applies only when one is no longer interested in any claim to his property. But the Jews asserted and reasserted their claim to "the land of Israel" (this is how they kept referring to it) since the beginning of their Second Exile. They remembered the land at least six times daily in prayers, at weddings and at funerals. They ordered their ritual observances in accordance with the seasons of what was once Palestine, refusing to adjust to the physical climate in the lands of exile, all because of their expectation that they would return.

It is a common misconception that for eighty generations the Jews sat still and waited for the messiah to realize this hope for them. Actually there was never a time when Palestine was without "mourners of Zion," as pre-Zionist pioneers called themselves. To be sure, they did not use modern techniques of political negotiation and scientific planning. But they never stopped trying to settle the land. At the first favourable turn in circumstances, immigration was instantly afoot. But their strength was slight and circumstance was always against them, so that they never achieved very much and it seemed that they never would.

Consider seeds falling on a sheet of bedrock, struggling to send out roots. The stone is unyielding. It is impossible that a living plant should establish itself upon it. Still, the rains fall, the winds blow and the sun shines. The rock heats. Then night comes and it cools. For a fleeting instant a fissure appears in the rock, and the seeds have their way at last, providing they are there at the opportune moment. In order to grasp the moment, the seeds must keep falling all the long, apparently hopeless seasons, so that, though millions be wasted, there may be a seed present when the rock cracks.

So it was with the Jews and Palestine. Two thousand years of trying to return, and always circumstances were against them. Then for a short while, for a few decades in our century, conditions turned. For a moment in eternity there was a chance of reclaiming the land. For that moment the Jews were ready, waiting and ready. That is how the state of Israel came into being. The process was a constant pressure against the wall of circumstance until a breakthrough was achieved.

Robert McClure and others in the United Church cannot see this process. "It is an odd fact of history," McClure says, "that Lord Balfour could give away a chunk of land not his to give." The odd fact is not that Balfour gave away somebody else's property but that he recognized the rights of two owners of the same land—the Jews and the

Arabs—for that is what his Declaration of 1917 says, a concession few people in his time and ours are willing to make. It is important not to deny the Palestinian Arabs their claim, but it is equally important not to deprive the Jews of theirs.

McClure will not grant ancient Jewish rights to the land, but he concedes that since the Jewish state is a fact of life now, Jews have a right to maintain it, and he acknowledges an obligation to see that right upheld together with that of the Palestinians.

Some United Church leaders, however, are convinced the state of Israel has no right to be in business because it is the product of a purely secular, political movement which displaces others. But Zionism—the process of Jewish return to Palestine—is both spiritual and political.

What is the justification of the Jewish claim to a part of the territory of ancient Palestine? Is it simply that Jews need a haven of refuge, a home where, as Robert Frost has said, "when you have to go there they have to take you in"? If that were the only consideration, Jews would be safer in a country like Canada. The claim of the Jews rests on their historic memory and their long connection with the land. It was the land of Israel that gave the children of Israel their original peoplehood and their hope of rendering service to mankind.

The ancient dream was that all men would acknowledge the true God, that all Jews would be brought back to the land of Israel, that God's kingdom of justice and peace would be established throughout the earth, that the unrepentant wicked would be destroyed and that the righteous would enjoy eternal life, because death would be abolished. Today every detail of that dream is no longer applicable, but that the land of Israel would be associated with ethical and moral peoplehood is. If Jews were to give up their claim to the land, which is essential to their spiritual yearnings, their life as a people would lack meaning and relevance. The long hope of return, associated with the redemption of all mankind, would be cancelled.

So long as the hope of returning to Palestine was a dream, Jews could be as imaginative as they wished, but now that it is a reality they must not go beyond the bounds of what is possible. They cannot build on injustice to others, for that instantly robs their peoplehood of its ethical quality. For this reason Jews, in Canada as elsewhere, must, like the United Church, support the right of Palestinian Arabs to an independent state parallel to the territory where a majority Jewish population can flourish. Within the Jewish territory Jews must possess enough political independence to embody their ideals of social justice in legal and economic institutions of their own and encourage creativity in the arts and sciences.

Israel today falls short of Jewish prophetic ideals in many ways, but this should not mean that Jews do not deserve a chance to develop their ethical peoplehood in the land. The prophets noted that ancient Jews were capable of wrongdoing; modern Jews have that capability also. But they, like other peoples, must be given the opportunity to rise above weaknesses and to live in a spirit of commitment and dedication.

The General Council of the United Church has recognized the right of the Jewish people to such an opportunity. But it also recognizes the right of the Palestinian people to a similar opportunity. To many Canadian Jews this sounds like a contradiction; hence their quarrel with the United Church.

CHAPTER SEVEN

The Anti-Semitic Label

United Church leaders object to the easy use of the term anti-Semite. At least three former moderators, among others, have been so labelled—E. M. Howse, Robert B. McClure and N. Bruce McLeod.

Howse feels helpless in the face of charges of anti-Semitism. He hears Jews saying: "You hate Jews. You don't know you do, but you do because it's in your ancestry." Once you assume hate, he says, the cause is lost.

McClure's "great regret" as moderator was that he accomplished little in building understanding with the Jews. He had all the qualifications—experience in being a member of a minority (he was born in China), a refugee and a resident of the Middle East, roles that few moderators before him had known, and a large circle of Jewish friends. Yet he was not only unable to bring the United Church and the Jews closer "but by my miserable efforts I seemed to have widened the gap. My deep and sincere disappointment in this has mistakenly given me the label of being anti-Semitic."

McLeod has been familiar with anti-Semitism since his schooldays in Toronto. He was disturbed, in his two years as moderator, by "the amount of viciously anti-Semitic stuff there is." At the beginning of his term letters poured in, simultaneously accusing him of being a "Jew-lover" and an initiator of "criminally anti-Semitic activities." He has learned not to look for logic in this ambivalent manifestation, but it never ceases to sadden him.

Few would deny the existence of some anti-Semites in the United Church, but an overextensive and too ready use of the label affords the genuine anti-Semites a comfortable feeling of belonging to a popular group and a justification for dismissing their accusers as hysterical.

Some leading Jews too are concerned over the quick use of the anti-Semitic label by Jews. Dr. Nahum Goldmann, president of the

World Jewish Congress, has said: "We are inclined to regard every gesture made by the non-Jew that may be distasteful to us as a display of anti-Semitism, often when it is not intended. . . . This distrust explains Israel's mistrust of the international guarantees proposed for her future. . . . We have begun to feel that the only real danger to the Jews' survival comes from the outside. We ignore the fact that since World War II anti-Semitism has lessened and cannot be compared to the sufferings we had to endure during the Nazi period or under the former anti-Semitic regimes of Czarist Russia, Rumania and Poland. We are and have been inclined to devote our major efforts to the fight against anti-Semitism, sometimes presenting insignificant signs as a grave danger and other times fighting windmills."

Jews have always been anxious about anti-Semitism even when it was slumbering. History has taught them that a mere circumstantial spark is enough to inflame it. That is one reason why they are quick to react to anything that might be seen as anti-Semitism and are not always careful in their judgment concerning it.

There is another and more profound reason. Jews grow up with the knowledge that the roots of anti-Semitism are ancient. In pagan antiquity, in Hellenistic Egypt, there lived the anti-Jewish publicist Apion who infected the world that was later to become Christian with his accusations that Jews were guilty of ritual murder, worship of money, atheism and sedition, charges that have been made against Jews for more than two millennia.

Before the nineteenth century, anti-Semitism was largely religious in nature, growing in great part out of Christian dislike for the Jews "who crucified Christ." The term "ghetto" originally referred to segregated sections in European cities where Jews settled or were forced to live. Such segregated areas appeared in Europe as early as the year 70. In that year the Romans conquered Palestine and in the Second Exile which followed, Jews were dispersed throughout the Roman Empire and beyond. Many settled in Europe. They lived together in separate streets or localities by choice so they could more easily practise their religious and cultural traditions. They also huddled together because they feared other groups. Later, governments forced the Jews, who were a minority in the nations of Christian Europe, by law to live in segregated areas.

By the fourteenth century ghettos were increasingly common as religious and political leaders demanded that the Jews be segregated. The reason generally given for compulsory living areas was that the faith of Christians would be weakened by the presence of Jews. The first compulsory ghettos were established in Spain and Portugal at the end of the fourteenth century. In 1555, Pope Paul IV decreed that the Jews in the Papal States, the area around Rome governed by the Roman Catholic Church, had to live in separate quarters. Authorities throughout the Christian world followed this example. The crowded neighbourhoods that developed were usually surrounded by walls, and the gates were locked at night.

These years were marked by sporadic persecutions and expulsions—notably the expulsion from Spain under Ferdinand and Isabella at the beginning of the Spanish Inquisition—by severe economic and personal restrictions and by fictions such as ritual murder by Jews of Christian children. As Jews were excluded more and more from the economic life of their host countries, they increasingly found themselves limited to unpopular professions, such as money-lending. As a result, anti-Semitism took on economic overtones as well. Before the nineteenth century and the Enlightenment, however, anti-Semitism remained largely religious in character and was inspired and promoted mainly by Christian princes and rulers and by the Christian Church.

In the opinion of some Christian, as well as Jewish, theologians, the New Testament is "tainted" and a source for anti-Semitic material. It may not be classed as a definitive guide for anti-Semitism, but it contained enough material to feed the fires of anti-Semitism among later Christian generations.

The cry of the mob in Matthew 27:24, "His blood be on us and our children," became the text of anti-Jewish preachers throughout the Christian centuries. The diatribes against the Jews in the fourth Gospel have brought John the title of "father of anti-Semitism," and they were the inspiration for Good Friday sermons which drove medieval mobs to the Jewish quarter to pillage and murder. For Jews these are dangerous texts because they are usually taken at face value. Save for the scholars, the average Christian reader possesses no training to keep the historical circumstances in mind so as to avoid drawing unwarranted conclusions.

To the New Testament may be added the theological literature from the first century onward as a source of anti-Semitism. American theologian Rosemary Ruether has described anti-Semitic Christian theology as "the left hand of christology." The left hand infected the right hand with its simultaneous upgrading of Christianity and derogation of Judaism.

Arie Lova Eliav, a member of Israel's parliament, the Knesset, a liberal who is careful in his judgment of non-Jews and has battled for the rights of Palestinian Arabs, says: "Since the first centuries of the

Christian era, the Jews have been homeless wanderers in Christian Europe. They were regarded as the crucifiers of Christ. The young Christian governors, kings and princes expelled them from one country after another. Jewish history in Europe is the history of Christian anti-Semitism and Jewish martyrdom. There is not a single people, not a single state in Europe that at one time or another has not maltreated the Jews, from the Crusades and the Spanish Inquisition to the Nazi ovens at Auschwitz."

One can trace the fourth-century fusion of Roman power and Christian faith and the resultant combination of the anti-Semitic ingredients of both; the Middle Ages, with its emphasis on the belief of the demonic nature of the Jews and the folkloristic acceptance of a Jewish conspiracy against the Christian world; and the birth of racism in sixteenth-century Spain, when even conversion to Christianity did not help the Jews because they were regarded as inferior by blood.

Then came Luther, the "moral hero" of the Protestants, who possessed a gigantic blind spot for the Jews. Like Mohammed, whom the Jews rejected, thereby earning his animosity, Luther turned on the Jews because they did not flock to his banner. In his work, *Concerning the Jews and Their Lies*, he recommended the burning of synagogues and the banishment of Jews as mad dogs. Jules Isaac, the modern French educator who has had a profound influence in bringing many Christians to recognize their responsibility in "the teaching of contempt," has called the great Protestant reformer "the Christian precursor of Auschwitz." The Jews were a perverse people to Luther. He appeared to believe that they knew Jesus was the messiah but rejected him deliberately. Luther's influence on German Christianity in this field was disastrous for Jews.

With the emancipation following the Enlightenment and the French Revolution, most of the enforced segregation of Jews ended. But anti-Semitism persisted—although in a new form. As nations turned their attention away from thoughts of the hereafter to a concern with the here and now, the overtly religious overtones to anti-Semitism were secularized. The coming of the modern age and its science produced in its place the pseudo-scientific ideology of anti-Semitism. It was at this time that the term "anti-Semitism" was first used.

As we saw in Chapter 5, the promises of the Enlightenment and liberalism were not fulfilled for the Jews. Despite their new-found political, economic and social rights, they continued to be looked on by most peoples as intruders and aliens. This was due in part to the rising tide of nationalism throughout Europe, but it was also due to the continuing preservation by Jews of cultural and religious barriers that isolated the Jewish minorities from their fellow citizens. Jews remained unpopular, a group apart, on whom all evils could be blamed. As in the past, governments and political and religious leaders looking for an outlet for popular discontent exploited this unpopularity.

This line of modern, secularized anti-Jewishness is direct through the German pamphleteer Wilhelm Marr, who in 1879 was among the first to use the word anti-Semitism out of a misunderstanding of social anthropology, to the strange English-German scholar Houston Stewart Chamberlain, who saw history in terms of Aryan peaks and Jewish valleys, to German historian Heinrich von Treitschke, the German philosopher Friedrich W. Nietzsche, the French diplomat and man of letters Comte Arthur de Gobineau, to Richard Wagner the composer, whose concept of German folkmasses helped to paganize German Christianity, and finally to Hitler and Auschwitz.

Jews and Christians have a special connection because of the crucial role the Church and Christian nations played in the spread of anti-Semitism. The onus rests heavily on Christians, according to United Church theologians Alan Davies, Robert Bater, Bruce McLeod, and others. It is an opinion not unpopular among Jews.

Many United Church ministers, aware that the alienation of Christians and Jews goes back centuries, are torn by the suggestion that texts from Matthew and John produced anti-Semitism. They cannot be sure it is not so, and therefore bend all their efforts in an exposition of the New Testament toward a greater appreciation of its Jewish content. But many make no such effort and thereby add to Jewish suspicions.

The suspicions are strengthened by contemporary events. Every decade or so produces alarms over Jew-hatred. In the last twenty years they have proved false, but Jews do not find this reassuring. In Germany the Naumann conspiracy, General Remer's Socialist Reich Party, General Ramcke's S.S. Party and Von Thadden, who became familiar to Canadians through extensive CBC and press coverage, all overt manifestations of anti-Semitism, have proved a flash in the pan. The M.S.I. (Momento Sociale Italiano) rose in Italy only to decline again, and the current modified fascist manifestations are having a hard time. In the south of France the movement launched by Pierre Poujade bore many resemblances to the tide which Hitler set in motion in the south of Germany. It was anti-Semitic and demagogic; it appealed to disgruntled shopkeepers, promising to capture the country for them. Who remembers it now? In Britain there was the old comedian Oswald Mosley, an outspoken anti-Semite, but few took him seriously. A younger fascist and anti-Semitic movement spurted under Colin Jordan, but he was slapped into prison.

Despite the failure of all these would-be stormtroopers, Jews do not feel secure. In 1924 Hitler was in prison. Many people thought he was finished. In 1929 one worthy professor even went on record with the statement that "thereafter he faded into oblivion." Four years later Hitler became dictator of Germany. It shows how careful professors—and writers—have to be. And it proves to Jews that even the experts can be off the mark in assessing anti-Semitism and that there is no substitute for vigilance.

Anti-Jewish manifestations in Canada in recent decades also reinforce Jewish fears. In the years between the two world wars, there were the fulminations of *Action catholique*, a newspaper sponsored by Quebec's majority Church and with which famous French-Canadian names like Pelletier, Roy and Bourassa were associated. The paper printed Nazi preachments—that Jews were in an international conspiracy to subvert Christianity, take over the world and bend it to an immoral will—as if they were gospel truths. The fact that *Action* worked in tandem with the official Roman Catholic *Semaine Religieuse de Québec* endowed the anti-Semitic concepts with unusual authority. Quebec also produced Adrien Arcand and his National Social Christian Party of the 1930s, whose favourite theme was the demonic influence of the Jew in Canadian society. What gave Arcand credence, as Lita-Rose Betcherman details in her book, *The Swastika and the Maple Leaf*, was his flirtation for a period with the Conservative Party led by R. B. Bennett. Although Quebec was the centre for the twin existence of fascism and anti-Semitism, in part because popular discontent, the feeding-ground for anti-Semitism, was more widespread in that province, other provinces—Ontario, Manitoba and Saskatchewan—also had their share of the movement.

Jews in their forties and fifties remember the "Gentile only" signs and restricted housing advertisements in the newspapers. Those who fought in World War II and returned to look for homes, while still in uniform, negotiated for the purchase of a house in a restricted area. The deal went easily until mention was made of the buyer's origins, when suddenly the bargaining would be broken off, the real estate agent explaining that he was bound by a "gentleman's agreement" not to sell to Jews.

In pre- and post-World War I days department stores in Toronto and Winnipeg hired only *Judenrein* staffs. Ben Kayfetz, director of the Canadian Jewish Congress-B'nai B'rith Community Relations Committee, recalls only two Jewish members on the University of Toronto faculty in the 1930s. A Jew could not reach the Elysian level of high school principalship unless he had certain visible "markings," a Gentile wife, for example.

Robert McClure remembers that "in medical school the Jewish doctor was made fun of and resented by many of our WASP teachers. This even applied to making fun of their Jewish medical students. Having been raised as a member of a minority group of whites in China, I was quite allergic to these demonstrations of prejudice. The small number of Jewish doctors on hospital staffs was obvious to all."

In the years between the two world wars non-Jews looked askance at Jewish peddlers invading commercial, professional and residential areas formerly dominated by the Anglo-Saxon Protestant elite. McClure recalls talk at Toronto's Harbord Collegiate that the foreigners with "Jewish accents" were "taking over." Palmerston Blvd., with its canopy of trees and ornate streetlamps, became almost totally Jewish in character, the spacious homes built by non-Jews sold, in a Gentile exodus, to rabbis and Jewish doctors. College and Bloor Streets became the magnet for Jewish business enterprise.

All this changed as human rights laws in Canadian provinces became an established fact. The messianic era has not yet come to the teaching profession in this country, but one has only to look at the rosters in university faculties—history, economics, political and social sciences, natural sciences, law, English and foreign literature—and at the occupants of university presidential offices in western Canada, to realize the radical change.

In the 1930s, Jewish engineering graduates, because of the depression and prejudice, became jewellers and retailers of ladies' dresses. Today the deans of engineering faculties take care not to schedule examinations on Jewish holidays so that orthodox students are not prevented from writing. Such students no longer find their origins an obstacle to employment. At one time many Jewish medical graduates, faced with impossible barriers, immigrated to the US. Today Jewish doctors are members of hospital staffs across the country.

In the 1970s department stores boast that their salespersons speak a dozen European and Asian languages, even Yiddish. The complexion of politics has undergone a revolutionary transformation, Anglo-Saxon constituencies being represented by Jews and Jewish ridings by Anglophones and Francophones.

Yet these developments do not reassure Canadian Jews. They recall the gangs of hoodlums, encouraged by what was happening in Nazi Germany, forming swastika clubs to keep Jews away from recreation areas. The years have expanded and embroidered the tales and reminiscences, but incidents did happen. Trucks did pick up the Jewish "militia" at the corner of Spadina and Dundas in Toronto to take them to the Gentile battlegrounds in an "operation counter-swastika."

The bloody incidents on the Canadian scene belong to the past, yet polite bias still exists in social clubs and on the executive levels of corporations, banks and insurance companies. Jews applaud the gains but wonder how secure they really are. Jews do not see anti-Semitism as just another prejudice. Its long, long history and deep, deep bias, culminating in the scientific extinction of more than one-third of their people, makes it a plague that will not soon be eradicated.

Will the depression incidents and practices of the 1930s be repeated in the difficult economic years of the 1970s? In April 1976, the leader of the Ralliement Créditiste, Camil Samson, before a committee of the Quebec National Assembly, singled out Jews performing abortions as "artisans of destruction" who threaten the Quebec people. Canadian Jews ask: Why this incorrigible identification of Jewishness with what people fear? The year 1976 was also marked by the circulation of anti-Semitic cartoons in Toronto, the defacing of synagogues and the intensified activities of the anti-Semitic Western Guard, all noted by the daily press.

Aren't present circumstances in Canada the tinder box which can be set ablaze by anti-Semitic sparks, constantly emerging from the flint of the Gentile-Christian character? Should not the anti-Semitism just below the surface of the Canadian polity, acknowledged by many United Church leaders, be taken seriously?

It may be argued that the young are not so addicted to the old anti-Semitic beliefs as their fathers, that they are not so devoted to the ancient Christian dogma in which the first anti-Jewish seed is usually planted. All the post-1945 neo-Nazi parties in Germany, for instance, have been of this type—old survivors keeping in touch with other old survivors and regurgitating stale froth in familiar beer halls. No doubt it is a pity that some still survive, but it is consolation that they are old. By their existence they do not prove that a new Nazism has been born but that certain old Nazis have not yet died.

The same can be said of similar parties which have appeared in Latin America. In Argentina and Brazil neo-Nazi cells are continually being unearthed, but on examination most of them prove to be the products of large German colonies there, colonies swollen by fugitive war criminals.

Younger disgruntled elements of the population, however, can draw their inspiration not from old propaganda or old experience but from the realities of the 1970s. Might not the real facts of today prove as inflammable tinder to these sparks as those of yesterday did to Hitler?

In the United States, economic depression combined with national frustration, compounded by an ineffective regime in Washington, provides fertile soil for the haters. But the strong libertarian momentum, bred into American institutions, and an historic awareness that all Americans were originally foreigners could cause anti-Semitism to billow only regionally not nationally.

Canada generally follows the US pattern, as it often does in economic and social matters, with the most visible anti-Semitic outcroppings in Quebec where frustration is greatest.

Jews do reflect on the enormous differences between the 1930s and the 1970s, on the widespread resentment against Arab totalitarians brandishing a cruel and self-centred weapon, and on the fact that almost everybody in Canada now belongs to some kind of minority group. Surely the fossil survivals of Hitler Germany cannot be resurrected here. But twentieth-century experience compels the Jews to take no chances. The Canadian Jewish Congress continues to study every manifestation of anti-Jewish bias.

Since 1967 Jewish anxiety has risen because of the anti-Israel manifestations of the American Left, which spilled over into Canada, and the radical theologians like the Berrigan brothers, as well as the street Jew-hatred that erupted in the US Black revolution. The 1973 Middle East war accented the anxiety through the political pressure of the Arab oil embargo and the resulting energy crisis throughout the industrialized nations, many of which had heretofore supported Israel.

These circumstances have produced a new concept of Jew-hatred, which has been given exhaustive treatment in a B'nai B'rith Anti-Defamation League-sponsored study by Arnold Forster and Benjamin A. Epstein. Their thesis is simple: the old anti-Semitism came from active hatred; the new comes from insensitivity and unconcern. "It includes often a callous indifference to Jewish concerns expressed by respectable institutions and persons, people who would be shocked to think themselves or have others think them anti-

Semites." It is this kind of hostility Jews discern in some United Church leaders and in the policy of *The Observer*.

However, not all who are indifferent to Jews are anti-Semitic. If a person is indifferent to Jews because they are Jews, then he may be classed as an anti-Semite, but if he is indifferent to them because he is self-centred and uncommitted to human rights he is not necessarily a Jew-hater. In an ADL survey in the US, respondents were asked whether they would support an anti-Semitic candidate for president. Only a few would, but one-third said it would not make any difference, and they meant just that. If the candidate produced bread-and-butter results or an effective foreign policy, it would make no difference to them how he treated Jews. Such people do not necessarily hate Jews; they just do not believe enough in human rights.

The same kind of indifference characterized Britain and France in their policy toward Israel during the Yom Kippur War. They wanted oil, and since the Arabs had it, that is where their sympathies lay. Moral principle was less important to them than the need for energy. If the Israelis had been sitting on rich oil deposits instead of the Arabs, there would have been no hesitation in siding with them. That kind of indifference is certainly not anti-Semitism. As for United Church leaders, most of them are not that cynical. Those who criticize Israel do so out of a sense of moral responsibility. They cannot be considered indifferent to Jewish concerns, callously or otherwise. Therefore, they do not fit the Forster-Epstein analysis.

Some social scientists suggest a more relevant definition of the new anti-Semitism—the willingness to grant Jews rights as individuals but not as a group (see Chapter 5). "Modern Europe," says American writer Earl Raab, "never really accepted the legitimacy of the corporate Jew, although it was at its best willing to grant full civil rights to the individual Jew. That for the Jews was an impossible paradox, a secular version of Christian demands to convert. In neither case—giving up his religion or giving up his communal identity—could the Jew comply without ceasing to be a Jew." Inevitably failure to accept the right of Jewish group existence results in an assault on the civil rights of individual Jews. Hence, Jewish suspicion in Canada of those who are critical of Zionism, Jewish nationalism and the state of Israel. For Canadian Jews ethnic consciousness has become co-extensive with the existence of Israel. No wonder, then, that they have difficulty separating anti-Zionism from anti-Semitism.

American writer Cynthia Ozick expressed it best for Canadian Jews: "Moralists of the world! Here is the way it is. This is the only way it is. You cannot separate parent from child, the Jews from Zion.

And if you do, you are known for what you are."

If the United Church and the Jews of Canada are to reconcile their differences, they must recognize that they are in a unique relationship and that criticism of Israel is legitimate, but that it should be undertaken with sensitivity and care.

Canadian Jews must openly grant the right of criticism of Israel. Masses of Jews may be unhappy about any criticism, but Jewish intellectuals generally do not deny that right. Says Emil Fackenheim: "Of course, Christians have the right to criticize Israeli policies. On occasion they may even have the duty."

On the United Church side, critics must be careful not to give the impression that they are saying, as Canadian Jewish Congress president Sydney Harris phrases it: "What are those Jewish bastards doing to those Arabs over there?" That could be anti-Semitism as well as anti-Israelism. Many Jews see that attitude in the policy of *The Observer*. To say, as some United Church ministers do, that "Jews are hysterical and blind when anyone questions the absolute righteousness of Israel" is also unhelpful. Because different concepts of group loyalty are involved, care must be taken by both sides in the language used and the attitudes struck. Criticism of Israel by Christians should always be couched in language conveying the conviction that the Jewish state has as much right to continue to exist as any other political organism.

Why such care and caution? Why should Jews be treated differently? All people are sensitive to criticism; why special consideration for Jewish sensitivity? Granted that their suffering was great, but did not the Russians suffer millions of casualties in the same war that generated the Holocaust? And do not the Palestinians have their Diaspora, though many never left home?

Obviously there is need to have compassion and to make every effort at understanding any people who have borne pain and misery. We must search for the causes of all conflicts and the part we may have played in them. But it is still true that Jewish-Christian history is different from Russian-Christian and Arab-Christian relations, though there was the dread of the eastern menace from the steppes in one case and the Crusades in the other. The reasons for Jewish-Christian alienation and the persecutions of the Jews in which that alienation so often resulted make the relationship unique.

Some United Church leaders will not accept the special Jewish-Christian relationship. They refuse to assume the blame for what Christians have done to Jews in the past. But the issue is not that of bearing the sins of the fathers. It is a question of the ancient bitterness rising again through constant contact with the old image of the Jews in sacred texts and associations. "We're not like that any more," say United Church leaders. But in pre-World War II Germany and elsewhere the feeling there, too, was that former generations were not "like" the present one, and the tragic Jewish history was repeated again and again. Robert Bater is emphatic on this point: "I think there is every reason to say this is not a past problem but one which we can repeat very readily and are always in the greatest danger of repeating. To me, that's one of the fundamental points in this whole struggle between Christian and Jew."

To argue thus is not to make the Christian the sole villain and the Jew the whitewashed victim. The persecuted are as capable of hatred, bitterness and discrimination as are the persecutors. Howse is right to claim that there are two sides in any discussion on anti-Semitism. "As soon as you talk with me about anti-Semitism, you're talking only about my failings. Shouldn't we talk about racism? Just as there is a capacity in Christians to create anti-Semitism so there is within Jews a possibility of creating hostility to Gentiles. Isn't one as bad as the other?"

The issue here, however, is also the power of the strong over the weak, and for 2,000 years Christians have had power over Jews, a dominant position sanctified by theology. Today Jews are faced with the same problem of power in relation to Palestinian refugees (not the Arab states), as we shall see in Chapter 9.

Father Gregory Baum, the Canadian Roman Catholic theologian, is helpful in revealing the moral component in power relationships. He says that a majority which has derived benefits from a minority through power over it cannot follow objective standards of behaviour toward it. For example, it would be unjust for Americans to look upon Blacks as just another minority. They were brought to the US as slaves, exploited and dehumanized for profit, and their problems must be remedied with these historic facts in mind. For Americans to be objective about Blacks would be to deny "the whole historical truth."

Similarly a Christian cannot classify Israel as just another of many national entities. When Christians criticize Pakistan, India or China, they are not necessarily revealing latent hostility to Muslims, Hindus, Confucians or Buddhists. But when they criticize Israel, they are in danger of demonstrating a secret antipathy to Jews. "For accompanying Christian preaching almost from the beginning," says Baum, "were hostile and prejudicial views, not against Muslims,

Hindus and Confucians, but against Jews. They have entered our ecclesiastical tradition, our language of worship; they have nourished a popular symbolism and generated hostile feelings."

Jews must be discriminating in judging their assenters as well as their dissenters. They would be wrong to make an easy identification of anti-Israel opinion and anti-Semitism, for one can be pro-Israel and anti-Semitic. "I know people that are all for Israel," says Bruce McLeod. "They're backing her up with every bit of energy they have. They think the Jews should have a homeland and that *every* Jew should go there—and get off their street. And they mean it. That's a clear relation of anti-Semitic and pro-Israel feeling."

Many fundamentalist Christians are pro-Israel. Their reasons come from a literal interpretation of the Bible—they feel that the Jews are being gathered in the Promised Land for a single purpose, so that Christians may go there and convert them into Christians. Many Jews in Canada and elsewhere, including Israeli government officials, are enthusiastic over the fundamentalists' favourable response to the existence of the Jewish state. But no Jew of integrity should accept this kind of support.

It is understandable that Jews, being on the defensive, look for allies wherever they can get them, even for the wrong reasons. The resolution of the United Church-Jewish quarrel, however, can only be achieved through rationality and humanity on both sides, not expediency. Jews must understand their own weaknesses in any attempt at reconciliation. United Church leaders, on their part, must realize that stress on the Christian right to criticize Israel leads to alienation. Jews concede that right, some reluctantly, but it is not the main issue. United Church leaders should rather be concerned that criticism of the Jewish state be free—and is seen to be free—from the taint of anti-Semitism.

CHAPTER EIGHT

The Holocaust

Canadian Jews often complain that non-Jews do not understand the meaning of the Holocaust—the systematic murder of six million Jews under the Nazis—its unprecedented character and profound effects, so profound that Jews will feel its trauma for generations. This complaint is a familiar grievance in the bill of particulars against United Church leaders.

If a United Church-Jewish reconciliation is to come, there must be a clear understanding of why the Holocaust holds Jews in its grip more than three decades after its gruesome details were first revealed to an incredulous world. On March 14, 1975, the *Canadian Jewish News* could still write: "Given the circumstances in which two and a half million Jews still find themselves a quarter of a century after the birth of the modern state of Israel, there are few who would challenge the practicality and propriety of a vigorous campaign to remind the world that six million Jews died in the Nazi Holocaust."

For Jews that reminder is very realistic advice. It has to do with survival or extermination. That is why Jewish thinking is usually apocalyptic. One can be pessimistic or optimistic about an economic depression, but one can only be apocalyptic about the threat of annihilation.

Avoiding another Holocaust is an everyday business with Jews. There was no need for an explanatory announcement when in February 1975 the Canadian Jewish Congress called a conference of professional community workers and academics to work out the most effective techniques for educating people in the meaning of the ruin of European Jewish communities. Holocaust seminars are frequently held in Montreal, Ottawa, Toronto, Vancouver and Winnipeg. Everybody knows of the threat to Israel, which is seen as the danger of another massive destruction comparable to the Nazi act of genocide. Canadian Jews understand Yoram Kaniuk, one of Israel's best known writers, when he says: "There may be a time in history when the little Jewish state will not be able to perform miracles for the television-watchers of the world, and we'll vanish—right in front of three hundred million colour TV sets."

Jews, therefore, have taken up the task of concerted remembering, transmitting to their children the horror-filled details of the Europe of 1933-45. The events have entered the prayer books of synagogues on Yom Kippur, the most sacred day in the Hebrew calendar. How deeply they have stamped their dread on Jewish consciousness may be seen from the following excerpt from a prayer by Rabbi David Polish in the *High Holiday Prayer Book* of the Reconstructionist synagogues of New York, Montreal and Toronto.

> Almighty God, raise up a man who will go peddling through the world.
> Let him gather us up and go through the world selling us as trinkets.
> Let the peddler sell us cheaply. Let him hawk his wares and say:
> Who will buy my souvenirs? Little children done in soap,
> A rare Germanic parchment of the greatest Jew in Lodz.
> Men will buy us and display us and point to us with pride.
> A thousand Jews went into this, and here is a rare piece
> That came all the way from Crakow in a box car.
> A great statesman will place a candle at his bedside.
> It will burn but never be consumed.
> The tallow will drip with the tears we shed.
> And it will glow with the souls of our children.
> They will put us in the bathrooms of the United Nations
> Where diplomats will wash and wash their hands
> With Polish Jews and German Jews and Russian Jews.
> Let the peddler sell the box of soap that was once buried
> With Kaddish and Psalms by our brothers.
>
> Some night the statesman will blow upon the candle
> And it will not go out.
> The souls of little children will flicker and flicker
> But not expire.
> Some day the diplomats will wash their hands and find them stained with blood.
> Some day the citizens of the German town
> Will awake to find their houses reeking
> With all the vapors from all the concentration camps,
> From Hell itself, and the stench will come from the
> Soap box.

Then they will all rise up, statesmen, diplomats, citizens,
And go hunting for the peddler: You who disturb our rest
And our ablutions, you who haunt us with your souvenirs,
You who prick our conscience, death upon you!

But the peddlers shall never cease from the earth
Until the candles die out and the soap melts away.

The Holocaust has changed the character of many Jews. It has transformed them from pacifist believers in non-aggressive nationalism to parochial proponents of conventional nationhood.

Poets usually thrive in a crisis atmosphere, and Hebrew poets since the Nazi period have found a ready audience. In recent years the poet clothed with prophetic grandeur has been Uri Zvi Greenberg, the genius who came to Palestine from a Galician village in 1924. When World War II broke, he was in Poland on a mission for the Zionist-Revisionists, a rightist group, then escaped to his adopted country. His parents and sisters, among six million others, did not escape.

Jews identify with Greenberg and his lyric out-pouring of wrath and anguish over the Holocaust as with few other poets. He sees the Jewish people as a great irreversible tide, flowing from Abraham past the hostile settlements of the Gentile world. Its fate is to be hated and persecuted. Yet it alone has standards of vision and conduct which are unique, a legacy transmitted through blood of loved ones spilled.

Greenberg is defiantly and openly racist. He sees humankind divided into two camps—the Jews, who have the gift of true compassion, and the Gentiles, whose inner nature makes them ravenous beasts, only occasionally lulled by the music of a Beethoven and the insight of a Goethe and Kant. For him all things are touched by Holocaust nightmares.

It is not the morning star
  ascending in the east.
Look Brother,
It is a skull, a Jew's skull whose
  skin has been stripped,
Still in its fresh redness
  burning brightly
As in the Creator's thought before
  the creation of man.

The most frightful event in history since Creation—for Greenberg and for millions of Jews—is the fiery death of six million innocents.

Other peoples, when they imagine the most terrifying thing that could happen to the world, think of a nuclear war. Jews think of another Holocaust. To them the Hitler period is the ultimate in destruction. The "bomb" is impersonal death activated by a button. The Holocaust was death by design, accomplished by cold intellectuals honed in savagery, than which there is nothing more terrible.

The European experience of the 1930s and forties has driven so deeply into Jewish lives that many of them no longer seem capable of reacting to hatred and attack in the traditional way. The historic Jewish martyr went to his death with *Sh'ma Yisrael* (Hear, O Israel) on his lips, affirming his faith, though reality disputed it, in the unity of mankind. Jewish lives today are ruled by the slogan, "Never again!" Some Jews are determined to outdo the Gentiles; they will play the game of violence and beat them at it.

Holocaust writer Elie Wiesel explains the change in Jewish character in a dramatic way. In his passionate novella, *Dawn*, which is like a single scream, he tells of Elisha, a young member of the Jewish terrorist movement in the Palestine of the 1940s, who has been selected to kill a captain kidnapped from the British army in retaliation for hangings by the Mandate government. A Jew with blood on his hands? He has just escaped from the Nazi murderers, and now he must commit murder himself. The whole night long he prepares for the violence he must do. Before him come the visions of his dead friends, teachers and relatives. They are the witnesses of his conscience, and he justifies to them the brutal act he is about to commit.

His mother appears. "I said to her that I wasn't a murderer, that she had not given birth to a murderer but to a soldier, to a fighter for freedom, to an idealist who had sacrificed his peace of mind—a possession more precious than life itself—to his people's right to the light of day, to joy, to the laughter of children. . . ."

His dead father then appears, and Elisha says: "Do not judge me. Judge God. He created the universe and made justice stem from injustice. He brought it about that a people should attain happiness through tears, that the freedom of a nation, like that of man, should be a monument built upon a pile, a foundation of dead bodies. . . ."

Elisha shoots the British officer. His new arguments for violence triumph over the teaching of his parents and the power of traditional ideals.

Even in this condensed and mutilated form it is possible to understand Wiesel's exposition of the adjustment of Jewish character to the so-called realm of necessity. It is this change of character that permits the militant Masada syndrome, the determination to fight to the death: Our pain and sorrow are so huge we have grounds for dropping the bomb ourselves. Let Armageddon come.

Norman Podhoretz, editor of *Commentary* magazine, in a dour assessment of the Middle East in July 1976, says that Israel might well be forced by the superpowers into a Munich-like agreement with the Arabs, but unlike the South Vietnamese in 1975 and the Czechs in 1938, the Israelis would not surrender without a fight. They would fight first with conventional weapons and then "if the tide were turning decisively against them and if help in the form of resupply of arms were not forthcoming, it is safe to predict that they would fight with nuclear weapons in the end." In a Samson-like farewell they would go down and bring the world down with them.

Not all Jews accept this argument. For all the uniqueness and horror of the Holocaust many argue that there are still no grounds for changing the pacifist, anti-competitive Jewish character, formed in ancient times and transmitted through the centuries by precept and example. Such character is a practical matter for Jews; it is the only assurance they have for the viability of the Jewish group. As it alone was productive of the past—of making the Torah into "a portable homeland" and the Diaspora Jewish community an imperishable government-in-exile—it alone is reliable for the future.

Jews are dealing with realities when they attribute physical survival to character. Without an army and its weapons of violence, they not only preserved their communal life for two millennia but produced literary and spiritual creations that raised mere existence to moral power and influence. Take any people anywhere, reduce them to poverty, subdue them to exploitation, punish them with persecution, and they will emerge scarred, wounded and brow-beaten, dirtied and degraded. The Jews have suffered a more dreadful poverty, a more cruel exploitation, a more merciless persecution than any other people in the whole history of Christendom. What wonder that they have manifested, perhaps to an extreme degree, all the qualities shared by all peoples who have at any time been forced to bear these ills. And yet they have been able to rise painfully to their feet and win their place as self-respecting men and women. They have behind them centuries of persecution but at the same time centuries of inner freedom, culture, enlightenment, family devotion and high pursuits of mind and spirit. It may well be true that there has been no other people in the world to compare with this record. Out of their history of degradation the Jews have produced the three most influential minds of the twentieth century—Marx, Einstein and Freud. All this they did without resort to even defensive force or violence.

It is the so-called realists, the shortsighted worldlings, believing that reliance on conventional nationalism will save the Jew, who are the romantics. Certainly, the assurance of the future of the Jewish people, as of the whole human species, is relative. One can speak only of a maximum guarantee not an absolute. But when Jews tamper with the spirit that brought them so far, when they insist that the times call for an emphasis on militancy and force, they are interfering with the primal source of Jewish meaning and the Jewish sources of strength.

When I argue this way with death-camp survivors, they chafe. I did not know the Holocaust first-hand; therefore, I am not privy to its horror. But being a victim of violence does not make one an expert in human relations. The experience of unspeakable terror does not make counter-violence the ineluctable answer. There are Jews, witnesses of death-camp horrors, whose experiences have made them uncompromisingly anti-violence.

Viktor E. Frankl, the Viennese-Jewish psychiatrist, who spent World War II in Auschwitz and Dachau, has said: "We who lived in concentration camps can remember the men who walked through the huts comforting others. They may have been few in number, but they offer sufficient proof that everything can be taken from a man but one thing, the last of the human freedoms—to choose one's attitude in any given set of circumstances, to choose one's own way." Frankl, the Israeli artist Yehudah Bacon and the philosopher Martin Buber, all victims of Nazi violence, chose the way of non-violence.

Moreover, it is not correct to distinguish between death-camp survivors and other Jews. Hitler's plans were designed for the entire Jewish people. The Jews of Canada were also in his plans. The reader will permit a personal reference to make this point clear.

Like Uri Zvi Greenberg's family, my relatives also perished in the orgy of death of the 1940s. I have never seen the town of Slonim where my father was born. I know that though it was a small town of 16,000 with 14,000 Jews, it made up in poverty for what it lacked in size. Even in its best days it was so poor that black bread and herring brine often made a full-course dinner.

It had its limitations, Slonim did; but it had its virtues also. There was piety in Slonim and reverence for learning. Bread might be scarce there but not books. What is more, the townspeople of Slonim, as befitted the disciples of scriptural prophets and rabbinic sages, had a keen sense of justice, so keen that, according to an ancient practice, anyone who had been wronged was entitled to interrupt public worship until the iniquity had been righted.

And it was a merciful place. The poorest of Slonim, even those who themselves lived on alms, gave something regularly for charity's sake. It was also a place of great spiritual earnestness.

And now Slonim, as a Jewish town, is wiped out, expunged by a ruthless hand, for it was directly in the path of the German army invading Russia (see Notes on Chapter 8). Its old, old synagogue, where my ancestors worshipped for uncounted generations, is no more. Its *yeshivah* (Talmudical school) that was its major industry was converted into a stable by the Nazis. The books it composed and treasured are now ashes. Even the cemetery, where my forefathers sleep, has, I suppose, been erased.

As for the 14,000 Jews—some saints, some sinners, some learned, some untutored, some wise and some foolish, but all eager to live, all undeserving of the fate that overtook them—I do not want to think of them. Yet think of them I must.

They haunt me. But for some unexplained grace and a capricious decision by my father to come to Canada, I would be cold and still, like them. The thought takes on further poignancy when I reflect that, though I did not know them, many were my kin, bearing names common in my family—the Meir to which my father answered, the Leah to which my sister responds. What is more, being kin to me, they may actually have resembled members of my family in appearance and character.

That is why these Jews haunt me. I feel that I know them and their fate. Are they not flesh of my flesh and blood of my blood?

And it is inconceivable to me that these gentle people, knowing violence only in the sense of being victims of it, could say with the Israeli writer Ephraim Kishon: "We are madmen capable of smashing the world to bits if not given a place in the sun." Only the desperate Israeli and the Diaspora Jew, cut off from Jewish roots, talks like that.

Of course, the Jew should keep remembering the Holocaust and rise in indignation with each remembrance. Indignation is an old Jewish art which should be revived. Jews should wear it like a badge, as if it were one of the most honourable of human traits. While Judaism is a religion of love, its heroic figures were men capable of great indignation: Moses, indignant against the taskmaster beating the Hebrew slave, indignant even against his own people for worshipping the golden calf; or the prophets, from Elijah to Malachi; or even Christianity, the daughter of Judaism, for though the Christian religion started out to portray Jesus as the personification of pure love, it quickly gave up the attempt, realizing that its picture of him could not be kept moral unless it included indignation also. But Jews, like their forbears, should also be capable of embracing the world, though the world forsakes them.

The Holocaust has brought a profound crisis of faith to today's Jews. The best known confrontation between Jews in their belief and unbelief was that of theologian Richard L. Rubenstein and author Elie Wiesel at the International Scholars' Conference, Wayne State University, in 1970. In the presence of a learned fraternity from Germany, Canada, Israel and the United States, the protagonists squared off.

Said Rubenstein: "I have to decide whether to affirm the existence of God who afflicts Auschwitz on his guilty people or to insist that nothing the Jews did made them more deserving of Auschwitz than any other people, that Auschwitz was in no sense a punishment, and that a God who could or would inflict such punishment does not exist. In other words, I have elected to accept what Camus has rightly called the courage of the absurd, the courage to live in a meaningless, purposeless cosmos rather than to believe in a God who inflicts Auschwitz on his people."

Wiesel responds with his own anguish: "And here I will tell you, Dick, that you don't understand them [the Jews] when you say it is more difficult to live today in a world without God. No! If you want difficulties, choose to live with God. Can you compare today the tragedy of the believer to that of the unbeliever? The real tragedy, the real drama is the drama of the believer."

Even Jews who come to Wiesel's conclusion—that they must believe though it break their hearts—sympathize with Rubenstein. They understand well his idea that a God worthy of human adoration who could have inflicted Auschwitz on what was allegedly his people is obscene.

Jewish tradition characteristically does not give first place to belief or faith but to action. What a person believes about the world is not so important as what he does for the world. The Holocaust has served further to de-emphasize belief.

This may be seen in the mythology that has grown up around the memory of the six million. The hero of one myth is Reb Bunem, a *shamash* or sexton. The *shamash* was not high in the social scale of the East European *stetl's* (town) prayer-and-study house, but he was more essential to its operation than the rabbi. It is told that as the Nazis spread over the Russo-Polish countryside, Reb Bunem could not endure their presence; he went mad.

Every day he would mount the altar, open the cupboard where the Torah scrolls were kept, pound the table where they were read, and say: "*Ribono shel olom*, master of the universe, I want you to know that I am still here." And every day the number of Jews would grow smaller as the conqueror transported them to the camps. Still Reb Bunem would continue his daily ritual, drawing aside the curtain of the ark to reveal the scrolls, pounding the table and saying: "Master of the universe, I want you to know that I am still here."

Finally, all the Jews were taken except Bunem. The Nazis did not bother with madmen. Alone, Bunem mounted the altar, opened the ark, banged on the table and said: "Master of the universe, I want you to know that I am still here." Then he paused and added: "But you, where are you?"

Bunem was in the tradition of the reverent agnostics that populate Jewish history—the biblical Job and the Hasidic Levi Yitzhak of Berdichev—who refused to bow to injustice and demanded an answer of God himself. Justice must always be done, and if God will not do it, then the Jew must do it for him and on his behalf.

In questioning the divine lapses, the Jew of the past did not bother much with theology or systems of belief. He was preoccupied with ethics, action.

The Holocaust has deepened this distinction. After Auschwitz, Jews have become more addicted to *hutzpah* (audacity). They will have none of the compliant attitude of those who entered the gas chambers with bowed head. It is said that some German Jews were so passive that when they were told to fold their blankets a certain way before going to the "showers" they meekly obeyed. No more, say the post-Auschwitz Jews, "never again!"

No one can explain the Hitler period without taking this spiritual torment into account. One cannot approach this terrible time without a sense of dreadful mystery.

The crisis of faith and changes in Jewish attitudes are true of Jews around the world, but they are especially evident in Canada, a fact United Church leaders must reckon with in their relations with the Canadian Jewish community.

British and American Jews have been able to combine urbanity with their sensitivity to the Nazi period. Canadian Jews favour the passionate response, disproving the impression that those who settle into the Canadian milieu assume the alleged blandness of its character.

One example should be enough to show how deeply Jewish

emotions in this country can run in contrast to Jewish equanimity in other countries.

In the winter of 1972, Robert Shaw's *Man in the Glass Booth* was performed in Montreal's Sadye Bronfman Centre. Its theme was the trial in Jerusalem of Nazi Adolf Eichmann. London and New York critics received the play with indifferent reviews—it is no *tour de force*—and the audiences seemed to take the Holocaust theme in stride.

But in Montreal the reaction shook the community to the roots. The survivors' associations found the play morally objectionable because in their view the Nazis and their victims were presented as equally culpable.

Why the uproar in a Canadian city and not in other world capitals? Some American observers concluded that Canadian Jews lack sophistication. A more valid reason, cited by Canadian Jewish Congress officials, is that the "graduates" of concentration camps are a more active and influential entity in Canada than in larger Jewish centres where the trend to integration is more advanced. This situation must be considered in any dialogue with Canadian Jews.

Is it fair to say that United Church members do not understand the meaning of the Holocaust? Surely that cannot be said of W. Clarke MacDonald, secretary of the Committee on the Church and International Affairs, whose feelings represent a large segment of United Church leadership. He recalls visiting the Holocaust exhibit in the Jewish Pavilion at Expo in Montreal in 1967, where the most touching presentation was a tiny pedestal displaying a child's pair of worn shoes.

The inscription noted that the shoes were found outside the Auschwitz complex, probably kicked off as the last act of a youngster who disappeared, with a million others, into the Nazi death factory.

"My five-year-old daughter was by my side," says MacDonald, "and I can affirm that I held her hand more tightly at that point. If someone had spoken to me as I came out, I would have found it difficult to reply, because I was so deeply moved by what I had seen, heard and felt in that experience. If I—as a person who at that time had never set foot in Europe, had never visited Israel (as I have done twice since), knew only a limited number of Jews on a personal level, could feel that way—then I can well imagine why the Jews feel as they do."

Similarly, E. M. Howse acknowledges that the slaughter of six million Jews might well be judged "the single worst crime in history."

But neither MacDonald nor Howse is willing to concede that it is a unique crime. It is simply different in degree from that of the Assyrians who flayed their enemies and that of Joshua who demolished his foes without a trace. Whether extermination is by knife, crossbow, bullet, flaying alive or burning, says Howse, the history of the annihilation of all minorities is almost a normal part of human shame. "To that extent Hitler did only what Joshua did."

To regard the Jews as unique victims, according to Howse, might disguise the fact that Jews, too, are capable of animosity. "In the early days before [the defeat of the Jewish war party at] Masada and the destruction of Jerusalem, Jews were merciless to all their enemies. There is nothing to suggest they are less merciless than the rest of us."

As for MacDonald, the shame of Auschwitz is in the same category as the shame of the rape of a quarter million Bangladesh women in that country's war not long ago.

Both men contend the sorrow of the world is universal and therefore indivisible, that Jews are identical in their failings when in power, and in their suffering when powerless, with all mankind and deserve no special concern. They should be content to accept the genuine sadness of other people over what happened to them, coupled with a determination that such a thing should not happen again to anyone, anywhere, on the face of the earth. But they should not expect that others should experience a sense of guilt for the Holocaust.

There is universalism and spirituality in this attitude, but it tends to split hairs. In the Judeo-Christian tradition, sorrow and guilt for the sins of humankind are closely related. All Christians and Jews must feel guilty because of what they fail to do to rescue humanity from injustice. Factually they may not be guilty but morality demands that they feel guilty. Elie Wiesel said it: "I live and therefore I am guilty. I am still here, because a friend, a comrade, an unknown died in my place." Without a sense of guilt there can be no confession, no repentance and ultimately no constructive action.

We should feel guilty that we have done little to lessen the sorrows of the Bengalis, but how can we acknowledge our responsibility to them if we haven't yet recognized failure at Hitler's death camps? The way to Bangladesh leads through Auschwitz. Especially because Christians and Jews have been in a 2,000-year confrontation, the fact of Auschwitz refuses to be bypassed. For Christians and Jews, therefore, the Holocaust is unique, whatever else it may be to others.

John W. Burbidge of Trent University challenges the United Church on this issue: "For anyone who wills to enter into dialogue with the Jewish tradition, the uniqueness of the Holocaust must be faced squarely, not only in terms of the act itself but its background within the traditions of Western Europe and Christian theology. This ultimate responsibility of the Christian tradition and the Western European culture for what happened there is a matter of disturbing self-examination. Few are mature and strong enough to do that with honesty."

The Holocaust will always be a barrier for Christians and Jews to overcome. One remembers the pre-war struggle of the Protestants in Germany to unite against tyranny. In 1934 representatives of Lutheran, Reformed and United Churches met at Wuppertal-Barmen to oppose the "German Christians" who were trying to reform church government in conformity with Hitler's wishes.

But of the combined forty million Christian adherents in Germany, Dietrich Bonhoeffer alone, according to his biographer, publicly "viewed the Jewish problem as the first and decisive question, even as the only one." He befriended Jews, helped them to flee the Third Reich and announced to his fellow Christians: "Only he who cries out for the Jews may sing the Gregorian chant."

Bonhoeffer was hanged in a concentration camp three days before the Allies reached it and his remains cremated. He was among the fractional minority willing to face up to a sense of guilt over the Jews and follow its consequences!

After Hitler's death, European Christians wrestled with the spectre of guilt. The synod of the German Evangelical Church on April 27, 1950, announced: "By dereliction of duty and in keeping silent we are also guilty of the crimes committed towards Jews. We pray all Christians to rid themselves of all anti-Semitism whatsoever, to resist it earnestly where it raises its head again."

Such confession may be valid for Christians who lived through the Nazi period and were silent, but why should Canadians, and specifically United Church people, flagellate themselves? The only reply is that some Christians even on this side of the Atlantic see the connection between the Holocaust and the centuries of false teaching about the Jews in Christian churches, and are prepared to share in what Franklin Littell of Philadelphia's Temple University has called "the terrible guilt of Christendom." They insist that the facts of the Holocaust be built into formal confessions of faith and remembered in church hymns and prayers.

Accordingly, they have devised a *Yom Ha-Shoah* (Holocaust Day) Liturgy for Christians, prepared by Dr. Elizabeth Wright of Queens College, Charlotte, N.C., and distributed by Christians Concerned for Israel. It is a collection of readings from Jewish Holocaust literature, with explanatory transitions. These Christians believe that Auschwitz and their part in it must be recognized for the sake of Jesus the Jew, for the sake of the credibility of the Christian religion.

Guilt for the Holocaust is an awesome thing. Jews themselves are not free of it, knowing in their heart of hearts their sins of omission during the days when the boast of a 1,000-year Reich rang out in Munich's halls.

No man can demand of another that he feel a sense of guilt. It must come from within or it is nothing. A Jew cannot say to a Christian, of the United Church or any other denomination: *J'accuse*. He can only hope for a special effort at understanding once the "commanding heights" of Auschwitz are scaled and the facts and effects of its uniqueness are seen. If United Church members will share the hope with the Jews, their dialogue can begin again.

CHAPTER NINE

The Palestinians

Although it is fueled by the events and attitudes of two thousand years of conflict and lack of real contact between the Jewish and Christian communities, the current quarrel between the United Church of Canada and the Canadian Jewish community was, as we have seen, ignited by their fundamentally differing attitudes towards the Middle East. In particular, controversy exploded over the Palestinian refugees, many of whom fled their homes in the new state of Israel to the West Bank of the Jordan River following the Arab-Israeli war of 1948 and then to the East Bank following the Six Day War in 1967.

United Church leaders charge that Jews are not considerate enough of the pain and sorrow of Palestinian refugees; the plight of these Palestinians is so similar to that of the Jews through the ages that United Church people find the Jews' failure to empathize astonishing.

I. F. Stone, the American journalist, has said: "To be a Jew is not quite to belong. Every society has its Jews. Israel's Jews are her Arabs."

This point is even more effectively made by Palestinians themselves. In June 1969, in the *Middle East Newsletter*, a Palestinian refugee wrote: "Zionist leaders have said the Jews must go to Palestine because it was a land without a people for a people without a land. I cry, I sorrow, for that land was mine. I am people. The Palestinians are people. And you who have suffered such persecutions have forced us to pick up your ancient cry, 'Next year, Jerusalem!' "

From the United Church viewpoint, this is the crux of the Middle East problem—that two peoples cry, "Next year, Jerusalem!"

Canadian Jews generally refuse to accept this approach. Many are militants who refuse even to cede the name "Palestinian" to those Arabs who once lived in Palestine, now known as Israel. At one time, they point out, Menahem Beigin's Irgun Z'vaei L'umi, the core of the civilian Herut Party which used terrorist tactics against the British Mandate authorities, was also known as Palestinian. In addition, militants claim the West Bank, captured from Jordan in the Six Day War, as ancient Judea and Samaria and thus as integral a part of the land of Israel as Jerusalem. The usual phrase "occupied territories" is therefore not only historically inaccurate for them but an unwelcome challenge to the Jewish right of possession. The government of Israel has taken to using the term "administered" rather than "occupied" as a concession to these historical claims, as well as to lessen the unpleasant connotation of conquest.

Apart from names and terms, Jewish militants will not accept the Palestinian Arab claim to a national identity, which they regard as fiction. Samual Katz, the Herut Party ideologist, has detailed the argument against Palestinian Arab nationalism. When the United Nations in 1947 offered the Arabs then living in the British Mandate of Palestine an independent state of their own alongside the proposed new state of Israel, they refused it. They reinforced this refusal after the armistice of 1949 by accepting Jordanian King Abdullah's conquest of the West Bank. They also refused to serve as a base for their exiled fellow-countrymen who wanted to liberate Arabs under Israeli rule. It was not only Israel's efficiency that kept West Bankers and the Arabs who remained in the new state of Israel in line, says Katz, but the absence of Palestinian Arab fervour.

His words strike a strong chord in the Canadian Jewish militant, including Canadian Zionists: "The fiction simply refuses to become a fact. The Arabs of Palestine are not a nation. There is no 'Palestine Arab' nation. They were and have remained a fragment of the large Arab people. They lack the inner desire, the spiritual cement and the concentrated passion of a nation. Though their number has grown in the past half century, they have not developed a specific national character. Their constant merging in the plots and sallies of the pan-Arab policy-drivers has exhausted their ardour. Their personal attachment, moreover, is not to the country but to a family, a clan, to a village or to a city. In this they do not differ from 1918, when T. E. Lawrence discovered the situation for himself."

From the beginning, the organized Zionists in Canada were militant and rightist. In the 1920s and thirties, Canadian Zionism was dominated by two matriarchal figures, Lillian Freeman of Ottawa and Rose Dunkelman of Toronto. Both women possessed the wealthy husbands and personal drive essential to voluntary careers in the promotion of the Zionist idea and the collection of funds to support the campaign for a Jewish home in Palestine. Of the two, Rose Dunkelman was the more militant. She not only guarded the organizational hearth and kept the fires of zeal burning, but censored Jewish outpourings to keep them in tune with what she believed was sacred biblical and orthodox Zionist doctrine.

After the Palestine Arab riots of 1929, Maurice Eisendrath, the late rabbi of Toronto's Holy Blossom Temple, who was once described by the American Jewish publicist Meyer Weisgal as "a furious anti-Zionist" serving "rich, assimilated Jews," displeased Rose Dunkelman by writing anti-Zionist columns in the *Canadian Jewish Review*. She bought a moribund weekly, made it into the *Jewish Standard* and hired New Yorker Weisgal, then editor of the influential *New Palestine* in the US, to transform it into a journalistic weapon against the Holy Blossom antagonist (who was later to embrace Zionism) and all others who attacked Jewish national aspirations.

The Toronto Jewish community as exemplified by Rose Dunkelman never lost its aggressiveness. It set the tone for Jewish militants across Canada. The case for the Palestinians has, therefore, never received a cool hearing from Canadian Jews, though it is understood and discussed compassionately by hundreds of thousands of Israeli Jews.

Even more moderate Canadian Jews are indifferent to Palestinian identity. Says Canadian Jewish Congress president Sydney Harris: "The Arabs are responsible for the troubles of the Palestinians; they've got scads of territory and uncounted millions in their treasuries. They could very simply have taken care of the refugees the way the Jews took care of theirs. And more easily, because they have all kinds of unsettled land. This may be highly immoral for me to say, but the greater immorality belongs to the leaders who started the war when they didn't have to."

The view of the organized Zionists of Canada, as well as most Canadian Jews, is that the Palestinian plea for national identity is an artificial tactic intended to eliminate the state of Israel. The refugees have a case as suffering Arabs but not as Palestinians, and their problems can eventually be solved by compensation, resettlement and partial repatriation. That is why, they argue, the Palestine Liberation Organization must, on no account, be recognized. It is a substitution of the burly Palestinian exile for the frail refugee, and that changes the terms of the argument.

On April 13, 1970, the Canadian Zionist Federation, representing factions from left to right, distributed a reprint of an article—"Who are the Palestinians?"—by the American Zionist writer Marie

Syrkin. Syrkin argues that Israeli recognition of the Palestinians as a dispossessed people or nationality would demand compromises from Israel other than those required for dislocated refugees; even the withdrawal of Israel to the pre-1967 borders would not lessen the force of the Palestinian nationalist's demand for the entire land of Palestine. Therefore, the existence of the Jewish state cannot be predicated on the Palestinian's claim that his national home has been taken from him. The dislocation or resettlement of individuals as an aftermath of war is another matter, a familiar and acceptable process in the Europe and Asia of the twentieth century.

Syrkin finds a moral case in the classic Arab sources for the contention that Palestinian nationalism is not historically genuine. All the declarations of the nascent Arab nationalist movement from 1880 on emphasized "the unity of Syria"(which before World War I included what became Lebanon and Palestine) and made no references to Palestine other than "south Syria": the Arab Congress of 1919 in Jerusalem; historian George Antonius in his book *The Arab Awakening*; the extremist Mufti of Jerusalem in 1947; and the Arab scholar and statesman Charles Malik in the magazine *Foreign Affairs* in 1952. As late as 1956, Ahmed Shukairy, then head of the newly organized Palestine Liberation Organization, contradicted the whole concept of Palestine liberation by announcing to the United Nations Security Council that "Palestine is nothing but southern Syria."

Syrkin, along with most Canadian Jews, concludes from all this that for Arabs "Palestine" was just an inaccurate name for an area in the Middle East which was politically and geographically separated from other Arab lands after World War I by imperialist plotters against Arab independence. In Arab eyes it never played the role the Jews gave it as the cradle of a nation and a holy land: "In the lexicon of Arab nationalism the independent existence of a Palestine state, like the existence of an independent Lebanon, represented a violation of the Arab national will."

Thus the concept of Palestine as a separate national identity is a very recent mutation, arising among Arabs as a purely negative reaction to Zionism, after the Balfour Declaration in 1917 recognized the Jewish right to a national home in Palestine.

It is not true, say Syrkin and Canadian Zionists, that the Jews proceeded to take over Palestine with a total disregard for a Palestinian presence, since there was no such presence. Nor is it true that the Jewish pioneers in Palestine were unaware of a native population. They came with agricultural studies and demographic charts, showing that soil reclamation in Palestine would make room for more Arabs as well as Jews and would provide an improved life for both (an argument some United Church leaders in the 1930s echoed, v. Chapter 1). Moreover, the early Zionists had due regard for sensitive Arab feelings. The late Chaim Weizmann, for example, recognized that "national sentiments of Palestinian Arabs would centre in Baghdad, Mecca and Damascus and find their natural and complete satisfaction in the Arab kingdoms which would result from the Peace Treaty settlement in the Near East."

Before the Jewish return, Palestine was a dying land, according to the Canadian Zionist-Syrkin argument. In 1883, Claude Reigner Conder in his book *Heth and Moab* called Palestine "a ruined land," and Mark Twain shocked American readers of his *Innocents Abroad* with the description of the Holy Land as "desolation." The transformation came when the Jewish National Fund reclaimed much of the wasteland from absentee Arab landlords at fancy prices and at an even greater expenditure of Jewish lives and labour. In 1891 only a dozen Arabs lived on the waste of Rehovot where the Weizmann Scientific Institute now stands. When Tel Aviv was founded in 1909 the only ones displaced were the camels who paraded along the beach.

But what about the post-1948 Jewish resident of a former Arab house in Jaffa or Jerusalem? Was not an Arab displaced thereby? If the resident is an oriental Jew, says Syrkin, he may point to the house of which the Arabs despoiled him when he fled from Iraq. If he is a Western Jew, he stands ready through the government of Israel to discuss compensation for abandoned Arab property any time the Arabs want to negotiate a peace settlement.

In sum, the argument runs, there is no moral imperative behind the Palestinian cause. When the Arabs fled in the war of 1948 and again in 1967, part of the speed was due to the panic of hostilities and the assurance of return after Arab victory, "but it was undoubtedly abetted by the subconscious or conscious feeling that flight to a village on the West Bank or across the Jordan was no exile." People picked themselves up "as though they were going from the Bronx to Brooklyn not as though they were abandoning a homeland." Any differences between them and their new neighbours were due to local antagonisms not national alienation. Clearly, argue most Canadian Jews, the new Palestinian nationalism is a contrived political tactic against Israel. The Palestinian refugees are not, as United Church leaders insist, a distinct people who have been separated by war from their national homeland.

For many Canadian Jews the most reasonable solution to the Middle East impasse—the one that would do least violence to parties concerned—would be to set up an entity for Palestinian Arabs on the

West Bank and East Bank of the Jordan River. That is where most refugees already live. It would also satisfy newborn Palestinian nationalism. Above all, it would mean that the Palestinian homeland was already in Arab hands and that it would not have to be liberated.

Canadian Jews see no moral or logical compulsion to recognize the Palestine Liberation Organization in coming to such an arrangement. Israel's business is with Arabs who never before thought of themselves as Palestinian but who now want a state, not with those who have invented the fiction of a dispossessed nation. The real intention of the latter is to do away with the Jewish state.

All these arguments leave open the question of how King Hussein, who rules the East Bank, will fit into the picture. Hegemony by a Hashemite monarch whose grandfather Abdullah was imposed on the area by Britain after World War I is not Palestinian independence. Certainly the PLO would not accept it. And that is the crux of the difference between the Canadian Jewish and United Church approaches to a solution of the Palestinian problem. The former would bypass the PLO; the latter see the organization as the only political representative the Palestinians have.

Canadian Jews have another objection to the PLO. They point to the organization as a terrorist gang unfit to represent anybody. United Church leaders do not condemn PLO nihilism strongly enough, say the Jews. Only in the case of Maalot, where in May 1974 children were cold-bloodedly shot by members of a radical PLO affiliate, did leaders in the United Church react with appropriate indignation.

But if the United Church denounced every terrorist attack against Israel, it would likewise be morally bound to decry every retaliatory bombing of Lebanese villages by Israeli planes, a balance not always welcomed in the Jewish community. Such bombings have occurred since 1970, the year King Hussein had a showdown with the PLO, killing thousands of its members and demolishing its training centres from which PLO attacks were made across the eastern border into Israel. PLO groups then moved to southern Lebanon and established themselves in villages in an area the Israelis called Fatahland, which the Lebanese army, weaker and smaller than the forces of its unwelcome Palestinian guests, could not control. Israel attempted to check the terrorism through air raids on the Lebanese villages. Most of the casualties in the bombings were civilians, a fact United Church leaders felt they could not overlook.

If the United Church fails in vigorous castigation of terrorism, Jews also fail when they refuse to distinguish between moderate and extremist elements in the PLO. The tendency to lump all members of the PLO together has been reinforced since early in 1975, the start of the Lebanese civil war. PLO factions at that time fought on the side of the Moslems and against the Christians, who were in turn aided by an unlikely ally, Israel. The Israelis helped rescue the Christians from defeat in the spring and summer of 1976, by supplying them with Soviet-made weapons captured in previous Israeli-Arab wars and Western arms (see Notes on Chapter 9). This has widened the gulf between Israel and the PLO and further influenced Canadian Jews towards an uncompromising stand against the Palestinian organization.

To most Canadian Jews there is no such thing as a moderate PLO element. I do not deceive myself either. I have met hundreds of Palestinians in the West Bank and Gaza, in Lebanon, Jordan and Canada. Not one among them loves Israel and would not be happy to see her disappear. They have their own version of "the ingathering of the exiles" and "a return to Zion."

They differ, however, on how to achieve their goals (see Notes on Chapter 9). Some radical offshoots—like Habash's Popular Front, Hawatmeh's Popular Democratic Front and Jabril's General Command—are uncompromising, ready to fight "a two-hundred-year war against Israel" after the fashion of the struggle between the Muslims and the Crusaders. Others have become reconciled to a smaller Palestinian state, arguing that sovereignty is more important than the size of the national territory, much as the Zionists had argued in the early 1940s.

There are still other factions: those who are for a small state in the hope it will become federated with Israel and through a rapid birthrate overcome the Jewish majority; and those who accept a small state as a springboard for military operations against Israel.

Yasser Arafat, leader of the PLO, is ambivalent on the issue. He demands—as he did at the twelfth conference of the Palestinian Council in Cairo—Palestinian rule over areas to be evacuated by the Israeli army in the event of an agreement, yet refuses to relinquish his vision of "a whole Palestine." Arafat is ambitious to lead the new state and supports contradictory views in a bid to keep the loyalty of all factions within his organization.

Arafat impressed me at a press conference in Beirut in 1974 as an inscrutable leader, careful not to tip his hand on theoretical Palestinian issues lest he alienate any of the PLO's diverse factions. Others, however, have found him positive in his approach to Middle East accommodation. Lord Caradon, British representative at the UN and author of the famed Security Council Resolution 242 on the Middle

East, met him in 1975 and came away convinced that "in Yasser Arafat the Palestinians have a leader who would eagerly seize any opportunity to make effective progress in their interests, that he would infinitely prefer peaceful to violent advance, that he would react favourably to any genuinely helpful approach and that he would regard the restoration of occupied Arab territories and the establishment of an Arab state in Palestine as far more valuable than the perpetuation of violence."

The PLO is not only made up of terrorists. These are the minority, although admittedly the minority has stamped the entire organization with its image. For thousands of Palestinians in the West Bank and elsewhere, the PLO represents a hope for peaceful co-existence with Israel.

In 1974, at a seminar on the "Future of Palestine" in London, England, the London representative of the PLO, Said Hammami, outlined the "strategy of evolution and co-existence" that could replace the PLO's armed struggle against "the Zionist state."

As a sop to the extremists or because, like many Palestinians, he has not yet learned to separate argument from propaganda, Hammami spoke of Israel as "a settler-state" based on oppression, and of Zionism as "a racialist, reactionary, chauvinistic movement." This is the typical harshness of the dominant Arab voice and is hard to take for those Israeli Zionists who have devoted their lives to the struggle for equality and justice for Palestinian Arabs.

Yet as an official Palestinian leader, he also declared himself ready to consider a Palestinian state in a part of Palestine, side by side with Israel, maintaining with her economic co-operation, cultural exchange, free movement across borders and constructive dialogue about a common future.

Hammami said: "The possibility, even the likelihood, of occasional acts of violence by individuals ought not, I suggest, to discourage us from trying to follow a non-violent, evolutionary Palestinian approach to a tolerable form of co-existence between Israeli Jews and Palestinian Arabs, following the establishment of a limited or partial peace settlement."

In an interview in the Dutch daily *Trouw* on June 28, 1975, Hammami said: "I am not happy with the fact that the name of my people is associated with terrorism. In my opinion, violence occurs because there is no Palestine state. I do not want the future Palestine state to be a base for violence. I'll go even further. . . . The founding of a Palestine state will reduce the number of Palestinians who believe in the use of violence to a minimum. Nobody can give you guarantees that after the founding of such a state no hijackings will occur any more. Of course, there will remain some violence. But thousands and thousands of Palestinians, Arabs and Jews will not want to fight any more. There will be peace. We propose a Palestinian state for the sake of peace."

It is significant not only that the PLO permitted Hammami to state his views but that, according to evidence from other sources, they are shared by a number of leading Palestinian personalities.

In the 1975 summer issue of the quarterly *Journal of Palestine Studies*, Sabri Jiryis, Israeli affairs specialist in Beirut's PLO research centre, discussed possibilities for an Israeli-Palestinian peace arrangement to which he aspires, and stressed the importance of a political solution rather than reliance on violence. "I believe that the Palestinians will benefit from peace more than anyone else," he says. "I cannot see the Palestinian issue purely as one involving land. No doubt land is very important, but there are other issues which are important, too, especially the social, economic and cultural problems facing Palestinians as a result of their dispersal all over the world. I believe that if the Palestinians are granted a period of peace and stability they can make good use of it—to rebuild themselves like any other people, to have a normal social and economic life of their own. . . . The major gain from a political solution would be the realization of these objectives."

And Majed Abou Sharar, PLO information officer, adds: "We have outgrown the politics of refusal. We have abandoned the absolutist, all or nothing approach we held for decades. Our policy of resistance rules out neither discussions with King Hussein, nor diplomatic bargaining with the Israelis, nor peace talks in Geneva, nor the creation of a mini-state in the Palestinian area."

Canadian Jews thus should not fall into the trap of branding the entire PLO as criminal and murderous. They are wont to say that PLO leaders counsel terrorism; therefore they are as bad as the terrorists. Admittedly, within the PLO there are hard-liners, but there are also those who advocate flexibility and reconciliaton with Israel. One senses this ambivalence in the speech of PLO representative Farouk Kadoumi before the UN Security Council in January 1976. On the one hand, he described the "Palestinian tragedy" as the result of alleged Zionist crimes, paying the usual lip-service to PLO ideology. On the other, he called for the establishment of a Palestinian Arab state within the common homeland of Jews and Arabs. Israeli Arabist, Dr. Mattityahu Peled of Tel Aviv University, a reserve general in the

Israeli army, regards this as a signal that the PLO, through its official representative in the Security Council, has abandoned the paragraph in the Palestinian Covenant which demands the creation of a secular, democratic state in the entire land of Israel-Palestine (*New Outlook*, Tel Aviv, April-May 1976).

Palestinians like Hammami, Jiryis, Kadoumi and others have begun to opt for new channels of accommodation. From their standpoint, peace must inevitably mean the end of Zionism which, they believe, can subsist only on war, discrimination and oppression. Many Israelis, in and out of government, also believe in peace, not a peace secured by armaments but by the true value of Zionism, a national renaissance based on economic progress, universal equality and social justice. There is room for a meeting of minds in such a context, and United Church members and Canadian Jews together could play a valuable role in defining it.

The Palestinian problem has been complicated by many factors: terrorism, competition for the same piece of land, Arab indifference and Jewish inflexibility. *The Observer* could have made a greater contribution to the acceptance of the Palestinian plight if it had rounded out the problem and presented it in depth instead of publishing one-sided sentimental pieces which made victims out of the Palestinians and villains out of the Israelis. *The Observer* lost an opportunity of educating both Jews and Christians on the crucial issue of the Middle East conflict—Palestinian homelessness—and in so doing not only impeded Christian-Jewish understanding, but precipitated an open quarrel.

The Palestinian refugee is not just the product of war with Israel. He is the victim of a three-pronged onslaught—from Arabs, Israelis and Palestinians themselves. Few have explained this better than Fawaz Turki in his *Journal of a Palestinian Exile*. Growing up in Beirut as a stateless person, he was like a Jew in the Diaspora, "despised, persecuted or at best ignored," suffering the slings and arrows of his hosts: "Why don't you go back to where you came from, you Palestinian sons of whores who sold their land to the Jews!"

Turki relates that as a teenager he was once peddling chewing gum and came upon a street entertainer with a monkey who was instructed "to show us how a Palestinian picks up his food rations. I was a rough boy of fourteen, hardened to the street life, but I could not suppress an outburst of tears. For that was a microcosm of the world, and I was too weak, too alone to hit back at it, so I wept." Turki has no love for Israel, but much of his bitterness is reserved for

Arabs: "The irony of my plight was that as I grew up my bogeyman was not the Jew . . . nor was he the Zionist . . . nor the imperialist . . . but he was the Arab—the Arab in the street who asked if you'd ever heard the one about 'the Palestinian who' . . . the Arab at the police station who felt he possessed a *carte blanche* to mistreat you, the Arab who rejected you. . . ."

The Palestinians failed, too, says Turki. They lost chances in 1937 and 1947 to fulfill national aspirations. In the latter year they should have accepted UN partition; in the former it would still have been possible to work toward the formation of a binational state with Zionists like Weizmann, Magnes and Buber, who treasured the early dream of a secular, democratic Jewish government, with distinct separation of "church" and state and equal citizenship for Muslims, Christians and Jews, a dream to which the PLO ideal today bears great resemblance.

Instead of reducing the problem to "good guys" and "bad guys" and emblazoning the word "Injustice" across the top of a page, leaving the impression that Israel was responsible for all the troubles of the refugees, the United Church *Observer* should have given Christians and Jews the Turki picture—the outrage, shame, anger and humiliation that came to the Palestinians from several quarters, which can be eradicated only through the co-operative effort of Arabs, Israelis and Palestinians. It could have advocated a Palestinian Zionism to complement Jewish Zionism. Many Jews would have rejected such a plea; many would have accepted it; few would have resented it. The United Church-Jewish quarrel might have been avoided.

Jewish obligation to the refugees is not lessened, of course, because Israel is not alone in responsibility for their plight. It makes little difference who is responsible for their tragedy. It exists, and it is part of the burden of the Jewish people. As Christians have a unique relationship to Jews, so modern Jews have a special connection with the Palestinians. Golda Meir used to say that there has never been a Palestinian national entity. The consequence of this argument is that since there is no such people, there is no responsibility to deal with it. But this non-existent people is very much like the Jews. Both came from the same racial strains; it is difficult to tell a Sephardic Jew from a Palestinian Arab. Both trace their antecedents to the land of Canaan. Both came to national political awareness at about the same time in history. Return to the homeland, or Zionism, is the creed of both.

The responsibility of Canadian Jews to Israel should not be confined to unquestioning financial support of the Jewish state. Israel means little if she becomes a kind of church to which Jews give money in order to be redeemed. Redemption comes, says Jewish tradition, only through the righting of wrongs committed and the correction of injustices done.

Shulamit Aloni, member of Israel's Knesset and leader of the Civil Rights Party, has written: "I understand and sense in every fibre of my being the desire to possess Gaza, to hold on to the Beth El and Anatot, to Giv'on and Samaria. It is like a gnawing bug that allows us no peace. But then this is precisely why I should understand the strong desire of the Palestinian for Jaffa and Ashkelon, for Gaza and Ramle. This is the tragedy of our existence in this area, and since for the Arab there is no return to Jaffa, Acre, Ramle and Ashkelon, we should forego ownership to Beth El and Anatot. Whoever thinks he is a member of the chosen people and that we alone are possessed of the sentiment of love for country, longings for landscapes and lands in which our forefathers lived and worked, whereas others are obtuse and just Jew-haters, forces us to live by the sword until our strength runs out." Only such a spirit carries hope for the resolution of the Palestinian-Israeli impasse.

Jews should recognize Palestinian rights not only for moral reasons but for the sake of Israel's own security. It is in Israel's interest to break out of the vicious cycle of terror, retaliation, more terror and more retaliation. Israel, for her own sake, must take the first step in reconciliation with the Palestinians. Many Israeli spokesmen insist that terrorism can be contained. It is a vain belief. There is growing sympathy for the terrorists of the PLO in the occupied territories. Moreover, increasing numbers of Israeli Arabs, torn between conflicting loyalties, are being drawn into the unrest. From Israel's point of view, this is more alarming than the terrorism itself.

If terrorism does not succeed in wrecking Israel, it will surely ruin Israeli democracy, with the inevitable intensification of such measures as "collective punishment" (the dynamiting of houses), suppression of political activity, "administrative arrests" without charge and deportations to Jordan.

The highest price Israel will have to pay for prolonged terrorism is the loss of the spirit of her citizen army, over which Israeli writer Shimon Shamir has agonized. The young soldiers, the source of Israel's strength, visiting their paraplegic and quadraplegic comrades in veterans hospitals, are asking: "How long can we go on fighting with raging resistance to threats of extermination?"

Israel cannot afford to wait for terrorists to become humane.

Time and numbers are against her. She must break out of the framework of aggressive violence. She must not only seek peace but pursue it actively. She must take the initiative in peace as she has in war. She can proclaim willingness to negotiate with any Palestinian leaders who will renounce terrorism. Such a proclamation would not affect her security, and it is her road to survival.

Once a Palestinian state comes into being, it will have to build a government apparatus, with thousands of officials, ministers and ambassadors, each with a stake in the status quo. Any threat to that status will be a threat to those thousands. It will hardly be worthwhile to be a terrorist or revolutionary.

Such has been the experience of practically all emerging countries, including Israel. Yesterday's terrorist is today's establishmentarian. The supreme example is Menahem Beigin, leader of the terrorist Irgun Z'vaei L'umi during the British Mandate of Palestine and now leader of the Likud Party in Israel's Knesset, a conservative *par excellence*.

The gigantic undertaking of ingathering and rehabilitating the refugees, with the support of the international community, would engage the Palestinian state economically for a long time. The leader of such a state—Arafat or anybody else—would have to prove he is master in his own house. The task of quelling terrorism would thus pass from Israel to the Palestinian government.

Only the Palestinians themselves are capable of removing Palestinian terror. Our century has not seen a single instance of a military victory over a terrorist organization. Kenya's Mau Mau and Malayan guerrillas, the Irgun under Britain's Palestine Mandate and the FLN in Algeria, the Giap guerrillas of North Vietnam and the struggle in Portuguese Guinea—they all have a common denominator: none were overcome by military means. The accommodation was political, negotiations with the terrorists themselves as in Algeria, or talks with a moderate national leadership which itself halted the terror, as in Malaya.

The only way to terminate the Palestinian terror is, therefore, to find an arrangement acceptable to the majority of the Palestinian people, satisfying its new-found yearning for a national identity, for a national home called Palestine, flying the Palestine flag.

Such a state, free and sovereign in accordance with an accommodation with the state of Israel, would mean a movement toward law and order in the whole of the Middle East, bypassing the manoeuvres of the superpowers.

This is the kind of reasoning Canadian Jews need to adopt when trying to understand Middle East realities. The United Church can be helpful in promoting such understanding through statements and articles in *The Observer* which appeal to the intellect rather than the passions, which recognize the complexity of the problem rather than emphasize the rights of one side.

While Canadian Jews must concede the rights of Palestinians, they are entitled to ask that Palestinians recognize the legitimate fulfillment of Zionist aims. The United Church General Council has called upon the Arabs, including the Palestinians, to do so. It must continue to stress this call, especially in the light of recent developments at the United Nations. For years Palestinians and other Arabs have been saying that Zionism and racism are one and the same. Now they have won over most of the member-states of the UN to this view.

Saying Zionism is racism does not make it so. Simply stated, Zionism is the organized return of the Jews to Palestine, but this return was not meant to be achieved through aggression. As first conceived by the prophet 2,500 years ago—"For out of Zion [Jerusalem] shall go forth the moral law"—and by the first Zionists early in this century, authentic Zionism is the transformation of the Jewish people into a national organism devoted to the creation of non-competitive nationalism. It is the belief that the individual cannot be moral unless the nation is moral.

Theodor Herzl, the first political Zionist, conceived of the Jewish state as resting "squarely on the ideas which are the common stock of the whole civilized world. . . . It would be unethical for us to deny a share in our commonwealth to any man, wherever he might come from, whatever his race or creed . . . . If a man joins us, if he accepts our institutions and assumes the duties of our commonwealth, he should be entitled to enjoy all our rights. . . . Our slogan must be now and always: 'Man, thou art my brother!' "

Israel is often accused of racism because she has one immigration law for Jews and another for everybody else; she grants Jews instant citizenship whereas non-Jews must go through a process of naturalization.

These are inequities that stem from the founding of the state as a haven for persecuted Jews. Without the justification of persecution, Canada for years gave instant citizenship to British immigrants, yet escaped the label of racist. Given a period of security and peace, there is no reason why Israel, developing her ancient Zionist traditions, should not become a secular state, as Herzl envisioned her and as most of her citizens want her to be, with equal treatment for all who wish to settle in the land.

Israel also suffers the disadvantage of struggling with the burden of an image as a military occupier. The most benevolent conqueror is still an enemy. The fact that Israel applies the repressive measures of the old British Mandate law to the inhabitants of the West Bank adds credence to the inimical image. It does more. It tears the fabric of democracy in Israel herself, for you can't have full civil rights for one section of the population and restrictive regulations for another. This is an agonizing situation for many Israelis, reared in libertarian traditions, and it opens Israel to unpleasant charges and Zionism to misinterpretation.

That misinterpretation is furthered by Canadian Jews who were not interested in Zionism in pre-state days but have now become emotionally involved with Israel. For many of them the Jewish state has become what it was never meant to be, namely, expansion, occupation and power. The traditional Zionism that goes back to the biblical prophets and Theodor Herzl did not have these elements.

The tragedy of what used to be called Palestine is that there are two peoples, each of whom has a strong case, with valid claims to group rights on a single territory. That problem was always inherent in Zionism. It is an open question whether the problem could have been resolved, but there is no point in reliving the past.

Now that new opportunities for accommodation exist, I think that there are possible adjustments and settlements to the problem. In the long run it can be resolved and the Zionist image redeemed. But it surely cannot be resolved through the pursuit of a policy of repeated military confrontations against adversaries who can never really be finally defeated and who have growing influence and limitless resources. Israel cannot pursue such a policy without facing risks which will in time bring her closer to destruction, something no United Church or Jewish leader wants.

What has to be done at this point is to permit free political expression on the West Bank and then deal with whatever forces emerge.

In so far as we have any information about the Palestinians on the West Bank, they want independence both from Israel and from Jordan. The *Jerusalem Post* Mideast correspondent concluded on January 2, 1976, after talks with leading East Jerusalem political figures, that "the PLO has established itself too firmly as the voice of the Palestinians to be defied either in Jordan or the West Bank." At the moment, there is a deadlock, and that is dangerous. Measures should be taken to overcome that impasse. I suggest two: a withdrawal program, having in mind Israel's security, and a recognition of whomever the Palestinians choose to represent them.

Canadian Jews have reason to be suspicious that Palestinians and other Arabs would like to see the Jewish state ultimately disappear. The question is how to reduce the possibility of this happening. The best way would seem to be by slowly building up a system of political accommodation in which hostile feelings will be reduced and eventually eliminated and not by total reliance on military forces.

Such policies have to be undertaken cautiously but they can be pursued much more vigorously than in the past. These options are far more realistic than the general Canadian Jewish stand in that they contribute to the ultimate security of the people of Israel as well as to the preservation of their institutions, which embody the original concept of Zionism.

Canadian Jews have much to amend in their attitude toward the Palestinians, but so have United Church leaders in their attitude towards the Jews. The Palestinians are not the only homeless people in the world. Although millions of refugees still languish in southern and southeast Asia, *The Observer* has made the Palestinians its major concern. The pain of homelessness is deep whoever bears it, but one must remember that the aim is to solve both Jewish and Palestinian homelessness. The warning of theologians Alan Davies and Robert Bater should not go unheeded: "Christians, preoccupied with the [Palestinian] refugees as symbols of oppression, must guard against transforming the latter into comforting symbols for a troubled Christian conscience which, choosing not to dwell on Christian guilt with regard to Jews, dwells instead on Jewish guilt with regard to Arabs."

CHAPTER TEN

The Hostile Theologies

Theological differences constantly get in the way of Christian-Jewish interchange. With liberals predominant in both the United Church and the Jewish community, one might have expected theology to play a lesser role in their dispute, but it looms large. Indeed, according to some academics, it is as fundamental in United Church-Jewish relations as in general Christian-Jewish attitudes. George Johnston of McGill University asks: "Do you assume that Jews have the right to expect complete tolerance and acceptance from any group of Christians? There is, after all, a major stumbling-block in the position each accords to Jesus of Nazareth."

Canadian Jews brush up against Christian theology at an early age. Social scientist Albert Rose, who grew up in Toronto, received the impression as a boy that his schoolmates were taught not to trust Jews, on religious or any other grounds, particularly because of their involvement in the crucifixion of Christ. "The children I played with," says Rose, "consistently came back to that theme." The "Christ-killer" label is painfully familiar to masses of Canadian Jews. Yet in the Jewish community, as well as in the United Church, the work of theologians is often derided by activists as "ivory-tower stuff," unrelated to the average person's problems. It is, perhaps, this attitude that explains why members of the Jewish-Christian family get into trouble. Theology is not just the intellectual discipline of the few; it gets right down to the daily experience of all.

"It is commonly believed," says John W. Burbidge of Trent University, "that what is critical is what people do, not what they think. What we fail to see is that people will do the same thing for quite different reasons. Because Jew and Christian can work together on the civil rights question or the United Appeal does not mean that we are the same in our motivation. Until we begin to come to terms seriously with the theoretical structures which distinguish the traditions and are the determining condition of what we do, we cannot really come to terms with current problems. It is, after all, a question of the relation between religious perspectives." "Brotherhood" gestures, though better than wrangling, simply paper over the deeper accommodation that must take place if the United Church and the Jews are to find synchronization and trust.

Throughout the ages, Jewish and Christian scholars have attempted to promote one faith by denigrating the other. During the time of forced disputations in the Middle Ages, when Jewish leaders were compelled by the Christian kings and princes of Europe to debate the relative merits of Judaism and Christianity with Christian authorities, the Christians had the circumstantial, if not the substantive, advantage. In modern settings, many scholars from both groups have continued the disputation in the same spirit, each side claiming the superiority of its faith in accordance with its updated interpretation.

Some modernists, in an effort to tone down the hostility, have attempted to show that there are really no differences between the two faiths; only the terminology differs. One still hears this argument at brotherhood meetings and encounters it on the pages of popular church and synagogue periodicals. The scholars on both sides are right to dismiss such good will exercises as misleading. There are profound differences between Christianity and Judaism and they are carried over into the United Church-Jewish situation. But are they necessarily antagonistic and inimical?

In former times the view on both sides was that they were. Gregory Baum in *Is the New Testament Anti-Semitic*? and Alan Davies in *Anti-Semitism and the Christian Mind* have shown how absolute was the virulence of the Church fathers towards the Jews. On the Jewish side, the Hebrew prayer book contained anathemas against the Christians. One of the fragments of the Cairo Genizah (a storehouse of worn-out Jewish sacred texts discovered by the late Solomon Schechter) contains a curse against the Christians in the Eighteen Benedictions, which were recited three times daily.

Times have changed. The malediction is no longer found in Jewish prayer books, and the Vatican and the World Council of Churches seek to eliminate derogatory references to Jews in their literature and to fight anti-Semitism among their adherents. But difficulties and ambiguities remain. Not all Christian scholars are willing to abandon the ancient, hostile view of Judaism, and the New Testament is still a source of anguish for those who see it so easily misread as a source of anti-Semitism.

Morton Paterson of Laurentian University cites Acts 7:51 as fuel to the fire of Christian-Jewish hostility: "You stiff-necked people, uncircumcized in heart and ears, you always resist the Holy Spirit. As your fathers did, so do you. Which of the fathers did not your fathers persecute? And they killed those who announced beforehand the coming of the Righteous One, whom you have now betrayed and murdered." How do you get around this impression of absolute incompatibility between Judaism and Christianity? Is it possible to make of the two faiths, instead of ineluctable competitors, mutual challengers, with recognized equal roles for both? Is Jewish-Christian symbiosis within the realm of possibility? This is a crucial question for all Christians and Jews, and certainly must be considered in assessing the United Church-Jewish quarrel.

Two early twentieth-century Jewish philosophers—Franz Rosenzweig, an heroic figure who is becoming a legend among Jews, and Martin Buber, the Zionist-humanist as much revered by Christians as by Jews—attempted to show that Christianity and Judaism were not mutually hostile but mutually challenging. Both have left us celebrated letters exchanged with Christians in which their novel concepts of Christianity constitute guideposts for groping toward Jewish-Christian mutuality.

The young Rosenzweig wrote: "What Christ and his Church mean within the world, on this point we are agreed. No one comes to the Father except through him. No one *comes* to the Father, but the situation is different when one need no longer come to the Father because he is already with him. That is the case with Israel." The theology in this statement is somewhat confining for the liberal, but it indicates an attempt to define co-existence.

Buber wrote: "We understand the christology of Christianity throughout as an important event which has taken place between the world above and the world below. We see Christianity as something the mystery of whose coming into the world we are unable to penetrate. But more deeply, more genuinely, we know that the history of the world has not yet been shattered to its very core, that the world is not yet redeemed. We feel the unredemption of the world. The Church can or must understand this feeling as a conviction of our unredemption. But we understand it differently."

Buber wrote that letter in 1933, when Nazism began to affront the world. Was the outrage of the 1930s and forties just a social and political manifestation? No, says Morton Paterson in a paper to the Theological Union of Hamilton; it was "a word to the nations that a Christianity-without-Judaism was utterly incapable of bearing to the world the reality of God's love." Paterson boldly concludes that it was never intended Judaism should come to God through Christianity. Both seek occupancy in their Father's mansion as equals and as "fellow citizens."

To many Christians this argument will seem like "selling out," says Paterson, but it is a call for a kind of ecumenism that will break the "proud egocentricity of both Judaism and Christianity." Ecumenism is not only a process of overcoming the internal struggles of the Church. It is intended to "heal a broken fellowship" that reaches back thousands of years. If the United Church and the Jews are to find an accommodation, they will have to go back through the years, face the theological war and seek some kind of armistice. They should ride, not allow themselves to be ridden by, the stream of history.

In modest imitation of Buber and Rosenzweig, let us examine some basic differences in Jewish and Christian tradition, differences which appear to many to be irredeemably contradictory. This exercise may well be regarded as superficial, since there are limits beyond which it cannot go. The probings are simply indications of the depth Christian and Jewish scholars may plumb to mine the nuggets of dialogue.

The scholars are crucial in Christian-Jewish confrontation. They roam the vast expanses of ancient rabbinic and New Testament literature and can speak from familiarity with original sources. The fault of dialogue in the past has been that it consisted mostly of public relations. North American Jews, especially, have developed a remarkable talent in interfaith promotion. The Canadian Jewish Congress-B'nai B'rith public relations committee operated on this level for years. The realization is now dawning that Christian-Jewish understanding and United Church-Jewish reconciliation must engage the attention of the academic communities.

This is not to say that activist United Church ministers and Jewish clerics, and laymen of both groups, have no role to play in this field. They need first, however, to become acquainted with each other's basic attitudes. It is unusual to find even liberal rabbis familiar with the New Testament and United Church ministers with even a cursory knowledge of relevant sections of the Talmud. If the bitterness of the United Church-Jewish dispute is to be allayed, scholarship must go hand in hand with good will.

Let us consider the Christian concept of Jesus as a redeemer-saviour, the divine in human form, who dies for the sins of mankind; a concept still sacred to the liberal United Church as to other Christian churches. Such an idea in Judaism is unthinkable, and George Johnston is justified in saying that it is a major obstacle to mutual tolerance and acceptance.

Sholem Asch, in his novel *The Nazarene*, correctly marks the amazement of Jews at the suggestion there could be a man who is God. He portrays Jesus preaching to the congregation at Sabbath services in the synagogue of the Cyreneans. "And the strange rabbi opened his lips and said in a mighty voice: 'I am the bread of life. He that comes to me shall not hunger, and those that believe in me shall never thirst. I am the tree which God has planted, and those that are united with my roots shall blossom and prosper. . . . I am the bread which is come down from heaven. Truly I say to you that he who believes in me shall have everlasting life.' "

If the heavens had opened above the heads of the congregation, says Asch, and hosts of angels had descended to range themselves around the rabbi of Nazareth, the people could not have been more astounded and terrified. An old man rose and said: "There came to us Moses, telling us to believe in the Torah which he brought down from Sinai. There came to us the prophets, telling us to believe in the living God. This one tells us to believe in himself alone. Who is he? Is he greater than Moses, greater than the prophets?"

The people appealed to other teachers present: "You who are rabbis in Israel, how can you stand by while he blasphemes the Holy One of Israel and say nothing?" For Jews in the time of Jesus as today there is no place for a redeemer-saviour simply because God is the redeemer and saviour, and he would not have to die for the sins of the world by way of atonement.

Traditional Christianity stresses the saviour-mediator because of its concept of original sin, which means that every human being is tainted with the sin of Adam. The burden of this sin is so heavy that he cannot rise above it by his own ethical reformation. He needs a special act of grace, provided by the sacrificial death of Jesus. Thus the belief that no one is saved except through Jesus.

"Original sin" does not occur in Judaism. To the Jew this would have meant that he is not free to choose between good and evil, since he is weighted with evil from birth. "In Judaism the person rules sin; in Christianity sin rules the person." In the latter case there is no hope except through Jesus; in the former a person has the power to resist evil if he will only use it. The Talmud tells of a rabbi who found difficulty resisting the temptation of a beautiful woman. He was almost consumed with the fire of his passion, but he fought the "evil impulse" and drove it out of his heart saying: "Although you are fire and I flesh, yet I am stronger than you." Jews have found no other weapon against the evil inclination except the inner power of ethical choice.

Yet in a less dramatic and more humanistic way the idea that one person can atone for the sins of his fellow beings is not foreign to Jewish thought. *Tzadikim,* saints, voluntarily suffer for the sins of others. An entire section of the Yom Kippur liturgy in the synagogue is devoted to the story of ten martyrs of the second century, during the Hadrianic persecutions, who readily died for the sins of the sons of Jacob. The original motivation here was to arouse the compassion of the Deity; if God will not be moved by the prayers of ordinary people, let him remember the self-sacrifice of the saintly. The Talmud tells of Rabbi Judah the Prince, who was learned and wealthy yet suffered deeply and whose torments atoned for the sins of his generation.

While Christianity teaches that a person can achieve salvation only through Jesus, Buddhism teaches that he is expected to work out salvation on his own. But this idea, too, does not exist in Judaism. The ancient rabbis, who developed the character of the Jewish faith, did not believe that all a person had to do was to study Torah, the Law, and reward would come to him automatically, an impression Christians often get from the New Testament attitude toward Judaism. In traditional Judaism, the human being is dependent on God—but directly, without an intermediary. He can use the Torah or remember the righteous to open himself to God's help. He does not stand alone. A person needs God, who is ever ready to help and "is near to those who call upon him in truth." One need only visit the synagogue on High Holidays to hear how the ancient prayers repeatedly call upon God for help and forgiveness. Yet there is a general impression that Jews do not depend on God's grace as much as do Christians.

In short, while Judaism and Christianity vigorously part company on the person of Jesus of Nazareth and his power of salvation, they agree that God's help is essential to the human struggle. The difference is in the emphasis the Jew places on a person's freedom to approach God independently and God's evenhanded justice, and in the stress the Christian places on man's or woman's helplessness and their need of divine grace through Jesus. But without Jesus both Christian and Jew confront God and are aware of their human ambivalence. Both understand that a person is Godlike, "a little less than divine," if he affirms his partnership with God in the work that can be done on earth, but is dust and ashes, filled with pride, if he thinks he can operate on his own.

Let us examine another traditional concept which separates Jew from Christian—the Trinity, also sacred to the United Church. For the Jew, God is one and indivisible, and his unity is expressed in the *sh'ma*: "Hear, O Israel, the Lord is one." The traditional Jew prolongs the sound of the last word, *ehad*, one. The stories are legion of how Jewish martyrs breathed their last with the word *ehad* on their lips. For the Christian the Trinity is no less fundamental—God the father, God the son, God the holy ghost or spirit. No one has ever found the formula that would reconcile the two concepts.

Nonetheless, the unity of God for Jews did not rule out several divine aspects expressed in dual or even trinitarian terms. As every reader of the Bible knows, there are two names for God, *Elohim* and *Yahweh* or Jehovah. One, say the ancient rabbis, stands for compassion, the other for law. Or, as modern Jews would phrase it, one reflects the intimate relations in human nature, the personal, and the other the harmonious laws in the universe with which the physicists and astronomers are concerned. Judah Halevi, the medieval Jewish philosopher, explained the duality in terms of Greek and Jewish concepts. One was "the God of Aristotle" and the other "the God of Abraham, Isaac and Jacob." A philosopher, by the powers of reason and logic, may arrive at the conclusion that there is a prime mover in the universe (the Greek idea), but he could not independently experience the mystical bond, or love, between God and man. That would require faith in a divine presence (the Jewish idea). Another example is the phrase *avinu malkenu*, "our father our king," sung to a popular melody. The average Jewish worshipper in the synagogue knows the difference between the two designations. As king, God is the source of law, dispensing justice; as father, he responds in a personal way to move the heart and spirit.

Judaism has developed the concept of *shechina*, divine presence, as a connection between God and people. The *shechina* dwelt among them even when they were "unclean" and it accompanied them in exile. In some sources *shechina* becomes *ruah hakodesh*, spirit of holiness, which is not, like the Christian holy ghost or spirit, a definable presence, but a quality that can make the human being perceive truth. Thus, though it means something else, holy spirit is not absent from Judaism.

Finally, Jewish theology expresses itself in trinitarian style through the declaration that "God, Torah and Israel are one." Although we meet this series for the first time in a late mystical book, the three items are very old. Some scholars conjecture that the combination may have existed in the Jewish baptismal formula the early

Christians appropriated. It is tempting to suggest that Jesus the son was substituted for Torah and "holy ghost" for the community of Israel.

Unity and trinity, it is clear, are not irreconcilably contradictory. By recognizing several aspects of God, Jews enriched their understanding of him without disturbing their passionate affirmation of his unity.

By the same token, Christianity, though it is capable of asserting three absolutes, is a monotheistic faith. Christians would have no difficulty reciting the *sh'ma*: "Hear, O Israel, the Lord our God is one." How can three be one? That is a mystery in Christian belief, but it is no less real for the believer. Both Christians and Jews fought pagan gods in their loyalty to the one God; both endured martyrdom rather than surrender their monotheistic morality. Judaism and Christianity are committed to the understanding that all human values derive from one source, that God is the force of all that is good, true and beautiful to which all persons aspire, that since there is only one Father all men and women must be his children.

"Simplify, simplify" is the journalist's and the partisan's creed. Simplifying often brings clarity to an idea, but often as not it also brings distortion. So it is with the contrast usually made, particularly in United Church and other Christian pulpits, that Christianity is an affirmation of belief and Judaism an emphasis on the deed. From before Martin Luther and since, Christian teachers have said that if one has faith all things will come. Conversely, Jewish teachers have noted that in the biblical story of how the Torah was received at Mount Sinai, the Israelites did not say, "We shall heed and we shall do," but "We shall do and we shall heed." Ergo, Christianity stresses believing, Judaism doing.

It stands to reason, however, that good deeds presuppose some beliefs and that faith must find tangible expression in life. So the Talmud says. So it is written in the second chapter of James: "What doth it profit, my brethren, though a man say he has faith and have not works? Can faith save him?"

The balance between faith and deed is overlooked in both Judaism and Christianity by preachers who seem capable of propagating their faith only through invidious contrast. Because Jewish tradition prescribes *mitzvot*, commandments, 613 to be exact, the judgment is often made that Judaism is a kind of IBM machine, calculating a person's deeds, whereas Christianity may be defined as the unmathematical but sublime Sermon on the Mount. Another way the simplifiers put it is that in Judaism sin is an action, in Christianity it is a state of the soul.

So much in Judaism is beyond the slide-rule that it seems stressing the obvious to underscore the fact. For our purpose, let us concentrate on a statement by Simon the Just, a Talmudic sage who placed the importance of deeds and action in perspective: "The world stands on three things, on Torah, on worship and on deeds of loving-kindness." The end product is the loving act, says Rabbi Simon, but two conditions must be fulfilled before the action becomes meaningful; one must study and worship.

Torah, or teaching, is a cardinal element in the life of the professing Jew. "The ignorant man cannot be pious." Rabbis Hillel and Shamai, at the turn of the first century of the Christian era, debated at length on the relative importance of learning and deeds and concluded that good deeds of themselves were of little consequence; they require an intellectual accompaniment.

But the good life does not end there. It also demands an emotional component, what Rabbi Simon calls worship. "What is the service of the heart?" asks the Talmud. "It is prayer." The ancient Jews believed, as many do today, that by observing the 613 commandments one could reserve a place in heaven; yet Rabbi Judah the Prince, who edited the Mishnah, the authoritative commentary on the Bible, could say: "It is possible to acquire one's true portion in an hour" without the observance of all the commandments. Learning and heartfelt relationships are not subject to calculation or measurement and cannot be divorced from the true deed.

As untrue as the judgment that historic Judaism was just a process of bookkeeping is the assertion that historic Christianity was simply assent to a creed. The eighth chapter of Romans demands that people live in submission to "the law of the spirit." The Christian parallel of the Jewish "learning, worship and loving deeds" is faith, hope and charity, "but the greatest of these," says Paul in the First Letter to the Corinthians, "is charity." That entire thirteenth chapter is probably the grandest exposition of the ethical principle ever written, at once Jewish and Christian as the apostle himself. That ethical influence showed itself in Christian opposition to the evils of Roman society, helping to erase the gladiatorial contests, to curb sexual offences, to banish the exposure of unwanted children to the elements and the abandonment of the aged.

Christianity and Judaism are rich in both faith and deed; the basics are there, not to be disregarded. Unquestionably there were and are differences in emphasis. The Jews are inclined to the position that a person tends to be what he does, the Christian to the view that one tends to be what he believes. Judaism is more practical and balanced, Christianity veers toward the heroic. Both strive to capture the whole person, body and soul, and to make them part of the divine purpose.

We come now to the most common oversimplification of the differences between Judaism and Christianity, that the former is a religion of law and the latter a way of love. The contrast was made in the New Testament, as we shall see, and that accounts for its widespread acceptance. It was also helped along by a psychological factor. The young resent traditional restraints; Christianity, the new faith, thus threw off the fetters of the old. So the German philosopher Nietzsche identified the freedom of his new superman ethic with the struggle of Christianity against the enslaving codes of Judaism. Likewise in our day, the proponents of "situation ethics" consider themselves emancipators; those who are impelled by true love, they say, need not be shackled by the stated moral laws of the past.

In the New Testament, the contrast between Pharisaic law and the emancipating message of Jesus is sharp and dramatic. The Nazarene insisted that the sabbath was made for man and not man for the sabbath, indicating that love supersedes law. This principle had divided Rabbis Hillel and Shammai before Jesus, the consensus favouring the liberal Hillel. The ancient rabbis, in line with Hillel, permitted people to do on the sabbath all the things needed "for the saving of life," even if the danger to life could not be specifically defined. Jesus was simply enunciating the liberal interpretation of Jewish law, espoused by his teachers as part of the controversy with the conservatives of the day. He belonged to the school of Hillel which resisted the rigidity of the Shammai group. His arguments were not in support of a new religion but on behalf of one of the two interpretations of the old. His was not the minority view of love versus law, as the New Testament indicates, but the stand of the majority of the Jews of his time.

How does one, in the light of this exposition, explain Paul's contrast of the freedom of the spirit, emanating from love, with the bondage of the law? In a sense, Paul was living in an unreal world, though it was real enough to him, between the First Coming, marking the inauguration of the messianic age, and what he believed was the imminent Second Coming. "Behold, I tell you a mystery," he wrote in the First Letter to the Corinthians. "We all shall not sleep, but we shall all be changed in a moment, in the twinkling of an eye, at the last trump.

For the trumpet shall sound and the dead shall be raised incorruptible, and we shall be changed." In this interim age Paul was reflecting what his rabbinic contemporaries believed, that the old laws would be suspended and that the messiah would bring a new Torah, which the apostle called "the law of the spirit." The Talmud says that in the messianic era even the law prohibiting consumption of the flesh of the pig would be cancelled.

Once Paul passed from the scene and the Second Coming did not materialize, the Christian Church had to face reality and, instead of theorizing about the law of the spirit, proceeded to live according to laws. Indeed, the laws of the Church became more severe in the pursuit of the good life than those of the Pharisees had ever been. They forbade the sexual act for those "who would be perfect," something Pharisaic or rabbinic law would have found unnatural and unloving. The Talmud maintained that in God's design "there is no man without a woman and no woman without a man, and not the two of them without the divine presence or the *shechina*." Marriage in the mainstream of Jewish tradition has always meant the fulfillment of God's love. Adultery was a surrender to the weakness of the flesh, but never marriage.

A basic command in Judaism as in Christianity (for where did Jesus get it?) is to love God with heart, soul and might. The rabbinical commentaries are always specific in interpretation lest sentimentality disregard practical application. How does one love God—by feeling, by expressing the feeling? That would be merely sentimental. To love God with the heart, says the ancient tradition, is to establish schools for the young; to love God with the soul is to build one's house into a home until it, too, is a place of worship, a sanctuary; and to love God with all one's might is to bring his influence into the dealings of the marketplace and the courts, so that fairness and justice prevail.

Law and love in Judaism are twins. Law by itself cannot mould character, but it does create a setting and a climate for the good life. Thus laws work to build those social institutions and personal habits that promote the life of the spirit. A person who observes the laws perfunctorily is not fulfilling them. They must be observed with *kavanah*, the right intention. Always the feeling beyond the law has to be sought. "Jerusalem was destroyed only because people insisted on their legal rights," says the Talmud. They did not practise compassion, which cannot be governed by laws but which is essential for the proper performance of them.

For this reason the rabbis of the Talmud were willing to rearrange the laws to conform with changing circumstances, a fact which many fundamentalist Jews ignore. If it is the function of the law to seek the goals of stability and justice, it is no less the function of lawmakers to respond to the needs of the poor and oppressed and those who are subjected to injustice by archaic laws. Law must work as a flowing river. The living kernel must always be separated from the dead shell. This is the dynamic principle of Jewish law which liberal Jews today seek to revive. It cannot work without compassion and love.

To say, therefore, that Judaism is Law and Christianity Love has no meaning in the historical context. Both elements are present in both persuasions. Again, it is largely a question of emphasis.

As Judaism has been misunderstood by Christians to signify tyrannical law, so Christianity has been confused by modern Jews with primitive and medieval versions of the New Testament faith. In recent decades, liberal Jewish scholars, with the conviction born of the Church's inability to cope with the European Holocaust, have been condemning the romanticism of Christianity.

It was natural for Jews who experienced the Holocaust to wonder why Christianity did not prove itself a tangible force in opposition to Nazi savagery. As we have seen, the Christian churches in Germany, Protestant and Catholic, seemed to possess no saving spiritual resources to enable them to outface a clear satanic danger. There was Dietrich Bonhoeffer, but one martyred saint does not make a church. Many Holocaust survivors have dismissed Christianity as an impotent faith grown rigid with age. A more systematic critic, a rabbi of both Berlin and Bergen Belsen, was the late Leo Baeck who found Christianity too dreamlike to operate in the real world of radical evil. Unlike Judaism, rooted in the practical concerns of law and ethics, Christianity, Baeck argues, is given to an excess of mythology and miracles, to a preoccupation with mystery and sacraments. It is too utopian to be of any use in rescuing men and women from the slime, too self-intoxicated to be concerned with social justice.

The core of Christianity for Baeck is not Jewish but pagan, going back to the Dionysian revels and the myths of gods dying and being reborn. This is where the redeeming saviour originated, in the association of the worshipper with the mystery of death and resurrection. Whatever social concerns the Christian Church has periodically manifested, says Baeck, comes from Jewish influence. They were the exceptions that grew "on the Old Testament soil of Calvinism and Baptism." Essentially, the character of Christianity is Pauline, the apostle having merged "Jewish wisdom" with the mystery religions, submerging the former. "The generally romantic Pauline faith can confront a culture only as an outsider without real access to it." The classical religion, according to Baeck, is Judaism, the romantic, sentimental one is Christianity. It was no surprise, therefore, that Christianity was unable to meet the reality of Hitler.

Baeck was not the first to find strong pagan elements in Christianity. It would have been surprising, indeed, if anthropologists did not find a striking similarity between the ancient Dionysian myth and the New Testament crucifixion story, and between the Hellenistic mysteries in which the worshipper gains immortality through the rebirth of the dying deity and vicarious atonement in Christianity. All religions are indebted to paganism for some of their theology and ritual. The genius of great religion, however, is to refine the archaic concepts, to reinterpret the ceremonials, to maintain a continuity with the past though departing from it. Baeck, however, does not credit this talent to Christianity. As the pagan communed with divine forces without any application of the lesson to daily life, so does the Christian. Hence, the powerlessness of the faith when the Nazis struck.

Baeck's criticism of Paul as a romantic does not square with the practical things he did for the spread of Christianity. His mystical faith was undoubtedly the driving force against "the Greeks who seek wisdom and the Jews who want a sign," but he was no mere daydreamer. He believed the Judgment Day was near and set out to save the Gentiles and Jews in the dawn of its coming. He not only preached charity but practised it and became a vigorous fund-raiser for Jerusalem's poor. It was this example that set the Church to rival the synagogue in a network of philanthropic institutions which probably won, and continues to win, more adherents than preaching.

Once again there is danger in simplified contrast, in saying Judaism is classic, Christianity romantic. As well as dismissing the practical achievements of Christianity, this argument rules out the mystical, romantic notions in Jewish tradition. Were not the prophets of ancient Israel romantics, poets, visionaries? Were not the writers of the Psalms in dreamlike communion with God? And were not the ancient Jews, from the Exodus to the Exile, touched by the suffering myth? They had no resurrection mythology, but Isaiah's prophecy of the suffering servant was transformed to encompass the whole people.

In both Judaism and Christianity there are many strands—mystical and rational—which complement one another. In the stormy days of exile and persecution the Jews needed the romantics and the martyrs who sacrificed themselves because they thought ideas to be more significant than life itself, thereby assuring the survival of the Jewish people. For the day-to-day struggle Judaism provided laws, which were also a significant factor in survival. In a similar way, Christianity needed its martyrs and lawmakers.

The main barrier between Christian and Jew has been the Christian Church's dedication to missions in order to win converts to Christianity. Over the centuries, multitudes of Christians, United Church members among them, have gone out into the world to spread the gospel. They have done so because they are so commanded by their faith: "And he [Jesus] said unto them, 'Go ye into all the world, and preach the gospel to every creature' " (Mark 16:15). Their aims were of the purest and their lives often self-immolating. The United Church does not lack examples of genuine, even heroic, Christian service in the mission field, inspired by the appeal of the New Testament. Jewish tradition bids Jews be a "light to nations," but it does not encourage them to make others over in their own religious image.

The United Church's efforts at missionizing the Jews and others is no longer as strong as it was in pre-World War II years, but an attitude still persists that non-acceptance of Jesus carries a suggestion of spiritual blindness or intransigence. If what we think is as critical as what we do, as John Burbidge maintains, then it is important to re-examine the whole concept of Christian missions in the modern context.

To those who are the targets, missionizing is the religious analogue of political imperialism. Not always was imperialism a dirty word. The Romans believed they were bringing civilization with the spread of *Pax Romana*, and in a sense they were. Wherever Rome was strong, peace prevailed. It was not too long ago that Britain could boast of a sense of responsibility, of carrying "the white man's burden," in maintaining an empire on which the sun never set. The British through imperialism brought many nations from tutelage to independence. Imperialism or colonialism in the best sense meant the middle stage between parochial nationalism and international cooperation.

In the same way, missionizing religion represents a transitional step between those who profess parochial gods open only to members of the sect on the one hand, and the right of all men to worship God, each in his own way on the other. The religious imperialist, like the political imperialist, may be nobly motivated, intent on widening spiritual perceptions. Nonetheless, both are forms of imperialism, and imperialism involves injustice and war.

No one needs to be reminded that today's political imperialisms are constantly on the edge of war. They follow the example of the religious imperialism of the past, Christendom and Islam. When the Jews had power during the Hasmonean period, they became religious imperialists, imposing their faith on the Idumeans by force. The Thirty Years' War in the seventeenth century was a consequence of rival imperialistic claims encouraged by Roman Catholicism and Protestantism. Only when it ended in a stalemate did Europeans begin to understand the value of tolerance, today still only an ideal in most of the world.

Even when it proceeds by peaceful means, missionary activity tends to demean people, setting members of a family against each other and deriding the character and integrity of ancient cultures. No people has ever been missionized without feeling the implied insult to its history and culture. The pagan Romans hated Jews and Christians because of their missionary forays. The Boxer rebellion in China expressed itself in attacks against foreign missions.

If Christians and Jews, if Canadian Jew and United Church member, are to effect an understanding and acceptance of one another, missions must be relegated to history, for they are incompatible with the needs of a diverse humanity seeking a formula of co-existence. No religion should strive to be the universal religion. The aim should rather be to promote universal religion which is not denatured cosmopolitanism without recognition of group differences. Universal religion will become a reality when all the great religions accept three principles: (1) that every religious group is entitled to seek life's meaning according to its own historical experience and by use of its own culture; (2) that mankind itself can be saved only when it is recognized that God is equally accessible to all religious groups, seeking him in their respective ways; and (3) that in view of the foregoing premises, diversity is valid and the search for superiority unacceptable.

Jacob B. Agus has said it: "We have to accept the fact of diversity among the several streams of faith just as we acknowledge the differences within each faith. If it is through history that God brings us closer to himself, then we cannot doubt that he employs many and diverse pathways. Nothing is more characteristic of his glory, either in physical nature or in the history of humanity, than the rich diversity of its manifestations."

The above analysis of Christian and Jewish concepts and texts may not be wholly valid, but since it is based on the investigations of specialists into comparative rabbinic and New Testament sources, there is sufficient validity to suggest that nothing is gained through the maintenance of guarded solitudes. This discussion of contrasting fundamentals and oversimplifications of differences in Judaism and Christianity is not an attempt to blunt the distinction between the two faiths. No one should underestimate the sharpness or depth of the divergences. My aim has been to indicate that theological difficulties need not be a bar to open and fearless dialogue. It is not enough for the United Church and the Jews to be tolerant of one another or even to show positive good will. There must be the kind of trust and confidence that can withstand honest probing and testing.

At the same time, all derogatory allusions to dissenting faiths and groups should be eliminated from religious textbooks, rituals, prayers and teaching materials. This step is especially important for Christians and Jews whose traditions have been rivals for centuries. The process of removing pejorative references may seem like censorship or Bowdlerization, appropriate for fundamentalists but offensive to liberal United Church sensitivities. Yet every decent individual imposes on himself a censorship to refrain from insult and the commission of indignities, and so should the group.

There is no suggestion here to tamper with the Old and New Testaments. That would constitute mutilation of classical and sacred literature. There is an obligation, however, to place hostile references in both testaments in perspective. Teaching the Bible with proper regard for historical fact and sociological truth is also part of religious ethics. Scriptures must always be read and studied in depth. The Hasidic saint Raphael of Bershad, who took on as a special life-long spiritual assignment the seeking and speaking of truth, was asked: "Suppose you are faced with a situation where truth-telling would do harm, what do you do then?" He replied: "Then, I tell the deeper truth."

Yet even that is not enough. More affirmative exercise is necessary. The United Church and the Jews of Canada should encourage the development of rituals and prayers with the specific aim of overcoming the natural and acquired tendencies toward group antagonism. A beginning should be made in addressing the United Church-Jewish problem: "O Lord, guard my tongue from evil and my lips from speaking guile against the Jews (for the United Church) or the *Notzrim* (for the Jews) and to such as curse me let my soul be serene." The use of such liturgical and educational material should come to occupy an important part in the religious practice of both faiths.

The path of United Church-Jewish reconciliation is through the recognition of theological equality, the substitution of challenging mutuality for hostility, the elimination of all pejorative allusions and the acceptance of the principle of diversity.

CHAPTER ELEVEN

Will We Ever Learn?

Will the United Church and the Jewish community ever find an accommodation? Their quarrel is as old as Christianity and as new as *The Observer*'s last editorial criticizing Zionist attitudes; as old as the beginning of the Diaspora and as new as the condemnation by the Canadian Jewish Congress of *The Observer*'s editorial judgments. The quarrel has never looked so hopeless nor so hopeful; hopeless because liberals on both sides, who pride themselves on tolerance, are paradoxically as intransigent as the ancient believers; hopeful because tendencies toward conciliation and empathy have never been stronger.

Would it be better if the two communities left each other alone? Some believe so; to try for peace and understanding is futile, they feel, because the two faiths live in radically different worlds. Most orthodox Jews have long felt that Judaism and Christianity are planets apart, and that there is therefore no point in dialogue or other co-operative effort.

Non-orthodox Holocaust survivors are also deeply suspicious of the United Church. The survivor organizations are strong in Canada, and their membership would undoubtedly reflect the attitude of American orthodox writer Eliezer Berkovits who said: "All we want of Christians is that they keep their hands off us and our children." Berkovits speaks of "The spiritual bankruptcy of the Christian religion," and he would find few among Canadian Jewish survivors who would disagree.

In United Church-Jewish relations the suspicions have hardened into what W. Clarke MacDonald describes as "a failure of acceptance," typified by "the Plaut-Forrest syndrome." While Rabbi Plaut and Dr. Forrest may accept each other as individuals, "they are symbolic to many people in both the Jewish and United Church communities of two antithetical elements. I doubt if in some minds in the

Jewish community anything which Forrest may say is acceptable, as is also true within the United Church community in some places with regard to things which are said by Plaut."

Some experts do not consider United Church-Jewish relations crucial for Canadian harmony. Ben Kayfetz of the Canadian Jewish Congress-B'nai B'rith community relations committee says that Jews and United Church members are not just religious adherents. They have other roles as "taxpayers, newspaper readers, television viewers, voters, ratepayers, Rotarians, businessmen, workers, teachers, and so forth," and these are more effective levels on which to build an accommodation. Yet one must ask: If United Church members and Jews cannot meet on the religious level which, more than any other, should provide hope for opening the door to understanding, what expectation is there for an opening on any other front?

The United Church member and the Canadian Jew cannot avoid each other because of the contact between Christian and Jew in the New Testament, where the Jewish image is often the polar opposite of what is ideally Christian. This New Testament conflict is bound to be carried over into living attitudes and convictions, in imitation of the ancient rivalry and misunderstandings between Church and synagogue, unless new insights and new contacts between the two communities give Christian-Jewish differences depth and perspective.

David Demson of Emmanuel College has said that "the Christian is committed to the defence of the Jew, just as brother is committed to the defence of brother in the house of their father." The Christian who rejects the Jew would "do well to remember that he is also repelling the will of the Lord, who has invited both Jew and Christian into his house." The same judgment would have to be made against the Jew who rejects the Christian.

United Church people and Jews are shut out from each other's nature and purpose and are left to nurse antagonisms divorced from reality. This is bound to lead to greater bitterness and resentment. It is not possible to let the United Church-Jewish controversy die, as Kayfetz suggests, and turn to other areas of accommodation. The alternative to dialogue, the instrument of inter-group understanding, is not indifference or neutrality, but the impassioned quarrel. To turn away from the quarrel is to let it fester, escalate and ultimately to damage the social fabric of Canada. Through dialogue, the United Church member and the Canadian Jew must grope towards an understanding and acceptance of one another.

Understanding consists of appreciating how an opponent evaluates life, its meaning and its goals. That does not mean merely obtaining information concerning the ways in which the respective religions function, valuable as such information is. It means trying to determine how an opponent thinks of his relation to God, to other men and to the world. Understanding does not recognize any authority other than that of the thinking and experiencing human mind. This challenge to understand one's opponents may appear formidable to the layman, who might feel inclined to abandon the exercise to religious philosophers. But the standard of intellectual life has risen for everybody. At one time, the suggestion that everyone would have to study algebra and geometry seemed incredible. Communism has introduced average people to the intricacies of metaphysics. There is no reason why the general United Church member and Jew should not become acquainted with the ideas that will clarify the meaning and purpose of one another's existence.

United Church people and Jews must begin to reflect thoughtfully on their problems and avoid responding with uninformed passion to anything and everything the other says, as they have so often done in the past. Dialogue is difficult to begin because it means not only studying and learning the theoretical structures that mould Christian and Jewish faith and action; it requires first a serious examination of one's own tradition alone, a monumental task in itself, and then a consideration of that tradition in encounter with those of other faiths who have examined theirs. Professor John Burbidge believes that the Jews have had to perform this exercise more "than any religion in the world" because of their emergence from the ghetto, the pressures of old and new types of anti-Semitism and their experiences in this century. He suggests that as a result "they have a religious vitality and depth which is greater than Judaism itself had for many centuries before. It is also a vitality which other traditions might well envy. Until we are prepared to think seriously about why we are the way we are," Burbidge contends, "we cannot build bridges that have any solid foundation."

It would be an exaggeration to attribute to Jews generally the ferment of Jewish intellectual circles in the last half century. Jewish scholars have been engaged in a meaningful re-thinking process, but its effects have not yet trickled down to the general populace. In Canada, at least, most Jews are not yet ready to take a dispassionate look at what has happened to the Jewish people in the last five decades.

They are still in the "feeling" stage, in the visceral or "gut" state, as multitudes of them phrase it. They are not yet attuned to the sensitive ruminations of the Martin Bubers and Abraham Joshua Heschels.

We are not concerned here only with the leaders of the United Church and the Jewish community, who have been the featured players in the quarrel, but with the millions in the United Church and the hundreds of thousands in the Jewish community. Both camps are in need of Burbidge's intellectual standards in the tasks of understanding and accommodation. There is, of course, the danger here of vulgarization, as those who oppose the whole concept of Christian-Jewish dialogue point out. Dialogue can easily degenerate into gimmickry. Moreover, although masses of people are involved, dialogue of necessity cannot be a mass exercise. It must be carried on in smaller entities, as yeast in bread. Early Christians saw themselves in this role, and Jews since the days of the Talmud have regarded popular adult study groups as a sacred duty that never ends. But the point of reconciliation would be lost if the process of accommodation were left solely to high-ranking scholars. Moses faced the same problem in having to choose between preserving the Torah for his elite posterity or risking its vulgarization by giving it to the erstwhile worshippers of the golden calf.

As preparation for their dialogue with the Jews, I recommend to members of the United Church two classics, written early in this century—the precursors of the current Christian-Jewish attempts to coexist in intellectual and emotional realms. The first is a three-volume work by George Foot Moore, an American Presbyterian of Harvard University. The traditional Christian view of Judaism has generally been gleaned from those narrow items where Christianity and Judaism touched each other. The liberal Moore doubted the authenticity of a picture of Judaism fitted together from arguments intending to show the superiority of Christianity. He set about filling out the picture in its true dimensions in *Judaism in the First Centuries of the Christian Era, The Age of the Tannaim*, first published in 1927.

The three volumes, in a style simple and graceful, bring to life the Jews who were the contemporaries of Jesus by letting Judaism speak for itself. "Exhaustiveness," says Moore in his "Introduction," "I have not aimed at; inerrancy is the last thing I should pretend to; but I trust that no essential point has been altogether overlooked, and I am confident that those who know the material best will be the most considerate in their judgment." They were and still are. Jewish scholars hailed the work as a landmark in the authoritative investigations of their people. The remarkable feature of the volumes is not just their authenticity but the grasp of what rabbinic or Talmudic or Pharisaic Judaism means in all its divergent trends, the idiosyncracies of its sects, the methods of its interpretation of sacred texts and of life itself.

Moore explained, with the facility of a master teacher, the Jewish ideas of God, the nature of man and his relation to God, morals, piety and the hereafter, in addition to all the rituals and observances: circumcision, the sabbath, the fasts and festivals, the laws concerning prayer and study. He did not attempt to glorify Jews and Judaism but paid them the supreme compliment of telling the story as it is, with all its idiosyncracies, to use his word. The work has been reprinted at least seven times, and I am astonished that few in the United Church are familiar with it or have even heard of it. If one truly wishes to understand Jews of the first century and today, he must enter the New Testament through the portals of Moore's Tannaitic teachers, the representatives of authoritative Jewish tradition.

A smaller work but no less in mastery of original Jewish sources is R. Travers Herford's *The Pharisees*. The Pharisaic image in the New Testament is, to say the least, unfavourable. The words "Pharisee" and "hypocrite" usually go together in the Christian literature of the last nineteen hundred years. Few historic figures have been more unjustly maligned. According to some scholars, Pharisees were teachers of Jesus. Much of what the Nazarene said in precept and parable, even the images, come from them. To see them through the New Testament's eyes is to see "through a glass darkly." The word "Pharisee" comes from the Hebrew *p'rushim*, meaning dissenters from the aristocratic party of the Sadduces. They were the ancient rabbis who represented the masses of Jews against the elitists and priestly clan. They were among the early fashioners of the democratic tradition—the labourers and tradesmen who were also learned. Herford gives a full portrait of their condition, beliefs and ideals, how they viewed *Halachah* (the Way or the Law) as a moral discipline and how they interpreted and expanded the teaching of the biblical prophets.

Most important for Christians are the questions he raises about the picture of Pharisaism in the New Testament. For Herford the evidence of the New Testament on this subject is that of "outsiders" who could see the effects of Pharisaism but without the authoritative means of knowing what produced those effects. Lacking first-hand knowledge, they were in no position to judge what they did see. "It is, moreover," says Herford, "the evidence of partisan witnesses, honestly partisan no doubt, intensely convinced that they were in the right, but nonetheless partisan, even when not definitely hostile. This is not to say that they were on that account false witnesses; it is to say that their evidence is only of secondary value for deciding the question of the real meaning of Pharisaism and cannot be admitted till that of the Pharisees themselves has been heard."

The argument is nicely turned. One does not in fairness hear only the testimony of the accusing Christians. The accused Jews must also have their day in court, and both Herford and Moore give them that day as officers of the court, not as defence attorneys. Their volumes are, therefore, especially valuable for United Church people in their approach to the life and culture of the Jews, ancient and modern.

While it is surprising that more liberal Christians, in their search for truth, do not read books on Judaism where Christianity had its roots, it is not surprising that Jews do not read expositions on the Christian faith.

From the beginnings of the Christian Church Jews paid little attention to its theology. Their preoccupation was defence against attack by the Church. Some Christian scholars, trying to define the relation between Judaism and Christianity, assume that the ancient Jews reacted to the existence and challenge of the rising Christian faith. Jewish scholars, however, until very recent times, paid little attention to what Christianity actually taught and thought. Though the Talmud developed concurrently with the Christian Church for the first five hundred years of the Common Era, it was hardly aware of its contemporary. This was not arrogance or stubbornness, as some might judge, but the inward look of a minority striving to preserve its values. Alan Davies says: "No modern religious Jew would ever admit, or ought to admit, that Judaism as a religious faith owes even a fragment of its spirit to a stubborn or blind rejection of Christian claims. Judaism does not usually define itself in relation to Christianity at all. Rather it represents an autonomous biblical religion which has passed through many stages of growth quite independent of Christian assumptions of its character."

This isolation, combined with the anti-Jewish bias of the Church, placed the New Testament and Christian theological literature outside the literary Pale for Jews. In orthodox Jewish circles today the New Testament, though not officially proscribed, has no place within the intellectual perimeters of even a learned man. Liberal Jews do not usually read it unless it is included in a university survey course.

Even then it is read with a certain distaste because of its anti-Jewish reputation.

It is important for dialogue with the United Church that Jews read the New Testament. They must read the Hebrew Bible first, of course, as Burbidge suggests and as their own tradition commands, but it is also time for reorientation. If total openness is to be the policy, then the Christian scriptures must be read despite the discomfort caused by passages in the Gospels of Matthew and John.

The New Testament, like the Old, cannot be understood without commentary, and the literature on Jesus and the Gospels is vast. Understanding can be a complex problem for the uninitiated. But as with the books on Judaism for the Christian, there are classics that stand out for Jews in the maze of expositions on the Christian faith.

The Jew should first hear the arguments against him, and the classical text demonstrating Christian bias is that of Paul Billerbeck and Hermann Strack, whose voluminous work, *Commentary on the New Testament from the Talmud and Midrash*, is a comparative presentation of the sayings of Jesus and his rabbinic contemporaries. Written in German, the tone is unmistakably superior, the authors usually finding the Nazarene's statements to be of finer spiritual quality than those of the ancient rabbis.

More objective and lighter, but nonetheless authentic, are Ernest William Parsons' *The Religion of the New Testament*, E. F. Scott's *Varieties of New Testament Religion* and Frederick C. Grant's *An Introduction to New Testament Thought*. All three treat the background of the Christian faith and its main concepts with clarity and responsibility. An interesting twist to the period is given by Henry C. Cadbury in his work *The Peril of Modernizing Jesus*, in which he spells out the dangers inherent in interpreting Christianity for the modern world, dangers similar to those the Jew faces in trying to update his religion.

Jews should also read books on the New Testament written by Jews. *A Jewish Understanding of the New Testament* by Samuel Sandmel is fair-minded, but *The Jewish World in the Time of Jesus* by Charles Guignebert is unfair, with a strong anti-Christian bias. Trude Weiss-Rosmarin's *Judaism and Christianity, The Differences* is strongly pro-Jewish without being anti-Christian.

The classic in the field by a Jew is Joseph Klausner's *Jesus of Nazareth*, first published early in this century. It was translated from the original Hebrew edition into several languages and was eagerly read by Jew and Christian. Wide interest in the book derived from the anomaly that Klausner, a Lithuanian Jew and a Zionist who moved to what was then Palestine, would choose to treat such a subject in the reborn Hebrew language. In so doing, however, Klausner was demonstrating the principle of spiritual Zionism, that the land of Israel would radiate knowledge on universal themes to the rest of the world.

While Klausner's *Jesus* was a serious attempt to define the character of the Nazarene and pleased many Christians, it displeased many Jews. Jews found fault with its scholarship, both as to the Talmud and the Gospels, and with its conclusions. In treating Jesus from the Zionist position, "the national Hebrew standpoint," Klausner says that the Nazarene cannot be God or the son of God or even the messiah, because the "kingdom of heaven" is not yet a reality. Was he a prophet, then? No, because he failed to provide "consolation in the political national sense." Was he even a Pharisaic rabbi? No, because unlike the Pharisees, he did not bolster the national consciousness.

So far, though the arguments seemed rather contrived, Jewish critics were not aroused. However, Klausner went on to say that the morality of Jesus is of special grandeur. "If ever the day should come," he concluded, "and the New Testament ethical code be stripped of its wrappings of miracles and mysticisms, the Book of the Ethics of Jesus will be one of the choicest treasures in the literature of Israel for all time." But the time for such an assessment of Christianity and, in particular, of the teachings of the New Testament with its anti-Semitic overtones, by a Jew for Jews had not yet come.

Christians for their part have often cited Klausner in support of fundamentalist convictions concerning the divinity of Jesus, a fate which befalls most Jewish writers in the field though they disapprove of such use of their investigations. Despite the controversy, Klausner remains one of the first Jews with the courage to face up to the challenge of the personality and teaching of the New Testament's central figure. After more than half a century, his work, recently reprinted, still retains an audacious quality and should be read for at least that reason.

The books of Claude G. Montefiore should be read by Jews as a source of authentic information on the nature of Christian religion and for insight into the character of Jesus. A British Reform Jew writing in the 1920s and thirties, Montefiore undertook the three-fold examination every liberal Jew must perform in order to engage in dialogue with Christians. First, he studied the original Christian sources, and published his *Synoptic Gospels*. Then he looked at Jewish and Christian messages side by side, and produced *Rabbinic Literature and Gospel Teachings*. Finally, he studied the relation between Judaism and Christianity in a literary gem called *What a Jew Thinks about Jesus*.

The outstanding feature of Montefiore is his moderation. He can be critical of Christianity without being offensive. He can steer a middle course without blunting conviction. And he brings to Judaism and Christianity equally the demanding tests of humanism, though one is always aware of his unimpeachable loyalty to his own people. He appeared to regard himself as a popular expositor without technical expertise or originality in either Christian or Jewish areas, making heavy use of the authoritative investigations of both camps. His main thesis is that the closeness in spirit between Jesus and the Pharisees is so strong he must be judged a Jew rather than a Christian.

Montefiore, like Klausner, had trouble with Jewish critics who could not tolerate his gentle approach, and he hurled a word or two in their direction about pedantry. He is as fine a model of a Jewish loyalist seeking an honest accommodation with Christians and Christianity as I can recall.

Christians and Jews, of course, had been quarreling for a long time before the United Church-Jewish dispute erupted. Many books have been written chronicling accusations and counter-accusations and seeking reconciliation. British theologian James Parkes is the foremost writer in this area. His *Conflict of the Church and Synagogue* is a frank and constructive analysis of Christian-Jewish relations. The most influential book on the anti-Jewish hatred of the Christian centuries is by the French educator Jules Isaac whose study of anti-Semitism, *The Teaching of Contempt*, it is said, moved Pope John XXIII to initiate liturgical changes affecting Jews.

In North America Conrad Moehlman's *The Christian-Jewish Tragedy, A Study in Religious Prejudice*, and Malcolm Hay's *The Foot of Pride* are appeals from a Protestant and Catholic respectively for an end to bitterness. A. Roy Eckardt's *Your People, My People* and Franklin Littell's *The Crucifixion of the Jews* are passionate confessions of the wrongs committed by the Christian Church against the Jewish people. More calmly, Bernhard E. Olson in *Faith and Prejudice* investigates the Churches, but reassuringly charts the progress that has been made in building sensitivity to the problem. In Canada Gregory Baum attempted an answer to a long-standing question, *Is the New Testament Anti-Semitic?*, absolving the Christian scriptures, and Alan Davies proffered another answer in *Anti-Semitism and the Christian Mind*, where he implicates the New Testament in the spread of anti-Jewish animosity.

The books mentioned here constitute only a fraction of the twentieth-century literature on Christian-Jewish problems. They are not only valuable tools in preparation for dialogue but provide comforting evidence that earnest efforts are afoot to turn the trend of history. Dialogue needs the courage which comes from awareness that many minds and hearts are laden with concern.

Books are not only important as sources of information necessary for successful dialogue between Christian and Jew. They also provide a semantic aid. Some people have given up on the possibility of dialogue because the same words have different meanings for different people, thereby spreading confusion instead of clarification. This is especially true of Jews and Christians who read the same biblical words and come away with different meanings. Terms like redemption, sin, kingdom of God, the world to come, Israel, messiah, salvation, law, maiden-virgin are freighted with entire theological structures. The words instantly trigger pictures in the minds of Christian and Jew, pictures they live with for a lifetime, pictures more real than those that hang on a wall. Many Jews believe that the word salvation, to take but one illustration, has no Jewish meaning at all, because they associate it with soul-saving, an operation attributed to Christian missionaries. The semantic problem in dialogue is not to be underestimated. Still, it can be overcome by knowledge gleaned from Christian writers if one is Jewish and Jewish writers if one is Christian.

There is no suggestion here, of course, of disputation on articles of faith, which are subjective areas and beyond the scope of dialogue. The point is that we cannot make dialogue meaningful if we trade words which create different pictures for each side in the exchange. Our aim is to understand the past and to penetrate the myths and stereotypes which have cluttered the ancient relationship. That is an objective exercise requiring careful, and mutual, understanding of the words we use.

Absorbing a variety of written opinions on the meaning of Christianity and Judaism also helps to prevent the impression that one's antagonist represents a monolithic system. The United Church is very sensitive to the word monolith. It has become an accusation and counter-accusation between United Church and Jewish leaders. Jews generally are aware of the varieties of faith in Christianity and even within the United Church, but they tend to judge the United Church organization in terms of their own structure, which is formed essentially for defence. In turn, United Church people are familiar with the three popular denominations in Judaism, but since Jews prefer to speak and act toward non-Jews through community consensus the perception of Judaism as a monolith grows strong.

It is important, therefore, that United Church people understand—Jews themselves often forget—that Judaism was not a monolith in ancient or medieval times, nor is it today. "Normative" Judaism is no more a fact than normative Christianity. In the Talmudic schools of the first century diversity flowered in the soil of dialectics. It is told that one of the heads of a Palestinian academy, Rabbi Johanan, complained that one of his colleagues agreed too much with his opinions and wanted more challenge. The school of Hillel not only taught its own interpretation of the Bible but that of the opposing Shammaitic school. In the Middle Ages Jewish mystics and rationalists clashed in acrimonious disputes, and in modern times, relations among Reform, Conservative and Orthodox divisions, despite co-operative ventures, have often been acerbic.

Historically Jews, like Christians, were never of one mould. In striving for mutual understanding, Canadian Jews and United Church Christians must not lose sight of one another's inner diversity.

As we must come to dialogue intellectually prepared, that is, with open and informed minds, so obviously must we come with open hearts. Mutuality is not only a movement from the majority to the minority but from the minority to the majority.

It is often charged that Christians are indifferent to Jewish concerns. It is rarely said that Jews should be more heedful of the things that trouble Christians. One sees occasionally an article or letter in *The Observer* saying: "The majority has rights, too." Indeed, it has. But by the nature of things, since the majority has more power, a just society stresses the rights of the minority. We are concerned here, however, not with the rights of the majority but with its needs. Many United Church leaders feel that Jews brush aside too easily the Church's needs, and the feeling is understandable.

In the fiftieth anniversary issue of *The Observer*, January 1975, in which articles from the five decades were reprinted, the only piece by a Jew selected for republication was that of the late Toronto *Star* drama critic Nathan Cohen, "I Rejoice at Christmas, Too." *The Observer* was jammed with Jewish articles in the fifties, sixties and early seventies, but only Cohen's of December 15, 1966, was chosen. "I respect Christian teachings," said Cohen, "and they have helped me to enrich my appreciation of the meaning of life, and the dignity of each of my fellow men, whatever his colour, his faith, his rank. That is why, notwithstanding the history of anti-Semitism, despite my forebodings of the future, and speaking only for myself as a Jew, I find it well within my heart to consider the occasion of Christ's birthday a time for common rejoicing."

The reason for republishing Cohen's words is easily understood. Here is a Jew, for a change, offering a gift of heartfelt appreciation. Dialogue is a reciprocal exercise. It entails challenge, but there can be no meaningful challenge except through mutual acceptance. Despite the justifiable demand that Christians be on guard against anti-Semitism which so easily became the style of the Church in the past, Jews should understand that the thrust toward conciliation must come from both sides, from the Jewish community as well as from the United Church. Certainly one should not forget the power syndrome in Christian-Jewish relations, but it is also important to recognize that mutuality must precede reconciliation.

Liberals in the United Church and the Jewish community have special problems, but they also have extraordinary opportunities to explore a basis for mutuality. They can begin by working together on the important task of separating myth from faith. This is not just a theological exercise. It has to do with attitudes, which tend to confuse Christian-Jewish relations unless they are defined.

An established religion does not seem to live without myths. Both Judaism and Christianity make prolific use of the method to teach important truths. Myth is more than a parable or a metaphor. It is more than a beautiful portrayal. It works on the imagination, providing dramatic, readily understood pictures. It is not necessarily historical, yet it touches fact. The crucifixion is a myth, a wondrous story with a self-sacrificing hero, plenty of villains and a happy ending in the resurrection. The opening of the Red Sea for the Israelites as they fled from the ancient Egyptians is also a myth with heroes, villains and happy ending in the redemption of the chosen people.

Faith, in contrast to myth, is not so easily grasped. It is the quest for the ultimate reality, the search for meaning and truth, the sense of being part of the harmony in nature, the hunger for what is eternal in the midst of changing values, the hope of overcoming time through devotion to what is timeless, the thirst to be a free soul. These ideas are common to both Judaism and Christianity, and it is the business of the religious teacher and preacher to distil them from the myths.

In popular concepts, faith and myth run together, the combination often causing injury to the believer and undermining his relations with others. The danger of myth is that its details may become more important than its message. A person can become so chained to the details that he is drained of spiritual feeling. Yet it is impossible to eradicate myth because the human mind requires it for instant grasp of a lesson. A great religion aims at balance between faith and myth, something religious liberals in the United Church and the Jewish community have been trying to achieve, not always successfully.

The central myth in Christianity contains anti-Jewish bias, a fact that must be faced. Whenever the magic of the myth is enhanced, as at Easter time, the prejudice is intensified. A myth has great power of seduction so that its seeming reality can be transferred from one area of life to another, from the Church to the political arena, for example. The Nazis, aware of its power, perverted the Christian myth for their own purpose, impelling German theologian Rudolf Bultmann, outraged by the perversion, to call for the demythologization of Christianity. Yet out of the same myth comes the Christian faith at its grandest, the lesson of redemptive love, of the necessity to take great risks for truth, of surrender to the demands of the spirit, of self-immolation.

In Judaism the central myths are associated with the Jews and their unique role as chosen people, their acceptance of a divinely revealed law to govern a hoped-for ideal society in the promised land. There are Jews, entranced by this myth, for whom mankind is split into two rigid categories, the Gentiles and the Jews, the former representing evil and the latter righteousness. The trance is carried over into daily life where the two camps battle with no hope of respite. The perversion of the original myth gains currency with every outbreak of anti-Jewish feeling, leading at least one Jewish mystic to trace Gentile behaviour to a satanic source. On the other hand, the myth of chosenness has evoked from Jews sublime ethical principles and a social conscience, the combination sanctified by sacrifice for the common welfare.

The damage myths can do is clear. They must be examined from a humane perspective. Liberals among the Jews and in the United Church are in the most favourable position to move together in this purpose. Simultaneously, as they work on demythologization, they can together stress the deep need for faith in our time.

Everyone would welcome an interpretation of life which ensured indestructibility of human values; an insight that life is worthwhile despite suffering; a conviction that there is a real difference between good and evil and that it is well to identify with the good; a faith that history, despite the chaos of our social, political and economic life, is not meaningless but is a process of creation out of which will come a nobler breed of man and woman.

But Christian and Jewish liberals do not usually speak in this way these days. It sounds dreamlike, visionary. Religion today is urged to create a facile ideology, a special language, a popular slogan, a gimmick to catch attention. Technique is the order of the day. But there is really no need for Madison Avenue techniques in a co-operative effort to battle general disillusionment with the materialistic outlook on life. The times cry out for faith. Reliance on scientific control of natural forces and resources as a solution for human ills has proved a will-o'-the-wisp. All that is dear is imperilled for every man and woman today. The fear is universal. Our politics, our science, our social techniques, our government administration, our methods of distribution are out of kilter. All this is more than a question of depleting energy resources. There is a world-wide feeling that life's problems are insoluble.

Yet there is something in the spirit of the human being, some stubborn instinct of life which protests against letting the human drama end in a senseless farce. That instinct demands not only survival of the human race but of the values by which and for which men and women have lived, the values of truth, justice, mercy.

Young people beset by doubts in this disbelieving world cry out for a moral imperative that makes life worthwhile for those who obey it and which none can violate without injury to their deepest interests. They want to believe that in every situation there is a right and wrong, that in resisting the temptation to do wrong they are discarding a lesser satisfaction for a greater. Women today who would like to have children would welcome a faith that assured them that they will not regret having borne them, because their children will find life worthwhile in spite of the suffering it entails. Philosophers, scientists, educators and statesmen in the Western world are crying out for an ideological basis for the democratic way of life, one that would generate as much enthusiasm for democracy as Marxism and totalitarianism have aroused in most of the peoples of the world. Surely this demand testifies to the need for a spiritual faith in history as a meaningful process best expressed in the democratic ideal.

Those who accept the reality of spiritual values must lead people in their search for answers to the quest for a living faith. The leaders cannot do so as rivals and competitors. By themselves Christianity, Judaism or other great faiths no longer have much power. Their respective work is suspect because it is localized and gives the appearance of being sectarian. They must, therefore, work within the respective faith and beyond it in a kind of spiritual federation, for on the great questions of life's meaning and hope for the future they are allies. No one sees this better than religious liberals. Is not this a time, then, when United Church and Jewish liberals should begin to work in tandem? Are they not untrue to themselves in being untrue to each other? And in the process are they not untrue to the humanity they profess to serve?

If United Church and Jewish liberals take seriously their avowed obligations to their professed ethical and moral principles and to the need of finding answers to modern man's spiritual dilemma, they have the duty to curb their own natural tendency to use antagonism to one another as a means of enhancing their own importance in the eyes of respective adherents.

United Church and Jewish liberals can begin to try their co-operative wings in a marginal but significant area that touches the two historical religions, an area that cries for mutuality and compassion. In Canada and the United States marriage between Christians and Jews has become increasingly common. The Jewish minority has always set up "fences" against attack, and has long regarded assimilation as a more dangerous attacker than robust anti-Semitism, because it not only undermines the integrity of the group but does so insidiously. The assimilative tendency for a Christian-Jewish couple is obvious. Where the non-Jewish partner in such a union embraces Judaism the opposition of the Jewish family has become less formidable in recent years. Nevertheless, Jews who are enwrapped by the psychological tentacles of age-old persecution still find such intermarriage difficult to take. Where there is no conversion, that is, a mixed marriage, the opposition is inflexible.

United Church liberals find Jewish resistance to mixed marriage hard to understand. E. A. Howse tells of "a beautiful girl" who came to him weeping, in despair that she would have to postpone her wedding because of her mother's opposition. Her mother said if she married a Gentile "it would be as though she had not been born." Says Howse: "I cannot conceive that I could say to a child of mine: 'You will be as though you have not been born.' There must be deep-seated antipathy to do that." As Jew and Zionism became dirty words to Gentiles and Christians, so Christians and Gentile were anathema to Jews. Two thousand years of inimical Christian-Jewish relations have created this mutual malevolence. Once again the United Church liberal errs when he denies the special connection between the two religions.

What is the fate of the mixed couples? Most of them live in marginal anonymity. Their children grow up in a confusion of loyalty, usually believing themselves to be Jews by race, although there is no such thing, and interdenominational by persuasion, which also means little because it is bereft of spiritual content. Their spirit roams a wasteland between two religions, both indifferent to their welfare.

Precise statistics concerning such couples are not available (see Notes on Chapter 11). Since the situation in Canada is not too dissimilar from that of the US—some sociological factors may differ—an estimate can be made from a recent survey in Washington, D.C., which revealed that in four thousand Jewish homes an unconverted Christian formed part of the family. In roughly one-third of this number the wife was Jewish and the husband Christian. Jewish tradition regards the children of Jewish mothers as Jews, yet the children of mixed marriages usually have no connection with the Jewish community. The mixed couples in the US are a collection of an estimated half a million people. On a proportional basis, in Canada they would number from fifteen to twenty thousand human beings.

Fundamentalist Christians and Jews cannot be expected to have a message for these people. I cannot speak for orthodox Christians, but orthodox Jews would simply cite the dire consequences that come from the breach of inflexible tradition. The couples are, therefore, the particular responsibility of liberal Jews and the liberals of the United Church. Who else can bring them a sense of dignity, a feeling of belonging to a caring humanity, a confidence based on faith if not on myth, an awareness for the family that spiritual bonds must encompass the house or it cannot become a home?

From the liberal viewpoint, the essence of faith does not vary, whatever the form or the ritual of a particular religion. The different religions of the two partners, though tenuous, need not confront each other. Some Jews will say that this liberal attitude encourages mixed marriage, because it offers a basis for acceptance and legitimacy. What, then, should be the liberal's attitude? He cannot excoriate another faith as an abomination. He has no alternative but to find compatibility in the backgrounds of such a couple.

He must tell the Jewish partner that the Jew has earned his place in Western society by the fact of his humanity and has proved himself an extraordinary stimulant to enlightened thought and modern culture, that the Jewish heritage is important to the maintenance of the humanizing influence in the world.

The non-Jewish partner could learn to accept Jewish memories and loyalties as part of the atmosphere of the home. By the same token, the Jewish partner could learn to appreciate the Christian demand for heroism in a sorrowful world, for the knowledge that a man is not complete in himself and his true nature comes from that which is beyond himself.

As for the children, their need is to experience at home the positive, liberal attitude of both parents questing for the good and the true. In Jewish tradition the home is sacred not because it is set apart from life but because it is part of the struggle to attain the ultimate condition—personalities blending into one another to serve others. Humanism is implicit in the Judeo-Christian tradition, and for the child of a mixed marriage the aim must be to feel his humanness, so that when he reaches maturity he can have warmth and respect for the spiritual origins of both his parents. He might even be able to feel blessed that he was reared in a love unencumbered by the bias of myth and is therefore especially qualified to fight the prejudices and ill will that still beset society.

In serving mixed couples in a co-operative ministry, United Church and Jewish liberals could find their own liberalism enriched by the realization that the two faiths need less of disputation and more of dialogue.

Some, like Ben Kayfetz and B. G. Smillie of St. Andrew's College, Saskatoon, believe that United Church-Jewish orientation may have a better chance in the field of social action than in theology, that the possibilities of theological dialogue are restricted because of fundamental beliefs on both sides. The divinity and messiahship of Jesus are categorically denied by Jews, Reform or orthodox. For many Christians, fundamentalist and liberal even in the United Church, the acceptance of the state of Israel would be a denial of the core of their belief, in the one case in the inevitability of Jewish homelessness because of the rejection of Jesus, and in the other because for them the concept of Jewish nationalism is regressive. But in a country where the majority is Christian, Jews must find allies among Christians. To ignore them deliberately is to weaken the common struggle against violence and injustice in the world. Christians likewise, if they ignore Jews, will deprive themselves of valuable allies.

Certainly there are many non-theological areas where the United Church and the Jewish community could work as one—poverty, the breakdown of the family, the alienation of youth, the plight of the aged and the lonely, the irresponsibility of the new "situation ethics," the romanticization of violence and crime. United Church-Jewish co-operation could also be strengthened in common tasks to deepen the moral consciousness of Canada. B. G. Smillie says that "the relative silence of both our communions at the time of the application of the War Measures Act [during Quebec's separatist eruptions in 1970] indicates that we do not have a good record at saying the word of God in context."

Co-operation in social concerns is admittedly easier than theological dialogue, but one should not exclude the other. Rather should they go hand in hand, social action encouraging progress in dialogue, and vice versa.

Finally, if religious leaders are serious about an end to dispute and a beginning to accommodation, they must strip themselves of their representative roles, which are a towering barrier to dialogue in depth. In the past, United Church and Jewish officials have stood behind a title or a robe or a name on an office door, or they became "spokesmen for," to use Bruce McLeod's phrase. This was an error of *The Observer*, seeking a representative opinion among Jews, which is usually the lowest common denominator but not necessarily a reflection of authentic attitudes. A rabbi may be the poorest communal representative because he must hide his humanity behind the role of speaking for his people. He presents arguments, not always perceptions. The representative plays a competitive game, because all eyes are on him to win.

That is one of the difficulties in the United Church-Jewish quarrel. We choose sides and captains and step into the arena as adversaries to argue the issues. Each group assumes a fixed position and its representatives bend all their efforts to winning arguments about anti-Semitism, the Palestinian refugees, Israeli policy, the Holocaust, and theological insight. Winning is important, because the glory of the group must be maintained.

United Church and Jewish leaders, in a breach of their own Judeo-Christian philosophy, have succumbed to the sporting formulation of life, in which life is conceived of as a game. In so doing they have sublimated personal faith into group assertiveness, substituted the yes-or-no loyalty for the thoughtful approach to group patriotism, and made possible the triumph of easily manipulated emotions over intelligence.

We have combined gamesmanship and the Judeo-Christian ethic, thereby straddling two horses galloping off in opposite directions. But the Bible shows no trace of the sports fixation, either in the Old or New Testaments. The competitor as such is not exalted in the literature that is the basis for Judeo-Christian morality. We are reluctant to acknowledge the deep contradiction between the competitive and Hebraic-Christian codes which muddles our relationships. But the two strains exist, in our lives, in our morality and in the United Church-Jewish quarrel. We will be on our way to reconciliation once we face up to the game we are playing.

Feeling and emotion, combined with a lack of awareness of the facts, keep the United Church and the Jews apart. Reason says we must get together. To ignore reason would mean that we are either perplexed or hypocritical. In each instance that would defeat everything we stand for as Christians and Jews.

CHAPTER NOTES

See Bibliography for full listings of all titles.

THE SETTING: Why I Wrote This Book

A discussion on "Criticism of Israel in the Public Media" appeared in the monthly *The Jewish Frontier*, New York, October 1974.

In an article for *Commentary* magazine (December 1963) novelist Phillip Roth reduced Jewish criticism of Jewish authors writing about Jews for general consumption to: "What will the *goyim* [Gentiles] think?"

In the *Jewish Spectator*, New York, Summer 1976, Trude Weiss-Rosmarin laments "the shameful subversion of freedom of the press by Jewish Federations, which . . . have become the publishers and/or bosses" of most Jewish newspapers in the United States. The same lament may be applied to Canada's Jewish press.

Written sources: *Your People, My People* by A. Roy Eckardt; *Whose Jerusalem?* by Ronald Segal.

CHAPTER 1—How the Quarrel Escalated

Material for this chapter came from interviews with Rev. Dr. A. C. Forrest, editor, United Church *Observer*; Mr. Alfred Green, of Toronto; Very Rev. N. Bruce McLeod, former United Church moderator; Very Rev. E. M. Howse, also a former moderator; and Rev. Dr. George Morrison, former secretary of the General Council, United Church of Canada.

The agreement between officials of the United Church and B'nai B'rith (Appendix A) was reported in the Toronto *Star*, the Toronto *Globe and Mail* and was fully treated in the *Canadian Jewish News* and the *Jewish Standard*.

The statement of Roman Catholic and United Church clerics (Appendix B) appeared in the *Globe and Mail* and was distributed across

Canada by several Jewish organizations.

The statements by Rev. Dr. W. Clarke MacDonald and Prof. Lorne Kenny (Appendices C and D) appeared in the *Globe and Mail;* they were not distributed by mail.

The Salter ad (Appendix E) was published in the Toronto *Sun* before it appeared in *The Observer* and caused hardly a ripple of protest.

Written sources: Address by Prof. E. L. Fackenheim at St. Andrew's College, Saskatoon, May 1972; *Anti-Semitism and the Christian Mind* by Alan Davies; *The Catholic Church and Nazi Germany* by Guenter Lewy; *The Vatican in the Age of the Dictators, 1922-1945* by Anthony Rhodes; *The Yom Kippur War* etc., edited by Moshe Davis.

CHAPTER 2—The Plaintiff

Interviews: Father John Keating, now deceased, of the Catholic Information Centre, Toronto, and Judge Sydney Harris, national president of the Canadian Jewish Congress.

Telephone interview: Rev. Dr. Leslie Hunt of Wycliffe College, University of Toronto.

Conclusions on Jewish education and identity similar to those in this chapter were made by Harold S. Himmelfarb in an analysis, "Jewish Education for Naught," Institute for Jewish Policy Planning and Research of the Synagogue Council of America, Washington, D.C., September 1975.

For an analysis of how strongly the Jewish vote influences US elections, see "Implications of Electoral College Reform for American Jewry," Institute for Jewish Policy Planning and Research of the Synagogue Council of America, Washington, D.C., January 1976.

Written sources: Ya'acov Glickman's "The Organization and Governance of the Toronto Jewish Community"; "The Jewish Communities of Montreal, Ottawa, London, Hamilton, Winnipeg, Windsor, Edmonton, Calgary and Vancouver," Center for Jewish Community Studies, Philadelphia; Mel Fenson's "The Jewish Community of Canada," *American Jewish Year Book, 1974-75*; "American Jewry and U.S.-Israel Relations," Institute for Jewish Policy Planning, Washington, D.C., December 1974.

CHAPTER 3—The Accused

Interviews: Very Rev. N. Bruce McLeod, Very Rev. E. M. Howse, Rev. Dr. A. C. Forrest, Rev. Dr. George Morrison,

Dr. Albert Rose, Professor of Social Work, University of Toronto.

Written sources: Hertzel Fishman's *American Protestantism and a Jewish State*; *Europe Leaves the Middle East* by Howard M. Sachar; *Proceedings of the General Council*, United Church of Canada, and files of the United Church *Observer*.

CHAPTER 4—The Untamed

Interviews: Rev. Dr. A. C. Forrest, Very Rev. N. Bruce McLeod, Rev. Dr. George Morrison and Dr. Albert Rose.

Written sources: "The United Church *Observer* and the State of Israel," Basic Document of B'nai B'rith, mimeograph; *Proceedings of the General Council*, United Church of Canada, and files of the United Church *Observer*.

CHAPTER 5—Why Do Liberals Rage?

Interviews: Principal B. Robert Bater of Queen's Theological College, Kingston, Ontario; Very Rev. N. Bruce McLeod; Very Rev. E. M. Howse; Judge Sydney Harris; Dr. Albert Rose.

Answers to questions by mail from: Mr. Ben Kayfetz, executive director, Community Relations Committee of the Canadian Jewish Congress and B'nai B'rith; Mr. Julius Hayman, Q.C., editor and publisher, *The Jewish Standard*, Toronto and Montreal; Rev. Dr. George W. Goth of London, Ontario; Dr. Robert B. McClure, then of Malaysia; Prof. Morton Paterson of Laurentian University; Rev. Carl Zurbrigg of Simcoe, Ontario; Prof. Alan Davies of Victoria University.

The difficulty of defining liberalism is illustrated in *Commentary* magazine, September 1976, where sixty-four intellectuals invent various liberal subdivisions: early and late liberals, centre extremists, paleoliberals, tough-minded liberals, "rad-libs," and "trad-libs," etc.

Written sources: *History of the Jews* by Heinrich Graetz; *A History of the Jewish People* by Max L. Margolis and Alexander Marx; *A Social and Religious History of the Jews* by Salo Baron.

CHAPTER 6—The "Chosen" People

Interviews: Principal B. Robert Bater and Dr. Albert Rose.

Answers to questions by mail: Rev. George W. Goth and Dr. Robert McClure.

Written sources: *The Gospel and the Land* by W. D. Davies; *Religious Tradition and Myth* by E. R. Goodenough; *Judaism as a Civilization* by M. M. Kaplan.

CHAPTER 7—The Anti-Semitic Label

Interviews: Principal B. Robert Bater; Father Gregory Baum of St. Michael's College, Toronto; Judge Sydney Harris; Very Rev. E. M. Howse; Very Rev. N. Bruce McLeod.

Answers by mail: Rev. W. Goth, Dr. Robert McClure, Mr. Julius Hayman.

Dr. Nahum Goldmann's statement is quoted in *Israel and Palestine*, A Monthly Review, Paris, July-August 1975.

The quotation by Cynthia Ozick is from *Esquire* Magazine, November 1973.

Earl Raab's statement is from *Commentary* magazine, May 1974.

Written sources: Father Gregory Baum's sermon "Salvation is from the Jews," Eglinton United Church, Toronto, April 1972, mimeograph; Alan Davies' *Anti-Semitism and the Christian Mind* and "An Unresolved Issue Between Christians and Jews," address, Metropolitan United Church, Toronto, May 1974, mimeograph; Lucy S. Davidowicz's *The War Against the Jews, 1933-45*; Arie Lova Eliav's *Land of the Hart*; Emil Fackenheim's address to St. Andrew's College, Saskatoon, mimeograph; Forster and Epstein's *The New Anti-Semitism*; Ben G. Kayfetz's memoir to the Toronto Jewish Historical Society, May 1972, mimeograph; Margolis and Marx's *History of the Jewish People*.

CHAPTER 8—The Holocaust

Interview: Very Rev. E. M. Howse

Answers by Mail: Prof. John W. Burbidge of Trent University; Rev. Dr. W. Clarke MacDonald, secretary of the Committee on the Church and International Affairs, United Church of Canada.

The Holocaust prayer is by Rabbi David Polish in the *High Holiday Prayer Book*, ed. by M. M. Kaplan, E. Kohn and I. Eisenstein, Jewish Reconstructionist Foundation, New York 1948.

Yoram Kaniuk's statement is from an interview in the *New Outlook*, Tel Aviv, January 1975.

Uri Zvi Greenberg's poem is a translation by Robert Alter, which appeared for the first time in *Commentary*, Nov. 1973.

The debate between Richard L. Rubenstein and Elie Wiesel is recorded in *The German Church Struggle and the Holocaust*.

The story of Reb Bunem is told in *The German Church Struggle and the Holocaust* and in Elie Wiesel's *One Generation After*.

Viktor Frankl's words are from his *Introduction to Logotherapy: Man's Search for Meaning* whose title in the original German is *From Concentration Camp to Existentialism*.

An account of the destruction of the town of Slonim—how its houses were set to the torch and its men, women and children shot and buried in a common grave—is given in Leivy Smolar's *Lest We Forget*.

Written sources: Franklin Littell's *The Crucifixion of the Jews* and *The German Church Struggle and the Holocaust*, ed. by Littell; Elie Wiesel's novella *Dawn;* Eberhard Bethge's *Dietrich Bonhoeffer*.

CHAPTER 9—The Palestinians

Interviews: Judge Sydney Harris, Very Rev. N. Bruce McLeod.

I. F. Stone's quotation comes from his "Introduction" to Fouzi el-Azmar's *To be an Arab in Israel*.

Marie Syrkin's article, "Who are the Palestinians?" first appeared in *Midstream*, 1970.

Reports that Israel has been sending arms to rightist Christians in the Lebanese civil war appeared in the *Christian Science Monitor*, July 20, 1976; *The Washington Post* of July 21 and 27, 1976; and *Time* magazine, July 26, 1976.

A concise description of the PLO as an umbrella organization for diverse Palestinian elements was given November 12, 1975, by Harold H. Saunders of the US State Department to the subcommittee on international relations of the American House of Representatives. The statement was reprinted in the monthly review, *Israel and Palestine*, Paris, France, December 1975.

Lord Caradon's impression of Yasser Arafat is from an article in the *New Outlook*, Tel Aviv, December 1975.

Shulamit Aloni's statement is from the Tel Aviv daily *Yediot Aharonot*, August 9, 1974.

Written sources: Theodor Herzl's *Altneuland;* Eric Rouleau on "The Palestinians," *Le Monde*, Paris, May 21-25, 1975; Meyer Weisgal's autobiography, *So Far;* Samuel Katz's *Battleground: Fact and Fancy in Palestine; The Palestinians*, ed. by Michael Curtis, et al; Fouzi el-Asmar's *To be an Arab in Israel;* Arie Eliav's *Land of the Hart;* Fawaz Turki's *The Disinherited*.

CHAPTER 10—The Hostile Theologies

Interview: Dr. Albert Rose.

Answers by mail: Prof. John W. Burbidge; Prof. Morton Paterson; Prof. George Johnston of McGill University; Prof. Benjamin G. Smillie of St. Andrew's College, Saskatoon; Mr. Julius Hayman.

Martin Buber's and Franz Rosenzweig's statements are from *The Jewish-Christian Argument* by Hans Joachim Schoeps.

A Christian interpretation of loving God with all one's heart, soul and might was given by Leonard Griffith in the United Church *Observer*, January 1976. In the same issue, R. Gordon Nodwell discussed the seeming contradiction between the Trinity and monotheism.

On most issues Jesus seems to follow the liberal interpretation of Rabbi Hillel, but on the question of divorce he appears to side with Rabbi Shammai who held that a man could not divorce his wife except on grounds of sexual immorality. Hillel, so moderate on other matters, held the biblical position that the husband need not have any reason whatever to order a bill of divorcement.

Written sources: Jacob B. Agus' *Dialogue and Tradition*; Sholem Asch's *The Nazarene*; Leo Baeck's *Judaism and Christianity*; Gregory Baum's *Is the New Testament Anti-Semitic?*; Alan Davies' *Anti-Semitism and the Christian Mind*; Charles Guignebert's *The Jewish World in the Time of Jesus*; W. D. Davies' *The Gospel and the Land*; Joseph Klausner's *Jesus of Nazareth*; Claude G. Montefiore's *The Synoptic Gospels* and *What a Jew thinks about Jesus*; Morton Paterson's address to the Theological Union of Hamilton, Ontario, June 1966, mimeograph; Strack-Billerbeck's *Commentary on the New Testament from the Talmud and the Midrash* (German); Trude Weiss-Rosmarin's *Judaism and Christianity, The Differences*.

CHAPTER 11—Will We Ever Learn?

Interviews: Very Rev. E. M. Howse, Very Rev. Bruce McLeod.

Answers by mail: Prof. John W. Burbidge; Mr. B. G. Kayfetz; Rev. Dr. W. Clarke MacDonald.

Eliezer Berkovits' statement is quoted in Alan Davies' *Anti-Semitism and the Christian Mind* and is from Berkovits' *Faith After the Holocaust*.

Dr. David Demson's statement is from *The Ecumenist*, November-December, 1968.

Recent Canadian figures on intermarriage for the decade 1962-72 were compiled in Montreal by Dr. Jean-Claude Lasry and Evelyn Bloomfield-Schachter. In all these cases the non-Jewish partners became converts. No figures are available on mixed marriages in Canada, i.e., where both partners retain original identities.

Written sources: Samuel Sandmel's *We Jews and Jesus*; Conrad Moehlman's *The Christian-Jewish Tragedy*; Malcolm Hay's *The Foot of Pride*.

APPENDIX A

Statement by Officials of the United Church and B'nai B'rith, May 4, 1973:

"As representatives of the United Church Family and the B'nai B'rith in Canada, we have anguished over recent events that have driven deep wedges of misunderstanding and acrimony between us.

"As we in the Church recall the record of the centuries, we acknowledge the Church's sorry role in fostering hostility between the Christian and Jewish communities. We seek to ameliorate our relationship and pursue the future unfettered by intolerance, prejudice or rancour, with common goals directed towards the betterment of the society in which we live.

"We of the United Church deeply regret and disavow the insensitivity and inaccuracies contained in an article by John Nicholls Booth in the United Church *Observer* (March 1972). We of the B'nai B'rith deeply regret and repudiate invective as a form of expression and communication.

"We recognize and appreciate the interests of Jews everywhere, and of the United Church, for the events in the Middle East and in the survival of Israel.

"Though we may differ in opinion from time to time on some issues, we believe that cooperation and friendship can be achieved, and that criticism of each other can be constructive when offered in a spirit of mutual respect and integrity.

"As growing problems and challenges face us here in Canada, and throughout the world, members of the United Church and of B'nai B'rith need to meet one another, share insights, discover differences and cooperate, where possible, in social action for the common good; but communication cannot take place in an atmosphere of ambiguity or doubt regarding the respect of one party for the other.

"We jointly look forward to dialogue as the appropriate means whereby points of view can be expressed, reconciliation achieved and understanding established. We affirm that our combined energies shall be increasingly channelled in this direction.

Rt. Rev. N. Bruce McLeod, Moderator, United Church of Canada	Sydney Maislin, President, Canadian B'nai B'rith
Rev. Dr. George M. Morrison, Secretary, General Council, United Church of Canada	Herbert S. Levy, Executive Vice-President, Canadian B'nai B'rith."

APPENDIX B

Statement of Christian Concern About the Middle East, *The Globe and Mail*, October 19, 1973:

"We, the undersigned, a group of Christians in Toronto, moved by the tragic war now raging in the Middle East, wish to express our concern for the victims of this conflict, and wish, in particular, to share some Christian reflections both with the larger Christian community and with the community at large. The following observations are made with a deep sense of Christian contrition for the many past "silences" of the churches at those critical moments when the Christian conscience has been tested, and found wanting. We believe that another crisis of conscience has arrived, and that, on no account, must another silence be condoned.

"The Arab-Israeli struggle has for years been coloured by a mythology which continues to obscure the political and human dimensions of the collision of two peoples in the Middle East. This is the mythology of a Zionism consistently represented by anti-Zionists as a racist, imperialistic Nazi-type creed imposed upon the Middle East to dispossess and oppress non-Jews, and to establish presumably a 'Jewish Empire'. Many Christians, unfamiliar with the Zionist ideas, having been more or less persuaded of the basic truth of this mythology, tend as a result to interpret present-day events in its light. Thus, the current war is regarded as a war of liberation designed to remove the Zionist yoke in the name of humanity and justice. Such Christians are frequently disbelieving if informed that (a) Zionism is not a dirty word, like Nazism, but a complex phenomenon with its roots in both Jewish tradition and modern Jewish experience; (b) modern Zionism was born as the stepchild of Western Gentile anti-Semitism—the anti-Semitism of the Christian churches and a Christian culture—and was therefore an early liberation movement incorporating the response of disillusioned European Jews to the hostility of a Christian-Gentile world which refused to accept their presence; (c) the rhetoric of anti-Zionism is as old as the Zionist movement itself (that masterpiece of modern anti-Semitism, *The Protocols of the Elders of Zion*, was published about the time of the first Zionist Congress in 1897), and every important anti-Semite of this century has made repeated use of this rhetoric, from Henry Ford to Adolf Hitler to current Russian propaganda. One example illustrates this trend. In *Mein Kampf*, Hitler attacked (Zionist) Jews for seeking to build a Jewish empire in the Middle East as "a central organization for their international world swindle. . . ." Incidentally, the *Protocols* are presently in widespread circulation in the Arab-Islamic world, and definitely a factor in the Middle Eastern struggle.

"To understand the issues fairly, this mythology must be stripped away. When it is gone, one sees the tragic encounter of two peoples, each with legitimate claims and aspirations, over the same territory. Christians are involved on both sides of this encounter. They are involved on the Arab side, because modern Arab nationalism owes some of its roots to the Christian missionary presence since the last century. They are involved on the Jewish side, because Jewish nationalism is the stepchild of Christian prejudice, and because Israel, by its very existence, is both a reminder and a rebuke to Christians for their role in the Jewish plight in the twentieth century, with its Holocaust and its murdered children. Israel, to Jews, is more than another nation; it is a resurrection symbol following the near extinction of the Jewish people within living memory. For this reason, we believe, Christians must affirm Israel as the visible and tangible manifestation of both Jewish survival and Jewish security. For the possibility of a second Auschwitz is something which no Christian should view with equanimity and any semblance of moral neutrality. Indeed, as matters now stand, the option of remaining neutral in an apparent life-and-death struggle does not exist. To affirm Israel is not to pretend that Israel, as a nation-state, stands above the moral criteria derived from the canons of international justice and the conscience of rational man which apply to other nations. Clearly, no nation-state is innocent or can be innocent, since power, especially military power, is always subject to misuse, and nation-states by definition are vast impersonal concentrations of power. Once the Jewish state was born, it took upon itself the moral ambiguity of a world replete with power-struggles, and the moral dilemmas which are always entailed in the possession of power. Israel can be criticized as any other nation can be criticized, but it is profoundly wrong to oppose Israel because of its *Jewish* foundations, and to seek to dismantle its Jewish character, as the anti-Zionists invariably desire. In a military conflict in which the apparent object is not merely the recovery of occupied territory, but the destruction of the Jewish political community, and, if Arab rhetoric is to be taken literally, to 'drive the Zionists into the sea,' Christians must, in our view, stand with Israel, and stand without equivocation.

"The plight of the Palestinian refugees is a cause which has stirred much Christian sympathy, and which has become the focal point for the convergence of liberal sentiment (Christian and non-Christian) and the ideology of the Third World with its Marxist analysis. Israel has been identified by both groups as the oppressor, the Palestinian Arabs as the oppressed. This plight, in our view, is the other side of the tragic encounter between the aspiration of two peoples; tragic because injustice in one form or another is seemingly unavoidable. Christians are involved on this side of the conflict as well. In our opinion, however, the present attack of the Arab nations against Israel cannot be justified in these terms, because the former have themselves repeatedly revealed no small measure of indifference to the refugees during recent years. Moreover, in much Christian opinion, the refugees have unwittingly emerged as a comfort for a troubled conscience which, preferring not to dwell on Christian guilt with regard to the Jews, dwells instead on Jewish guilt with regard to the Arabs. Nor are the Churches in a position of moral objectivity whereby they can successfully play a mediatorial role between the Jewish and Arab worlds, balancing the claims and counter-claims of the two warring communities. We have long since disqualified ourselves for any such task, and should not adopt an attitude of moral superiority in a situation which exposes too many of our own failings.

Fr. Edward A. Synon	President, Pontifical Institute of Medieval Studies
Fr. Gregory Baum	Professor, St. Michael's College, University of Toronto
Sister Mary Jo Leddy	Teaching Assistant, Ph.D. (cand.) University of Toronto

Fr. John M. Kelly	President, St. Michael's College
John C. Meagher	Director: Institute of Christian Thought, St. Michael's College
Rev. Herbert Richardson	Professor, St. Michael's College
Fr. Arthur Gibson	Chairman, Department of Religious Studies, St. Michael's College
Alan T. Davies	Assistant Professor, Victoria College, University of Toronto
William O. Fennell	Principal, Emmanuel College, Victoria College, University of Toronto
David E. Demson	Associate Professor, Emmanuel College, Victoria University
Donald R. Keating	Teaching Assistant, York University
B. Robert Bater	Minister, Eglinton United Church
Sr. Donna Purdy	Executive Director, Canadian Committee on Social Ministry
Dr. G. S. French	Toronto"

APPENDIX C

Statement of United Church Official on Mideast, October 30, 1973, Toronto *Globe and Mail*:

"In recent days you have carried several letters from persons writing as Christians suggesting that in the Middle East struggle Christians should 'stand with Israel.' This is because in times past, nations calling themselves 'Christians' inflicted great evils on the Jewish people. One letter was signed by Father John M. Kelly of St. Michael's College and 13 others from St. Michael's (Catholic) and Victoria University (United Church). This letter stated: 'Christians must, in our view, stand with Israel and without equivocation.' Another writer, D. Keating, feels: 'There is no tragedy like the tragedy of Jewish lives lost in war.'

"We are deeply sensitive to the tragedy for both Jews and Arabs which the recent outbreak of hostilities has brought. We are hopeful that the present cessation of open warfare may be a prelude to an enduring and genuine peace. We deeply regret the shedding of the blood of both Jews and Arabs and pray for peace with justice in the Middle East.

"The tenor of a number of letters to the editor in your paper has served to polarize local feeling with regard to this matter. The letter by Father Kelly and 13 others in the October 19th edition contributed to this process. We feel that their statement is not adequate.

"The World Council of Churches, the Canadian Council, and major Protestant denominations officially support the U.N. Security Council Resolution 242, of November 22nd, 1967. This emphasized 'the inadmissability of acquiring territory by war. . . .' (Israel acquired a great deal of Arab territory by successful warfare in 1948 and 1967.) Resolution 242 also emphasized two principles: Withdrawal of Israeli armed forces from territories occupied in the recent (June 1967) conflict, and 'respect for and acknowledgment of the sovereignty, territorial integrity and political independence of every State in the area and their right to live in peace within secure and recognized boundaries free from threats or acts of force.'

"We believe in those principles. We believe if there is to be peace in the Middle East there must be a sincere attempt to achieve justice.

"In addition to pressing for a just peace and the security of Israel the churches have been deeply concerned with the plight of the Palestinian people.

"The Canadian Council of Churches has said officially: 'By establishing the State of Israel without protecting the rights of the Palestinians injustice has been done to the Palestinian Arabs which must be redressed.'

"The Anglican Church in Canada has called upon the Government of Canada to increase its contribution to UNRWA for the Palestinian refugees, to open Canadian doors to Palestinian immigrants.

"The Presbyterian Church in Canada has urged the government and the United Nations 'to seek deep-level solutions . . . which take full account of the needs and rights of all the peoples and nations involved, with particular reference to the plight of the Palestinian refugees.'

"The United Church of Canada resolved to 'urge the Government of Canada to back any action of the U.N. that, while guaranteeing the security of Israel, aims to secure justice and self-determination for the Palestinian Arabs.'

"In contrast to Donald Keating we feel that the loss of Arab and Israeli lives is equally tragic. It is fundamental for Christians to believe that God is no respecter of race or colour, and that in the eyes of his followers, the life of a Muslim, Christian, Jew, Buddhist or atheist is equally precious. We note with satisfaction that the cease-fire has been accepted by both sides in the Middle East conflict and that the peace-keeping force is to be composed of personnel from non-nuclear powers and those countries not on the Security Council.

"The State of Israel for reasons which seem valid to some Jews, but not to others, has different laws for Jew and non-Jew. We being among those who profess to be Christian, stand with many Jews in expressing our belief that the security of the Middle East must be founded in justice for all people.

W. Clarke MacDonald,
on behalf of the Committee
on the Church and International Affairs,
The United Church of Canada."

APPENDIX D

Fourteen University of Toronto Professors See Anti-Arab Bias in Pro-Israel Argument, October 24, 1973, Toronto *Globe and Mail:*

"The October 19 issue of *The Globe and Mail* contained what is in many ways a surprising apology for Zionism and an attempt, by Fr. John M. Kelly and 13 others, to commit Christendom to the support of the Zionist cause. The argument runs to the effect that, since the Christian world has been guilty of crimes against the Jews, it is therefore obligated to support Zionism willy-nilly, to the utter disregard of the wrongs done in the process to the Arabs, the original innocent bystanders.

"The letter in question is rife with prejudice, often subtle, but nonetheless virulent anti-Semitic prejudice against the Arabs (for they too are Semites and cousins of the Jews). The demand that we 'affirm Israel as the visible manifestation of both Jewish survival and security,' while at the same time denying Arab rights by omission or glossing them over, is clear evidence of bias.

"It is the perpetuation of the denial of Arab rights implicit in the Balfour Declaration and subsequently confessed to by Lord Balfour himself—that there never was any intention of safeguarding the rights of the non-Jewish majority of 90 per cent. This denial of Arab rights was repeated in the United Nations vote on the partition plan on November 29, 1947, while refusing the right of self-determination or even consultation to the Palestinians. Should Christendom not feel some guilt at this denial of rights that gave rise to the Palestinian diaspora?

"It is obvious bias to accuse the Arabs of wanting to perpetuate 'a second Auschwitz.' The Arabs have never had a first Auschwitz—that was an aberration of Western Christendom, and the learned signatories of the article should have known that historically the Jews have been much better treated by the Muslim Arabs than by Christian Europe. If the Voice of the Arabs radio station, run by the Palestinian

Liberation Organization in Cairo, threatened in 1967 to 'drive the Israelis into the sea,' no responsible Arab leader since that date has repeated such threats. Security Council resolution No. 242, of Nov. 22, 1967, accepted by Egypt and most of the Arab states, far from seeking to dismantle Israel affirms its right to secure borders.

"It is mere obfuscation to claim that Christian opinion is seeking solace in the guilt of the Jews with regard to the Palestinian refugees in order to absolve itself from its own guilt with regard to the Jews. If Israel bears any guilt for the plight of the Palestinian refugees, should not Israel face it? No accusation of Arab 'indifference to the refugees' can obviate this fact. If peace is ever to be attained, the wishes and rights of the refugees must be consulted.

"The World Council of Churches, in a meeting on the Island of Cyprus following the War of 1967, issued a declaration concerning the inadmissibility of the acquisition of territory by force. The Christian Church may not be guiltless with regard to Christendom's past treatment of the Jews but, if this is to keep it from mediating between Arabs and Jews, who in the world has the required clean hands to take up the task? Neither the Church, nor the United Nations, nor the Great Powers, nor the combatants themselves, have clean hands but this must not prevent one and all from working to bring peace to this cruelly war-torn area.

L. M. Kenny (and 13 other professors of the Department of Islamic and Near Eastern Studies), University of Toronto."

APPENDIX E

Excerpts from Salter Advertisement, *The Observer*, March 1974:

"HE AS GOD SITTETH IN THE TEMPLE OF GOD

". . . No organization of men, other than the nation of Israel is recognized in Scripture as an organization or body of people chosen by God. Other organizations may claim to be His temple but he does not acknowledge them. Ultimately, of course, the temple of God will be all mankind, when all have been transformed into the likeness of Christ and God is all in All.

"It follows then that the Catholic Church is not the temple of God. Neither are the Protestant churches, nor any of their offshoots. . . .

"The nation of Israel (all twelve tribes) is still the temple of God 'for the gifts and calling of God are without repentance' (Rom. 11:29). . . .

"So the great whore, the man of sin, the son of perdition, sits not only in the temple of God (the twelve tribes of Israel) but reigns also over the kings of the earth. By what power? No one will deny that it is by the power of money. And who controls the money of the world? Official Judah, with many individuals of the ten tribes and non-Israelites as their willing tools and collaborators until the whole earth is drunk with the worship of money and the power and corruption it brings. This has indeed been a mystery but what opposition could be more wicked and more deep-seated than that coming from those to whom God gave His law, who knew His will and opposed it? Who would suspect that some of the people whom God had chosen would set themselves up in opposition to Him and become His arch opposers? Only at the time of the end was this mystery to be revealed, the son of perdition exposed or identified. The whole history of Israel, the ten tribes, is one for forsaking God's word and law, being chastened for it and repenting, only to lapse into disobedience again. Judah, while having before them the example of Israel's punishment in being taken captive to Assyria, was even more apostate than Israel (Jer. 3:6—8:11) and at the time of Christ's first advent demanded from the Romans the crucifixion of Christ, for which they accepted full responsibility—'Then answered all the people, and said: His blood be on us, and on our children' (Matt. 27:25). They have never ceased their opposition to Christ and now, as the second advent of Christ draws near, they have secured control in Israel (the twelve tribes) and the nations of earth through the power of money and are about to proclaim their world government, a rulership promised by God only to Christ. But 'in one hour' her destruction comes. The merchants of the earth weep, but the poor and oppressed can rejoice: 'For true and righteous are his judgments: for he hath judged the great whore, which did corrupt the earth with her fornication, and hath avenged the blood of his servants at her hand' (Revelation, chapters 18 and 19).

"It is said that the Jews established the Catholic Church, and the facts seem to bear this out. Disraeli stated that the first Jesuits were Jews. Wherever Paul and the other apostles went in their ministry they were opposed by Jews or by Gentiles stirred up by Jews. Of necessity one who would rule a country must control politics, finance and religion. Hence the necessity of a false religion. One who would control the world must have a world religion, a system of world politics and world finance. We are well along the road to such complete control, to such complete slavery of the masses of mankind. Our only hope of release is the fall of Babylon—a fall that would seem to be due very soon for Britain (the leading tribe of the ten tribes of Israel) has now given her power unto the beast (Europe, ruled by Judah) by joining the European Common Market. . . .

G. J. Salter,
Haliburton, Ontario, Canada."

APPENDIX F

About Mr. Salter's Advertisement, United Church *Observer*, May 1974:

"We confess we were taken off guard by the reaction to G. J. Salter's ad in the March issue. This may be because we have never taken British-Israelism very seriously, although we have known some very fine persons who were preoccupied with the ten tribes and all that. Nor had it occurred to us that the B.I.'s would be considered anti-Semitic. In fact, we thought the reverse, that some Anglo-Saxons also wanted to be thought the Chosen People. With the result that when Mr. Salter's piece came in—as a tear sheet for an ad that had already run in the Toronto *Sun* (it appeared in a number of Canadian newspapers)—we saw it as a harmless expression of British-Israel opinion with which we didn't agree. However, we confess we didn't read it carefully, or we would have rejected it on the grounds of taste.

"Obviously some readers have been offended by it, including a number of official presbytery voices who take it very seriously. We were troubled about the anti-Semitic charges, so have checked with Mr. Salter who says: 'Anyone who would term my article anti-Semitic is reading into it something that is not there. On the contrary, it is very much pro-Semitic, for it shows that God has chosen the two tribes of Judah and the ten tribes of Ephraim-Israel (all of whom are Semites) as a special people unto himself above all nations of the earth.'

"We have also checked this out with British-Israel headquarters, and learned that Mr. Salter reflects their thinking. To those who found his interpretation of Scripture racist or anti-Catholic, we apologize. To those who object on the ground that it is anti-ecumenical or not in keeping with the theology of the United Church—well, we really don't think that our readers will be seriously damaged by such heresies, or that they need to be protected from hearing some of the strange ideas that British-Israelites and other enthusiastic minorities have been preaching for decades.

A. C. Forrest"

BIBLIOGRAPHY

THE UNITED CHURCH OF CANADA

PRIMARY SOURCES

Files of the United Church *Observer*, United Church House, Toronto.

Proceedings of the General Council, United Church of Canada, United Church House, Toronto.

BOOKS

"The United Church of Canada," *Encyclopedia Americana*. New York, 1963.

Kilbourn, William, Forrest, A.C., and Watson, Patrick, *Religion in Canada*. Toronto, McClelland & Stewart, reprinted 1968.

"The United Church *Observer* and the State of Israel." Toronto, B'nai B'rith Anti-Defamation League Basic Documents, 1969, mimeograph.

THE JEWISH COMMUNITY OF CANADA

Belkin, Simon, *Through Narrow Gates, Jewish Immigration 1840-1940*. Montreal, Eagle Publishing Co. Ltd., 1966.

Betcherman, Lita-Rose, *The Swastika and the Maple Leaf*. Toronto, Fitzhenry & Whiteside, 1975.

Chiel, Arthur A., *The Jews in Manitoba*. Toronto, University of Toronto Press, 1961.

"Canadian Jewish Congress," *Encyclopedia Judaica*, vol. 5. New York and Jerusalem, Macmillan Co.

Eisendrath, M.N., *Can Faith Survive?* Toronto, McGraw-Hill, 1964.

Elazar, Daniel J., *The Organization and Status of Contemporary Jewish Communities, 1970-71*. Philadelphia, Pa., Center for Jewish Community Studies.

Fenson, Melvin, "The Jewish Community of Canada," *American Jewish Year Book*. New York, 1974-75.

Figler, Bernard, and Rome, David, *A Biography of H. M. Caiserman*. Montreal, Northern Printing Co., 1962.

Glickman, Ya'acov, *The Organization and Governance of the Toronto Jewish Community*. Toronto, Canadian Jewish Congress, 1975, mimeograph.

Liebman, Charles S., *The Ambivalent American Jew.* Philadelphia, Pa., Jewish Publication Society, 1973.
Hart, A.D., *The Jew in Canada.* Montreal and Toronto, Jewish Publications Ltd., 1926.
Rosenberg, Louis, *Canada's Jews.* Montreal, Bureau of Social and Economic Research, Canadian Jewish Congress, 1939.
Sack, B.G., *History of the Jews in Canada.* Montreal, Harvest House, 1965; Volume 2, 1976.
Siegel, David, *Jewish Political Theory and Institutions.* Philadelphia, Pa., Center for Jewish Community Studies.
Weisgal, Meyer, *So Far, An Autobiography.* London, Weidenfeld & Nicolson, 1971.
Waller, Harold M., project director, *The Governance of the Jewish Communities of Montreal, Ottawa, London, Hamilton, Winnipeg, Windsor, Edmonton, Calgary and Vancouver.* Philadelphia, Pa., Center for Jewish Community Studies, 1975.

JUDAISM AND CHRISTIANITY

Agus, Jacob B., *Dialogue and Tradition.* New York and Toronto, Abelard-Schuman, 1971.
Asch, Sholem, *The Nazarene.* New York, J. P. Putnam's Sons, 1939.
Baum, Gregory, *Is the New Testament Anti-Semitic?* Glen Rock, N.J., Paulist Press, rev. ed., 1965.
Baeck, Leo, *Judaism and Christianity.* Philadelphia, Pa., Jewish Publication Society, 1958.
Borchsenius, Poul, *Two Ways to God.* London, Vallentine, Mitchell Co., Ltd., 1968.
Buber, Martin, *Israel and the World.* New York, Schocken, 1948.
Cadbury, Henry C., *The Peril of Modernizing Jesus.* New York, Allenson, 1962.
Davies, Alan T., *Anti-Semitism and the Christian Mind.* New York, Herder and Herder, 1969.
Davies, W.D., *The Gospel and the Land, Early Christianity and Jewish Territorial Doctrine.* Berkeley and Los Angeles, University of California Press, 1974.
Davis, Moshe, ed., *The Yom Kippur War, Israel and the Jewish People.* New York, Arno Press, 1974.
Eckardt, Alice and Roy, *Encounter with Israel.* New York, Association Press, 1970.
Eckardt, A. Roy, *Your People, My People.* New York, Quadrangle, 1974.
Finkel, A., *The Pharisees and the Teacher of Nazareth.* Leiden, Netherlands, E. J. Brill, 1974.
Fishman, Hertzel, *American Protestantism and a Jewish State.* Detroit, Wayne University Press, 1973.
Friedman, Saul S., *No Haven for the Oppressed.* Detroit, Wayne State University Press, 1973.
Glatzer, Nahum N., *Franz Rosenzweig, His Life and Thought.* New York, Schocken, 2nd ed., 1961.
Goodenough, E.R., *Religious Tradition and Myth.* New Haven, Conn., Yale University Press, 1937.
Graetz, Heinrich, *History of the Jews.* Philadelphia, Pa., Jewish Publication Society, 1941.
Grant, Frederick C., *An Introduction to New Testament Thought.* New York, Abingdon-Cokesbury, 1950.
Guignebert, Charles A.H., *The Jewish World in the Time of Jesus.* London, Routledge & Kegan Paul, 1951.
Hay, Malcolm, *The Foot of Pride.* Boston, Beacon Press, 1950.

Herford, R. Travers, *The Pharisees.* New York, Macmillan Co., 1924.
Isaac, Jules, *The Teaching of Contempt.* Toronto and New York, Holt, Rinehart & Winston, Inc., 1964.
Kaplan, Mordecai M., *Judaism as a Civilization.* New York, Macmillan Co., 1935.
Kaplan, Mordecai M., *The Religion of Ethical Nationhood.* New York and Toronto, Macmillan Co., 1970.
Kirsch, Paul J., *We Christians and Jews.* Philadelphia, Fortress Press, 1975.
Klausner, Joseph, *Jesus of Nazareth, His Life, Times and Teachings,* trans. from original Hebrew by Herbert Danby. Boston, Beacon Press, 1925 and 1964; New York, Macmillan Co., 1957.
Margolis, Max L., and Marx, Alexander, *A History of the Jewish People.* Philadelphia, Pa., Jewish Publication Society, 1927.
Moehlman, Conrad, *The Christian-Jewish Tragedy, A Study in Religious Prejudice.* Rochester, N.Y., Leo Hart Printing House, 1933.
Montefiore, Claude J.G., *The Synoptic Gospels.* London, Macmillan Co., 1927.
Montefiore, Claude J.G., *Rabbinic Literature and Gospel Teachings.* London, Macmillan Co., 1930; reissued New York, by Ktav, 1970.
Montefiore, Claude J.G., *What a Jew Thinks About Jesus,* 1937.
Moore, George Foot, *Judaism in the First Centuries of the Christian Era, The Age of the Tannaim.* Cambridge, Mass., Harvard University Press, 1954.
Parkes, James, *Conflict of the Church and Synagogue.* London, Soncino Press, 1934.
Parsons, Ernest William, *The Religion of the New Testament.* New York, Harper & Row, 1939.
Sandmel, Samuel, *We Jews and Jesus.* New York, Oxford University Press, 1965.
Sandmel, Samuel, *A Jewish Understanding of the New Testament.* Cincinnati, Hebrew Union College Press, 1956.
Schoeps, Hans Joachim, *The Jewish-Christian Argument.* New York and Toronto, Holt, Rinehart & Winston, 1963.
Scott, E.F., *Varieties of New Testament Religion.* New York, Scribner's, 1943.
Strack, Herman, and Billerbeck, Paul, *Commentary on the New Testament from the Talmud and Midrash.* Munich, Bech, 1922-1956 (German).
Weiss-Rosmarin, Trude, *Judaism and Christianity, The Differences.* New York, Jonathan David, 1943.

ANTI-SEMITISM AND THE HOLOCAUST

Bethge, Eberhard, *Dietrich Bonhoeffer.* New York, Harper & Row, 1970.
Baron, Salo, *A Social and Religious History of the Jews,* 15 vols. Philadelphia, Pa., Jewish Publication Society of America, 1937-1973.
Berkovits, Eliezer, *Faith After the Holocaust.* New York, Ktav, 1973.
Buber, Martin, *Eclipse of God.* New York, Harper & Row, 1952.
Dawidowicz, Lucy S., *The War Against the Jews, 1933-45.* Toronto, Holt, Rinehart & Winston, 1975.
Dawidowicz, Lucy S., *A Holocaust Reader.* New York, Behrman House, 1976.
Fackenheim, Emil L., *God's Presence in History.* New York, New York University Press, 1970.
Flannery, Edward H., *The Anguish of the Jews.* New York, Macmillan Co., 1964.
Forster, Arnold, and Epstein, Benjamin A., *The New Anti-Semitism.* New York and Toronto, McGraw-Hill, 1974.
Frankl, Viktor E., *Man's Search for Meaning.* New York, Pocket Books, 1973.

Glatstein, Jacob, Knox, Israel, and Margoshes, Samuel, eds., *Anthology of Holocaust Literature.* Philadelphia, Pa., Jewish Publication Society, 1969.
Lewy, Guenter, *The Catholic Church and Nazi Germany.* New York and Toronto, McGraw-Hill, 1964.
Littell, Franklin H., and Locke, Hubert G., eds., *The German Church Struggle and the Holocaust.* Detroit, Wayne State University Press, 1974.
Littell, Franklin H., *The Crucifixion of the Jews.* New York, Harper & Row, 1975.
Mark, Ber, *Uprising in the Warsaw Ghetto.* New York, Schocken, 1975.
Morse, Arthur D., *While Six Million Died.* New York, Random House, 1968.
Olson, Bernhard E., *Faith and Prejudice.* New Haven, Conn., Yale University Press, 1963.
Payne, Robert, *The Life and Death of Adolf Hitler.* Toronto, Popular Library, 1973.
Rhodes, Anthony, *The Vatican in the Age of the Dictators, 1922-1945.* Toronto, Holt, Rinehart & Winston, 1974.
Rubenstein, Richard L., *After Auschwitz.* Indianapolis, Ind., Bobbs-Merrill, 1966.
Ruether, Rosemary, *Faith and Fratricide.* New York, Seabury Press, 1974.
Samuel, Maurice, *The Great Hatred.* New York, Alfred A. Knopf, 1948.
Sartre, Jean-Paul, *Anti-Semite and Jew.* New York, Schocken, 1948.
Schlink, Edmund, *Der Ertrag des Kirchenkampfes (The Harvest of the Church Struggle).* Guetersloh, 1947 (German).
Sevenster, J.N., *The Roots of Pagan Anti-Semitism in the Ancient World.* Leiden, Netherlands, E.J. Brill, 1975.
Shirer, William L., *The Rise and Fall of the Third Reich.* New York, Simon & Shuster, 1960.
Smolar, Leivy, *Lest We Forget.* Washington, D.C., B'nai B'rith Youth Organization Judaism Pamphlet, 1967.
Swidler, Leonard, ed., "Jews and Christians in Dialogue." Philadelphia, *Journal of Ecumenical Studies,* Special Issue, 1975.
Wiesel, Elie, *Dawn.* Toronto, Ambassador Books, 1961.
Wiesel, Elie, *One Generation After.* New York, Bard Avon Books, 1972.

ISRAEL AND PALESTINE

Armanazi, Ghayth, "The Rights of the Palestinians: The International Definition." Beirut, *Journal of Palestine Studies,* Spring, 1974.
el-Asmar, Fouzi, *To be an Arab in Israel.* London, Frances Pinter Ltd., 1975.
Background to the Middle East Conflict. New York, Committee on New Alternatives in the Middle East, 1974.
Beigin, Menahem, *The Revolt.* London, W. H. Allen, 1951.
Ben-Gurion, David, *Israel, A Personal History.* New York, Funk & Wagnalls, 1974.
Ben-Meir, Alon, *The Middle East: Imperatives and Choices.* Mount Vernon, N.Y., Decalogue Books, 1975.
Brecher, Michael, *The Foreign Policy System of Israel.* New Haven, Yale University Press, 1972.
Chomsky, Noam, *Peace in the Middle East?* New York, Vintage Books, 1974.
Conder, Claude Reigner, *Heth and Moab.* London, Bentley, 1883.
Curtis, Michael, Neyer, Joseph, Pollock, Allen, and Waxman, Chaim I., eds., *The Palestinians, People, History, Politics.* Edison, N.J., Transaction Books, 1975.
Eliav, Arie Lova, *Land of the Hart.* Philadelphia, Jewish Publication Society, 1974.

Elon, Amos, *The Israelis: Founders and Sons.* New York, Holt, Rinehart & Winston, 1971.

Elon, Amos, and Hassan, Sana, *Between Enemies: A Compassionate Dialogue Between an Israeli and an Arab.* New York and Toronto, Random House, 1974.

Elazar, Daniel J., "Israel's Sephardim: The Myth of Two Cultures." Philadelphia, Pa., Research Paper, Center for Jewish Community Studies.

Epp, Frank H., *Whose Land is Palestine?* Grand Rapids, Mich., William B. Eerdmann Publishing Co., 1970.

Epp, Frank H., *The Palestinians, Portrait of a People in Conflict,* Photographs by John Goddard. Toronto, McClelland & Stewart, 1976.

Forrest, A.C., *The Unholy Land.* Toronto, McClelland & Stewart, 1972.

Friedlander, Saul, and Hussein, Mahmoud, *Arabs and Israelis, A Dialogue.* New York, Holmes and Meier Publishers, Inc., 1975.

Gendzier, Irene, *A Middle East Reader.* Indianapolis, Pegasus, 1969.

Ghilan, Maxim, *How Israel Lost Its Soul.* Middlesex, England, Pelican Books, 1974.

Harkabi, Yehoshafat, *Arab Attitudes Toward Israel.* New York, Hart Publishing Company, 1971.

Hecht, Ben, *Perfidy.* Toronto, Copp Clark Publishing Co., 1961.

Heikal, Mohamed, *The Road to Ramadan.* New York, Quadrangle, 1975.

Hertzberg, Arthur, ed., *The Zionist Idea: A Historical Analysis and Reader.* New York, Atheneum, 1973.

Herzl, Theodor, *Altneuland.* New York, Bloch Publishing Co., 1960.

Herzog, Chaim, *The War of Atonement, October, 1973.* New York, Little Brown, 1975.

Herzog, Ya'acov, *A People that Dwells Alone.* New York, Sanhedrin Press, 1975.

Jabber, Fuad, *Israel and Nuclear Weapons.* London, Chatto and Windus, 1971.

Joseph, Dov, *The Faithful City, The Siege of Jerusalem.* New York, Simon & Schuster, 1960.

Kapeliuk, Ammon, *La Fin Des Mythes.* Paris, Editions Albin Michel, 1975 (French).

Kaplan, Mordecai M., *A New Zionism.* New York, Herzl Press, 1959.

Katz, Samuel, *Battleground: Fact and Fancy in Palestine.* New York, Bantam Books, Inc., 1973.

Kenan, Amos, *Israel: A Wasted Victory.* Tel Aviv, Amikam Publishers, 1970 (Hebrew).

Kimche, Jon, *Seven Fallen Pillars, The Middle East, 1915-1950.* London, Secker & Warburg Ltd., 1950.

Laqueur, Walter, ed., *The Arab-Israel Reader.* London, Pelican Books, 1970.

Liebman, Seymour B., *The Middle East: A Return to Facts.* New York, American Zionist Federation, 1973.

Mansour, Atallah, *Waiting for the Dawn.* London, Secker and Warburg, 1975.

Meir, Golda, *My Life.* New York, G. P. Putnam's Sons, 1975.

Memmi, Albert, *Jews and Arabs.* Chicago, J. Philip O'Hara, 1975.

Parkes, James, *Whose Land? A History of the Peoples of Palestine.* Middlesex, England, Penguin Books Ltd., 1970.

Rodinson, Maxime, *Israel and the Arabs,* trans. by Michael Perl. New York, Pantheon, 1968.

Rouleau, Eric, "The Palestinian Quest." New York, *Foreign Affairs,* January 1975.

Sachar, Howard M., *Europe Leaves the Middle East, 1936-1954.* New York, Alfred A. Knopf, 1972.

Schleifer, Abdullah, *The Fall of Jerusalem.* New York, Monthly Review Press, 1975.

Schmidt, Dana Adams, *Armageddon in the Middle East.* New York, John Day, 1974.

Sefer Ha-Palmach (History of the Palmach Striking Force, Hebrew). Tel Aviv, 1962.

Segal, Ronald, *Whose Jerusalem? The Conflicts of Israel.* New York, Bantam Books, Inc., 1974.

Simon, Akiva Ernst, *Nationalism, Zionism and the Jewish-Arab Dispute in the Teaching of Martin Buber.* Israel, Centre for Arab Studies, 1975.

Slonim, Reuben, *Both Sides Now, An Encounter with Arabs and Israelis.* Toronto, Clarke Irwin, 1972.

Sykes, Christopher, *Crossroads to Israel.* Indianapolis, Indiana University Press, 1973.

Taylor, Alan R., *The Zionist Mind.* Beirut, Institute of Palestine Studies, 1974.

Tuma, Elias H., *Peacemaking and the Immoral War.* New York, Harper Torchbooks, 1972.

Turki, Fawaz, *The Disinherited: Journal of a Palestine Exile.* New York, Monthly Review Press, 1972.

Twain, Mark, *Innocents Abroad.* New York, Harper & Row, reprint of 1869 edition, 1975.

Vital, David, *The Origins of Zionism.* New York, Oxford University Press, 1975.

Ya'ari, Ehud, *Egypt and the Fedayeen 1953-1956.* Israel, Givat Haviva, 1975 (Hebrew).

INDEX